William C Godfrey

The voyage of the 'Fox' in the Arctic seas.

A narrative of the discovery of the fate of Sir John Franklin and his companions -

Vol. 1

William C Godfrey

The voyage of the 'Fox' in the Arctic seas.
A narrative of the discovery of the fate of Sir John Franklin and his companions - Vol. 1

ISBN/EAN: 9783337611354

Printed in Europe, USA, Canada, Australia, Japan

Cover: Foto ©Thomas Meinert / pixelio.de

More available books at **www.hansebooks.com**

NOTICE.

NO GIFT BOOK STORES

CAN GET

ANY OF OUR PUBLICATIONS

AT ANY PRICE.

☞ Every man should read this work carefully, and prepare to unite against the Republican party, ere the Union shall be rent asunder by their fanaticism.

HELPER'S IMPENDING CRISIS
DISSECTED.

BY JUDGE WOLFE, OF VIRGINIA.

ENDORSED BY MORE THAN TWO HUNDRED MEMBERS OF CONGRESS.

Cloth, $1.00.   Half Calf, $1.25.   Paper Covers, 50 cts.
244 8vo Pages.

The Most Powerfully Written Work in the English Language.

CONTENTS.

CHAPTER V.

Helper's ignorance of the feelings of the Non-Slaveholding Population of the South to their Country—The Negroes of the South true to their Masters—The Proofs given at Harper's Ferry—Not a Slave attempted to run away—The South have no fears of the uprising of the Negroes—How the Negroes aided their Masters to repel the British under Lord Cornwallis, and at New Orleans—Report of the Virginia Legislature on the Harper's Ferry Outrage.

CHAPTER VI.

Republican Party Ruining the Trade of the North—Trade Crushed—The Bankruptcy of the entire North Predicted—Helper's Advice to the North adopted by the entire South—Republican Party Responsible for the Withdrawal of the Southern Trade—"The Shoe commences to Pinch"—Helper's Statistics of the Prices of Land in the South demolished.

CHAPTER VII.

The Declaration of Independence quoted to prove that the Negro was not born "Created Free and Equal" with the White Man—Judge Taney's Decision in the Dred Scott Case quoted to prove the Author's assertions.

CHAPTER VIII.

Northern Testimony in regard to the Aggressions of the Republican Party against the South—Extracts from the Speeches of the Hon. J. A. Logan and Stephen A. Douglass —The Damage inflicted upon the Northern Merchants and Manufacturers by the Republican Party—The Proofs—The South in favor of Disunion in certain Contingencies—Eloquent Defense of the South by Hon. Horatio G. Seymour, of New York, and Col. J. W. Wall, of New Jersey.

CHAPTER IX.

The South united to a Man, ready to beat back the Northern Hordes with Cannon and Sword—Armories going up in the South—Manufactories increasing in every Southern State—The South could create a Bread Riot in the North any season, by withholding the Cotton Crop—Northern men should ponder well over these facts, before urging on this Republican Crusade against the South.

CHAPTER X.

Eloquent Defense of the South by the Hon. L. Q. C. Lamar, of Mississippi—Who introduced Slavery into this Country?—The Republicans—Their Hypocrisy—A Dissolution of the Union inevitable, if the Republicans succeed—A War of Extermination Predicted, if once commenced—Are the Northern People prepared for this?—Answer at the Ballot-Boxes.

CHAPTER XI.

The Bible sustains Slavery—Christ sustained Slavery—Slavery has existed in every age since the foundation of the World—The Proofs—The Negro as he is—His incapacity to govern himself—Free Negroes relapse into Barbarism—The Proofs—Conclusion and Appeal to the Northern People to sustain this Glorious Confederacy, by putting down the Republican Leaders.

~~~~~~~~~~

THE 'FOX' STEAMING OUT OF THE ROLLING PACK.

Drawn by Captain May.

The Voyage of the 'Fox' in the Arctic Seas.

A NARRATIVE

OF THE

DISCOVERY OF THE FATE

OF

SIR JOHN FRANKLIN

AND

PANIONS.

By CAPTAIN M'CLINTOCK, R.N., LL.D

WITH MAPS AND ILLUSTRATIONS.

PHILADELPHIA:

J. T. LLOYD,

1860.

DEDICATION.

There is no one to whom I could with so much propriety or willingness dedicate my Journal as to you. For you 't was originally written, and to please you it now appears in print.

To our mutual friend, Sherard Osborne, I am greatly obliged for his kindness in seeing it through the press—a labor I could not have settled down to so soon after my return; and also for pointing out some omissions and technicalities which would have rendered parts of it unintelligible to an ordinary reader. These kind hints have been but partially attended to, and, as time presses, it appears with the mass of its original imperfections, as when you read it in manuscript. Such as it is, however, it affords me this valued opportunity of assuring you of the real gratification I feel in having been instrumental in accomplishing an object so dear to you. To your devotion and self-sacrifice the world is indebted for the deeply interesting revelation unfolded by the voyage of the 'Fox.'

Believe me to be,

With sincere respect, most faithfully yours,

F. L. M'CLINTOCK.

London, 24th Nov., 1859.

(7)

LIST OF OFFICERS AND SHIP'S COMPANY
OF THE 'FOX.'

—————

F. L. M'CLINTOCK, . . Captain R.N.

W. R. HOBSON, . . . Lieutenant R.N.

ALLEN W. YOUNG, . . Captain, Mercantile Marine.

DAVID WALKER, M.D., . Surgeon and Naturalist.

GEORGE BRANDS, . . . Engineer, died 6th Nov., 1858, (Apoplexy)

CARL PETERSEN, . . Interpreter.

THOMAS BLACKWELL, . . Ship's Steward, died 14th June, 1859, (Scurvy)

WM. HARVEY, . . . Chief Quartermaster.

HENRY TOMS, ... Quartermaster.

ALEX. THOMPSON, . . "

JOHN SIMMONDS, . . . Boatswain's Mate.

GEORGE EDWARDS, . . Carpenter's Mate.

ROBERT SCOTT, . . . Leading Stoker, died 4th Dec., 1857, (in consequence of a fall.)

THOMAS GRINSTEAD, . . Sailmaker.

GEORGE HOBDAY, . . . Captain of Hold.

ROBERT HAMPTON, . . A. B.

JOHN A. HAZLETON, . . "

GEORGE CAREY, . . . "

BEN. POUND, ... "

WM. WALTERS, . . . Carpenter's Crew

WM. JONES, ... Dog-driver.

JAMES PITCHER, . . } Stokers.
THOMAS FLORANCE, . . }

RICHARD SHINGLETON, . Officers' Steward.

ANTON CHRISTIAN, . . } Greenland Esquimaux, discharged in Green-
SAMUEL EMANUEL, . . } land.

(9)

OFFICIAL ACKNOWLEDGMENT OF THE SERVICES OF THE YACHT 'FOX.'

————◄●►————

ADMIRALTY, LONDON,
24th Oct., 1859.

SIR,

I am commanded by my Lords Commissioners of the Admiralty to acquaint you, that, in consideration of the important services performed by you in bringing home the only authentic intelligence of the death of the late Sir John Franklin, and of the fate of the crews of the 'Erebus' and 'Terror,' Her Majesty has been pleased, by her Order in Council of the 22nd instant, to sanction the time during which you were absent on these discoveries in the Arctic Regions, viz., from the 30th June, 1857, to the 21st of September, 1859, to reckon as time served by a captain in command of one of Her Majesty's ships, and my Lords have given the necessary directions accordingly.

I am, Sir,
Your very humble servant,
W. G. ROMAINE,
Secretary to the Admiralty.

Captain Francis L. M'Clintock, R.N.

(10)

PREFACE.

THE following narrative of the bold adventure which has successfully revealed the last discoveries and the fate of Franklin, is published at the request of the friends of that illustrious navigator. The gallant M'Clintock, when he penned his Journal amid the Arctic ices, had no idea whatever of publishing it; and yet there can be no doubt that the reader will peruse with the deepest interest the simple tale of how, in a litttle vessel of one hundred and seventy tons burden, he and his well-chosen companions have cleared up this great mystery.

To the honor of the British nation, and also let it be said to that of the United States of America, many have been the efforts made to discover the route followed by our missing explorers. The highly deserving men who have so zealously searched the Arctic seas and lands in this cause must now rejoice, that after all their anxious toils, the merit of rescuing from the frozen North the record of the last days of Franklin has fallen to the share of his noble-minded widow.

Lady Franklin has, indeed, well shown what a devoted and true-hearted English woman can accomplish.

The moment that relics of the expedition commanded
by her husband were brought home (in 1854) by Rae
and that she heard of the account given to him by the
Esquimaux of a large party of Englishmen having
been seen struggling with difficulties on the ice near
the mouth of the Back or Great Fish River, she resolved to expend all her available means (already much
exhausted in four other independent expeditions) in
an exploration of the limited area to which the search
must thenceforward be necessarily restricted.

Whilst the supporters of Lady Franklin's efforts
were of opinion that the Government ought to have
undertaken a search, the extent of which was, for the
first time, definitely limited, it is but rendering justice
to the then Prime Minister* to state, that he had every
desire to carry out the wishes of the men of science†
who appealed to him, and that he was precluded from
acceding to their petition, by nothing but the strongly
expressed opinion of official authorities, that after so
many failures, the Government were no longer justified in sending out more brave men to encounter fresh
dangers in a cause which was viewed as hopeless

---

* Viscount Palmerston.

† See the Memorial (Appendix) addressed to the First Lord
of the Treasury, headed by Admiral Sir F. Beaufort, General
Sabine, and many other men of science, and which, as President
of the Royal Geographical Society, I presented to the Prime
Minister; and also the speech of Lord Wrottesly, the President
of the Royal Society, who, in the absence of the lamented Earl
of Ellesmere, brought the subject earnestly under the notice
of the House of Lords on the 18th of July, 1856.

Hence, it devolved on Lady Franklin and her friends to be the sole means of endeavoring to bring to light the true history of her husband's voyage and fate.

Looking to the list of Naval worthies who, during the preceding years, had been exploring the Arctic Regions, Lady Franklin was highly gratified when she obtained the willing services of Captain M'Clintock to command the yacht 'Fox,' which she had purchased; for that officer had signally distinguished himself in the voyages of Sir John Ross and Captain (now Admiral) Austin, and especially in his extensive journeys on the ice, when associated with Captain Kellett. With such a leader, she could not but entertain sanguine hopes of success when the fast and well-adapted little vessel sailed from Aberdeen on the 1st of July, 1857, upon this eventful enterprise.

Deep, indeed, was the mortification experienced by every one who shared the feelings and anticipations of Lady Franklin when the untoward news came, in the summer of 1858, that, the preceding winter having set in earlier than usual, the 'Fox' had been beset in the ice off Melville Bay, on the coast of Greenland, and after a dreary winter, various narrow escapes, and eight months of imprisonment, had been carried back by the floating ice nearly twelve hundred geographical miles—even to $63\frac{1}{2}°$ N. lat. in the Atlantic! (See the woodcut map, No. 1.)

But although the good litle yacht had been most roughly handled among the ice-floes (see Frontispiece), we were cheered up by the information from Disco, that, with the exception of the death of the engine-driver in consequence of a fall into the hold, the crew were in stout health and full of energy, and that, provided with sufficient fuel and provisions, a good supply of sledging dogs, two tried Esquimaux, and the excellent interpreter Petersen the Dane,* ample grounds yet remained to lead us to hope for a successful issue. Above all, we were encouraged by the proofs of the self-possession and calm resolve of M'Clintock, who held steadily to the accomplishment of his original project; the more so, as he had then tested and recognized the value of the services of Lieutenant (now Commander) Hobson, his able second in command; of Captain Allen Young, his generous volunteer associate;† and of Dr. Walker, his accomplished Surgeon.

Despite, however, of these reassuring data, many an advocate of this search was anxiously alive to the chance of the failure of the venture of one unassisted yacht, which after sundry mishaps was again starting to cross Baffin's Bay, with the foreknowledge that, when she reached the opposite coast, the real difficulties of the enterprise were to commence.

Any such misgivings were happily illusory; and

---

* Since his return to Copenhagen, Petersen has been worthily honored by his Sovereign with the silver cross of Dannebrog.

† Captain Allen Young, of the merchant marine, not only threw his services into this cause, and subscribed £500 in furtherance of the expedition, but, abandoning lucrative appointments in command, generously accepted a subordinate post.

the reader who follows M'Clintock across the "middle ice" of Baffin's Bay to Pond Inlet, thence to Beechey Island, down a portion of Peel Strait, and then through the hitherto unnavigated waters of Bellot Strait in one summer season, may reasonably expect the success which followed.

Whilst the revelation obtained from the long-sought records, which were discovered by Lieutenant Hobson, is most satisfactory to those who speculated on the probability of Franklin having, in the first instance, tried to force his way northwards through Wellington Channel (as we now learn he did), those who held a different hypothesis, namely, that he followed his instructions, which directed him to the S. W., may be amply satisfied that in the following season the ships did pursue this southerly course till they were finally beset in N. lat. 70° 05′.*

At the same time, the public should fully understand the motive which prompted the supporters of

---

* For a *résumé* of all the plans of research and the speculations of seamen and geographers, see the interesting and most useful volume of Mr. John Brown, entitled, "The North-West Passage and Search after Sir John Franklin," 1858. , In an Appendix to this work, we learn that, from the earliest Polar researches by John Cabot, at the end of the 15th century, to the voyage of M'Clintock, there have been about 130 expeditions, illustrated by 250 books and printed documents, of which 150 have been issued in England. Amidst the various recent publications, it is but rendering justice to Dr. King, the former companion of Sir George Back, to state that he suggested and always maintained the necessity of a search for the missing navigators at or near the mouth of the Back River.

Lady Franklin in advocating the last search. Put
ing aside the hope which some of us entertained, that
a few of the younger men of the missing expedition
might still be found to be living among the Esquimaux, we had every reason to expect that if the
ships were discovered, the scientific documents of the
voyage, including valuable magnetic observations,
would be recovered.

In the absence of such good fortune we may, however, well be gladdened by the discovery of that one
precious document which gives us a true outline of
the voyage of the 'Erebus' and 'Terror.'

That the reader may comprehend the vast extent
of sea traversed by Franklin in the two summers
before his ships were beset, a small map (No. †) is
here introduced representing all the lands and seas
of the Arctic Regions to the west of Lancaster Sound
which were known and laid down when he sailed.
The dotted lines and arrows, which extend from the
then known seas and lands into the unknown waters
or blank spaces on this old map, indicate Franklin's
route, the novelty, range, rapidity, and boldness of
which, as thus delineated, may well surprise the
geographer, and even the most enterprising Arctic
sailor.* For, those who have not closely attended

---

* The letter A in Baffin's Bay (fig. 1) indicates the spot where
Franklin was last seen. In fig. 2, B is the winter rendezvous
at Beechey Island; C, the greatest northing of the expedition,
viz., 77° N. lat.; Z, the final beset of the 'Erebus' and 'Terror';
the extreme north and south points of their voyage being represented by two small ships.

† See map on back of the large map in front of book.

to the results of other Arctic voyages may be informed, that rarely has an expedition in the first year accomplished more by its ships than the establishing of good winter quarters, from whence the real researches began by sledge-work in the ensuing spring. Franklin, however, not only reached Beechey Island, but ascended Wellington Channel, then an unknown sea, to 77° N. lat., a more northern latitude in this meridian than that attained long afterward in ships by Sir Edward Belcher, and much to the north of the points reached by Penny and De Haven. Next, though most scantily provided with steam-power, Franklin navigated round Cornwallis's Land, which he thus proved to be an island. The last discovery of a navigable channel throughout, between Cornwallis and Bathurst Islands, though made in the very summer he left England, has remained even to this day unknown to other navigators!

Franklin then, in obedience, to his orders, steered to the southwest. Passing, as M'Clintock believes, down Peel's Strait in 1846, and reaching as far as lat. 70° 05' N., and long. 98° 23' W., where the ships were beset, it is clear that he who, with others, had previously ascertained the existence of a channel along the north coast of America, with which the sea wherein he was interred had a direct communication, was the *first real discoverer of the North-West Passage.* This great fact must therefore be inscribed upon the monument of Franklin.

The adventurous M'Clure, who has been worthily honored for working out another North-Western pass-

2

age, which we now know to have been of subsequent
date,* as well as Collinson, who, taking the 'Enterprise' along the north coast of America, and afterward
bringing her home, reached with sledges the western
edge of the area recently laid open by M'Clintock,
will, I have no doubt, unite with their Arctic associates, Richardson, Sherard Osborn, and M'Clintock, in
affirming, that "Franklin and his followers secured
the honor for which they died—that of being the first
discoverers of the North-West Passage."†

Again, when we turn from the discoveries of Franklin to those of M'Clintock, as mapped in red colors on
the general map, on which is represented the amount
of outline laid down by all other Arctic explorers from
the days when these modern researches originated with

---

* In 1850.

† See a most heart-stirring sketch of the last voyage of Sir
John Franklin, by Captain Sherard Osborn, in the periodical
Once a week, of the 22d and 29th October and 5th November
last. Possessing a thorough acquaintance with the Arctic Regions, the distinguished seaman has shown more than his ordinary power of description, in placing before the public his
conception of what may have been the chief occurrences in the
voyage of the 'Erebus' and 'Terror,' and the last days of
Franklin, as founded upon an acquaintance with the character
of the chief and his associates, and the record and relics obtained by M'Clintock. This sketch is prefaced by a spirited
and graceful outline of all previous geographical discoveries,
from the day when they were originated by the father of all
modern Arctic enterprise, Sir John Barrow, to whom, and to
many other eminent persons, from Sir Edward Parry downward,
I have in various Geographical Addresses offered the tribute
of my admiration.

Sir John Barrow, we perceive that, in addition to the discovery of the course followed by the 'Erebus' and 'Terror,' some most important geographical data have been accumulated by the last expedition of Lady Franklin.

Thus, M'Clintock has proved that the strait named by Kenedy in an earlier private expedition of Lady Franklin after his companion the brave Lieutenant Bellot, and which has hitherto been regarded only as an impassable frozen channel, or ignored as a channel at all, is a navigable strait, the south shore of which is thus seen to be the northernmost land of the continent of America.

M'Clintock has also laid down the hitherto unknown coast-line of Boothia, southward from Bellot Strait to the Magnetic Pole, has delineated the whole of King William's Island, and opened a new and capacious, though ice-choked channel, suspected before, but not proved, to exist, extending from Victoria Strait in a northwest direction to Melville or Parry Sound. The latter discovery rewarded the individual exertions of Captain Allen Young, but will very properly, at Lady Franklin's request, bear the name of the leader of the 'Fox' expedition, who had himself assigned to it the name of the widow of Franklin.*

---

* In his volume before cited, p. 12, Mr. John Brown gave strong reasons (which he had held for some time) for believing in the existence of the very channel which now bears the name of M'Clintock. It is, however, the opinion both of that officer and his associates, as also of Captain Sherard Osborn, that

Neither has the expedition been unproductive of scientific results. For, whilst many persons will be interested in the popular descriptions of the native Esquimaux, as well as of the lower animals, the man of science will hereafter be further gratified by having presented to him, in the form of an additional Appendix,* most valuable details relating to the zoology botany, meteorology, and especially to the terrestrial magnetism, of the region examined.

Lastly, M'Clintock has convinced himself, that the best way of securing the passage of a ship from the Atlantic to the Pacific, is by following, as near as possible, the coast-line of North America: indeed, it is his opinion, founded upon a large experience, that no passage by a ship can ever be accomplished in a more northern direction. This, it is well known, was the favorite theory of Franklin, who had himself, along with Richardson, Back, Beechey, Dease, Simpson and Rae, surveyed the whole of that same North American coast from the Back or Great Fish River to Behring Strait. Thus, when Franklin sailed in 1845, the discovery of a North-West Passage was reduced to the finding a link between the latter survey and the discoveries of Parry, who had already, to his great renown, opened the first half of a more northern course from east to west, when he was

---

Franklin could not have reached the spot where his ships were beset by proceeding down that ice-choked channel, but that he must have sailed down Peel Sound.

* Much of this Appendix will be prepared by Dr. David Walker.

arrested by the impenetrable ice-barrier at Melville Island.

And here it is to be remembered, that the tract in which the record and the relics have been found, is just that to which Lady Franklin herself specially directed Kenedy, the commander of the 'Prince Albert,' in her second private expedition in 1852; and had that intrepid explorer not been induced to search northward of Bellot Strait, but had felt himself able to follow the course indicated by his sagacious employer, there can be no doubt, that much more satisfactory results would have been obtained than those which, after a lapse of seven years, have now been realized by the undaunted perseverance of Lady Franklin, and the skill and courage of M'Clintock.

The natural modesty of this commander has, I am bound to say, prevented his doing common justice, in the following journal, to his own conduct—conduct which can be estimated by those only who have listened to the testimony of the officers serving with and under the man, whose great qualities in moments of extreme peril elicited their heartiest admiration and ensured their perfect confidence.

In writing this Preface (which I do at the request of the promoters of the last search), I may state that, having occupied the Chair of the Royal Geographical Society in 1845, when my cherished friend, Sir John Franklin, went forth for the third time to seek a North-West passage, it became my bounden duty, in subsequent years, when his absence created much anxiety, and when I reoccupied the same position, ardently to promote the employment of searching expeditions, and warmly to sustain Lady Franklin's endeavors in this holy cause.

Imbued with such feelings, I must be permitted to say, that no event in my life gave me purer delight than when Captain Collinson, whose labors to support and carry out this last search have been signally serviceable, forwarded to me a telegram to be communicated to the British Association at Aberdeen announcing the success of M'Clintock. That document reached Balmoral on the 22d of September last, when the men of science were invited thither by their Sovereign. Great was the satisfaction caused by the diffusion of these good tidings among my associates (the distinguished Arctic explorers Admiral Sir James Ross and General Sabine being present); and it was most cheering to us to know, that the Queen and our Royal President* took the deepest interest in this intelligence—such as, indeed, they have always evinced whenever the search for the missing navigators has been brought under their consideration. The imme-

---

* At the Aberdeen meeting the Prince Consort thus spoke: "The Aberdeen whaler braves the icy regions of the Polar Sea to seek and to battle with the great monster of the deep; he has materially assisted in opening these icebound regions to the researches of science; he fearlessly aided in the search after Sir John Franklin and his gallant companions whom their country sent forth on this mission; but to whom Providence alas! has denied the reward of their labors, the return to their homes, to the affectionate embrace of their families and friends, and the acknowledgments of a grateful nation."

diate bestowal of the Arctic medal upon all the officers and men of the 'Fox' is a pleasing proof that
this interest is well sustained.

But these few introductory sentences must not be
extended; and I invite the reader at once to peruse
the Journal of M'Clintock, which will gratify every
lover of truthful and ardent research, though it will
leave him impressed with the sad belief, that the end
of the companions of Franklin has been truly recorded by the native Esquimaux, who saw these noble fellows "fall down and die as they walked along
the ice."

Looking to the fact, that little or no fresh food
could have been obtained by the crews of the 'Erebus' and 'Terror' during their long imprisonment
of twenty months, in so frightfully sterile a region as
that in which the ships were abandoned—so sterile
that it is even deserted by the Esquimaux—and also
to the want of sustenance in spring at the mouth of
the Back River, all the Arctic naval authorities with
whom I have conversed, coincide with M'Clintock
and his associates in the belief, that none of the missing navigators can now be living.

Painful as is the realization of this tragic event, let
us now dwell only on the reflection that, while the
North-West passage has been solved by the heroic
self-sacrifice of Franklin, Crozier, Fitzjames, and their
associates, the searches after them, which are now
terminated, have, at a very small loss of life, not only
added prodigiously to geographical knowledge, but
have, in times of peace, been the best school for test-

ing, by the severest trials, the skill and endurance of many a brave seaman. In her hour of need—should need arise—England knows that such men will nobly do their duty.

RODERICK I. MURCHISON.

CONTENTS.

CHAPTER I.

CHAPTER II.

CHAPTER III.

CHAPTER IV.

CHAPTER V.

CHAPTER VI.

CHAPTER VII.

CHAPTER VIII.

CHAPTER IX.

CHAPTER X.

CHAPTER XI.

APPENDIX.

LIST OF ILLUSTRATIONS.

SIR JOHN FRANKLIN.

CHAPTER I.

Cause of delay in equipment—Fittings of the 'Fox'—Volunteers for
Arctic service—Assistance from public departments—Reflections upon
the undertaking—Instructions and departure—Orkneys and Greenland—Fine Arctic scenery—Danish establishments in Greenland—
Frederickshaab, in Davis' Straits.

IT is now a matter of history how Government and private expeditions prosecuted, with unprecedented zeal and
perseverance, the search for Sir John Franklin's ships, between the years 1847–55; and that the only ray of information gleaned was that afforded by the inscriptions upon
three tombstones at Beechey Island, briefly recording the
names and dates of the deaths of those individuals of the
lost expedition, who thus early fell in the cause of science
and of their country.

In this manner were we made aware of the locality where
the Franklin expedition passed its first Arctic winter. The
traces assuring us of that fact, were discovered in August,
1850, by Captain Ommanney, R. N., of H. M. S. 'Assistance,' and by Captain Penny, of the 'Lady Franklin.'

In October, 1854, Dr. Rae brought home the only addi-

(31)

tional information respecting them which has ever reached us. From the Esquimaux of Boothia Felix he learned that a party of about forty white men were met on the west coast of King William's Island, and from thence traveled on to the mouth of the Great Fish River, where they all perished of starvation, and that this tragic event occurred apparently in the spring of 1850.

Some relics obtained from these natives, and brought home by Dr. Rae, were proved to have belonged to Sir John Franklin and several of his associates.

The Government caused an exploring party to descend the Fish River in 1855; but, although sufficient traces were found to prove that some portion of the crews of the 'Erebus' and 'Terror' had actually landed on the bank of that river, and traces existed of them up to Franklin Rapids, no additional information was obtained either from the discovery of records, or through the Esquimaux. Mr. Anderson, the Hudson Bay Company's officer in charge, and his small party, deserve credit for their perseverance and skill; but they were not furnished with the necessary means of accomplishing their mission. Mr. Anderson could not obtain an interpreter, and the two frail bark canoes in which his whole party embarked were almost worn out before they reached the locality to be searched. It is not surprising that such an expedition caused very considerable excitement at home.

Lady Franklin, and the advocates for further search, now pressed upon Government the necessity of following up, in a more effectual manner, the traces accidentally found by Dr. Rae, and, in fact, of rendering the seach complete by one more effort, involving but little of hazard or expense. It was not until April, 1857, that any decisive answer was given to Lady Franklin's appeal. (See Appendix No. 1.)

Sir Charles Wood then stated "that the members of Her Majesty's Government, having come, with great regret, to the conclusion that there was no prospect of saving life, would not be justified, for any objects which in their opinion could be obtained by an expedition to the Arctic seas, in exposing the lives of officers and men to the risk inseparable from such an enterprise."

Lady Franklin, upon this final disappointment of her hopes, had no hesitation in immediately preparing to send out a searching expedition, equipped and stored at her own cost. But she was not left alone. Many friends of the cause—including some of the most distinguished scientific men in England,* and especially Sir Roderick Murchison, whose zeal was as practical as it was enlightened—hastened to tender their aid, and soon a very considerable sum was raised in furtherance of so truly noble an effort.

On the 18th of April, 1857, Lady Franklin did me the honor to offer me the command of the proposed expedition; it was of course most cheerfully accepted. As a post of honor and some difficulty, it possessed quite sufficient charms for a naval officer who had already served in three consecutive expeditions from 1848 to 1854. I was thoroughly conversant with all the details of this peculiar service; and I confess, moreover, that my whole heart was in the cause. How could I do otherwise than devote myself to save at least the record of faithful service, even unto death, of my brother officers and seamen? and, being one of those by whose united efforts not only the Franklin search, but the Geography of Arctic America, has been brought so nearly to completion, I could not willingly resign to posterity the honor of filling up even the small remaining blank upon our maps.

To leave these discoveries incomplete, more especially in a quarter through which the tidal stream actually demonstrates the existence of a channel—the only remaining hope

---

* A list of them and their subscriptions to be given in Appendix.

of a practicable north-west passage—would indeed be leaving strong inducements for future explorers to reap the rich reward of our long-continued exertions.

I immediately applied to the Admiralty for leave of absence to complete the Franklin search; and on the 23d received at Dublin the telegraphic message from Lady Franklin : "Your leave is granted; the 'Fox' is mine; the refit will commence immediately." She had already purchased the screw-yacht 'Fox,' of 177 tons burthen, and now placed her, together with the necessary funds, at my disposal.

Let me explain what is here implied by the simple word refit. The velvet hangings and splendid furniture of the yacht, and also everything not constituting a part of the vessel's strengthening, were to be removed; the large skylights and capacious ladderways had to be reduced to limits more adapted to a polar clime; the whole vessel to be externally sheathed with stout planking, and internally fortified by strong cross-beams, longitudinal beams, iron stanchions, and diagonal fastenings; the false keel taken off, the slender brass propeller replaced by a massive iron one, the boiler taken out, altered and enlarged; the sharp stem to be cased in iron until it resembled a ponderous chisel set up edgeways; even the yacht's rig had to be altered.

She was placed in the hands of her builders, Messrs. Hall & Co., of Aberdeen, who displayed even more than their usual activity in effecting these necessary alterations, for it was determined that the 'Fox' should sail by the 1st July.

Internally she was fitted up with the strictest economy in every sense, and the officers were crammed into pigeon-holes, styled cabins, in order to make room for provisions and stores; our mess-room, for five persons, measured eight feet square. The ordinary heating apparatus for winter use was dispensed with, and its place supplied by a

few very small stoves.   The 'Fox' had been the property
of the late Sir Richard Stratton, Bart., who made but one
trip to Norway in her, and she was purchased by Lady
Franklin from his executors for £2000.

Having thus far commenced the refit of the vessel, I
turned my attention to the selection of a crew, and to the
requisite clothing and provisions for our voyage.

Many worthy old shipmates, my companions in the pre
vious Arctic voyages, most readily volunteered their ser·
vices, and they were as cheerfully accepted, for it was my
anxious wish to gather round me well-tried men, who were
aware of the duties expected of them, and accustomed to
naval discipline.   Hence, out of the twenty-five souls composing our small company, seventeen had previously served in
the Arctic search.

Expeditions of this kind are always popular with seamen, and innumerable were the applications sent to me;
but still more abundant were the offers to "serve in any
capacity," which poured in from all parts of the country,
from people of all classes, many of whom had never seen
the sea.   It was, of course, impossible to accede to any of
these latter proposals, yet, for my own part, I could not
but feel gratified at such convincing proofs that the spirit
of the country was favorable to us, and that the ardent
love of hardy enterprise still lives amongst Englishmen, as
of old, to be cherished, I trust, as the most valuable of our
national characteristics—as that which has so largely contributed to make England what she is.

My second in command was Lieutenant W. R. Hobson,
R.N., an officer already distinguished in Arctic service.
Captain Allen Young joined me as sailing-master, con-
tributing not only his valuable services but largely of his
private funds to the expedition.   This gentleman had previously commanded some of our very finest merchant ships,
the latest being the steam-transport "Adelaide" of 2500

tons : he had but recently returned, in ill health, from the Black Sea, where he was most actively employed during the greater part of the Crimean campaign. Nothing that I could say would add to the merit of such singularly generous and disinterested conduct. David Walker, M.D., volunteered for the post of surgeon and naturalist ; he also undertook the photographic department; and just before sailing, Carl Petersen, now so well known to Arctic readers as the Esquimaux interpreter in the expeditions of Captain Penny and Dr. Kane, came to join me from Copenhagen, although landed there from Greenland only six days previously, after an absence of a year from his family : we were indebted to Sir Roderick Murchison and the electric telegraph for securing his valuable services.

Like the Paris omnibuses we were at length *tout complet*, and quite as anxious to make a start.

Ample provisions for twenty-eight months were embarked, including preserved vegetables, lemon-juice, and pickles, for daily consumption, and preserved meats for every third day : also as much of Messrs. Allsopp's stoutest ale as we could find room for. The Government, although declining to send out an expedition, yet now contributed liberally to our supplies. All our arms, powder, shot, powder for ice-blasting, rockets, maroons, and signal mortar, were furnished by the Board of Ordnance. The Admiralty caused 6682 lbs. of pemmican to be prepared for our use. Not less than 85,000 lbs. of this invaluable food have been prepared since 1845 at the Royal Clarence Victualing Yard, Gosport, for the use of the Arctic Expeditions. It is composed of prime beef cut into thin slices and dried over a wood fire ; then pounded up and mixed with about an equal weight of melted beef fat. The pemmican is then pressed into cases capable of containing 42 lbs. each. The Admiralty supplied us with all the requisite ice-gear, such as saws from ten to eighteen feet in length, ice-anchors, and

FIG. 1.

JONES SOUND

NORTH DEVON

MELVILLE BAY

Sabine I.
Aug.

3RD NOV.

23RD OCT.

B A F F I N

Franklins supposed track

7TH DEC.

LANCASTER SOUND

C. Liverpool

1ST JAN 1858

B A Y

C. Walter

Ponds B.

Uternivi

1ST FEB.

COCKBURN

OMENAK FIORD

WAIGAT

Scott Inlet

ISLAND

DISCO I.

5TH MAR.

Godhavn

DISCO

S. Rater

1ST APRIL

CUMBERLAND

ISLAND

D A V I S

Walsingham

ARCTIC CIRCLE

S T R A I T

FOX CHANNEL

17TH APRIL

26TH APRIL

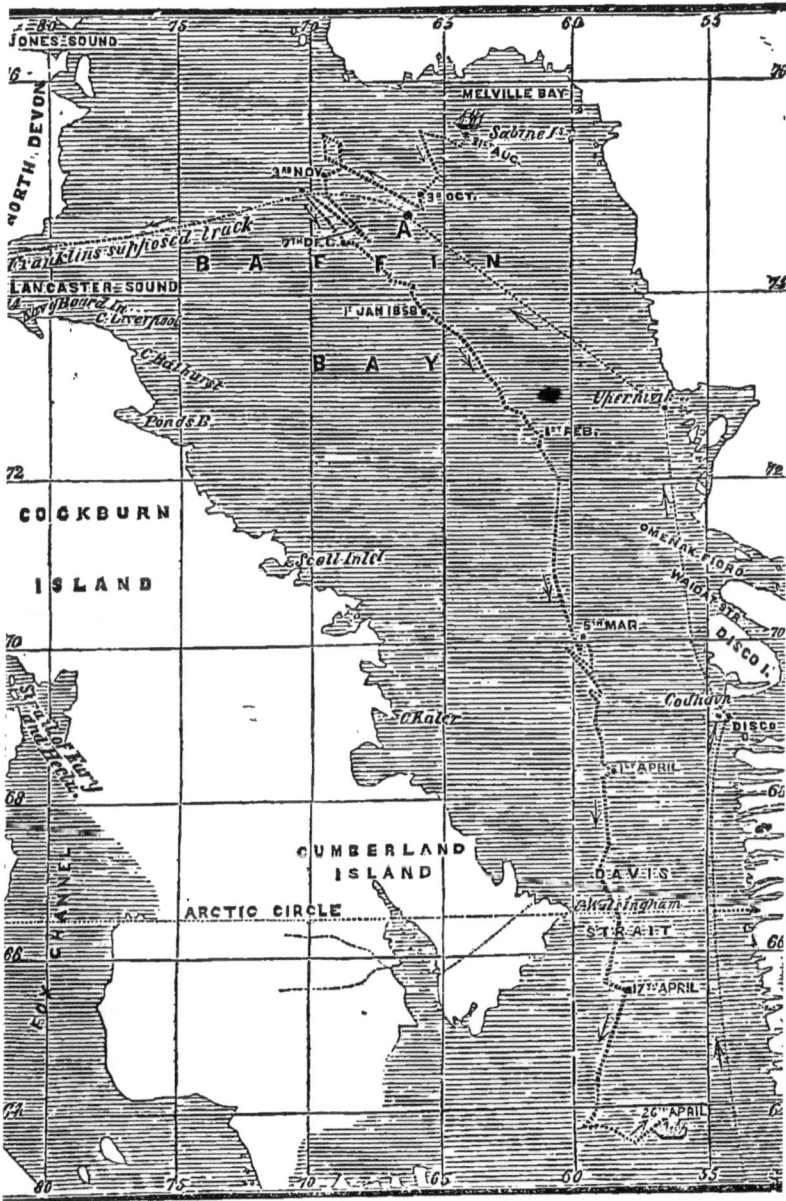

SKETCH MAP OF THE DRIFT OF THE 'FOX' DOWN BAFFIN'S BAY IN
THE FLOATING ICE.

ice-claws: also with our winter housing, medicines, pure lemon-juice, seamen's library, hydrographical instruments, charts, chronometers, and an ample supply of arctic clothing which had remained in store from former expeditions. The Board of Trade contributed a variety of meteorological and nautical instruments and journals; and I found that I had but to ask of these departments for what was required, and if in store it was at once granted. I asked, however, only for such things as were indispensably necessary.

The President and Council of the Royal Society voted the sum of 50*l.* from their donation fund for the purchase of magnetic and other scientific instruments, in order that our anticipated approach to so interesting a locality as the Magnetic Pole might not be altogether barren of results.

Being desirous to retain for my vessel the privileges she formerly enjoyed as a yacht, my wishes were very promptly gratified; in the first instance by the Royal Harwich Yacht Club, of which my officers and myself were enrolled as members—the Commodore, A. Arcedeckne, Esq., presenting my vessel with the handsome ensign and burgee of the Club; and shortly afterwards by my being elected a member of the Royal Victoria Yacht Club for the period of my voyage. Lastly, upon the very day of sailing, I was proposed for the Royal Yacht Squadron, to which the yacht had previously belonged when the property of Sir Richard Stratton.

Throughout the whole period required for our equipment, I constantly experienced the heartiest co-operation and earnest good will from all with whom my varied duties brought me in contact. Deep sympathy with Lady Franklin in her distress, her self-devotion and sacrifice of fortune, and an earnest desire to extend succor to any chance survivors of the ill-fated expedition who might still exist, or at least, to ascertain their fate, and rescue from oblivion their heroic deeds, seemed the natural promptings of every honest English heart. It is needless to add that this experience of public opinion confirmed my own impression that the glorious mission intrusted to me was in reality a *great national duty.* I could not but feel that, if the gigantic and admirably equipped national expeditions sent out on precisely the same duty, and reflecting so much credit upon the Board of Admiralty, were ranked amongst the noblest efforts in the cause of humanity any nation ever engaged in, and that, if high honor was awarded to all composing those splendid expeditions, surely the effort became still more remarkable and worthy of approbation when its means were limited to one little vessel, containing but twenty-five souls, equipped and provisioned (although efficiently, yet) in a manner more according with the limited resources of a private individual than with those of the public purse. The less the means, the more arduous I felt was the achievement. The greater the risk—for the 'Fox' was to be launched alone into those turbulent seas from which every other vessel had long since been withdrawn— the more glorious would be the success, the more honorable even the defeat, if again defeat awaits us.

Upon the last day of June, Lady Franklin, accompanied by her niece Miss Sophia Cracroft, and Capt. Maguire, R. N., came on board to bid us farewell, for we purposed sailing in the evening. Seeing how deeply agitated she was on leaving the ship, I endeavored to repress the enthusiasm of my crew, but without avail; it found vent in three prolonged, hearty cheers. The strong feeling which prompted them was truly sincere; and this unbidden exhibition of it can hardly have gratified her for whom it was intended more than it did myself.

I must here insert the only written instructions I could prevail upon Lady Franklin to give me; they were not **read** until the 'Fox' was fairly in the Atlantic.

ABERDEEN. *June* 29, 1857.

My dear Captain M'Clintock,

You have kindly invited me to give you "Instructions," but I cannot bring myself to feel that it would be right in me in any way to influence your judgment in the conduct of your noble undertaking; and indeed I have no temptation to do so, since it appears to me that your views are almost identical with those which I had independently formed before I had the advantage of being thoroughly possessed of yours. But had this been otherwise, I trust you would have found me ready to prove the implicit confidence I place in you by yielding my own views to your more enlightened judgment; knowing too as I do that your whole heart also is in the cause, even as my own is. As to the objects of the expedition and their relative importance, I am sure you know that the rescue of any possible survivor of the 'Erebus' and 'Terror' would be to me, as it would be to you, the noblest result of our efforts.

To this object I wish every other to be subordinate; and next to it in importance is the recovery of the unspeakably precious documents of the expedition, public and private, and the personal relics of my dear husband and his companions.

And lastly, I trust it may be in your power to confirm, directly or inferentially, the claims of my husband's expedition to the earliest discovery of the passage, which, if Dr. Rae's report be true (and the Government of our country has accepted and rewarded it as such), these martyrs in a noble cause achieved at their last extremity, after five long years of labor and suffering, if not at an earlier period.

I am sure you will do all that man can do for the attainment of all these objects; my only fear is that you may spend yourselves too much in the effort; and you must therefore let me tell you how much dearer to me even than

any of them is the preservation of the valuable lives of the
little band of heroes who are your companions and followers.

May God in his great mercy preserve you all from harm
amidst the labors and perils which await you, and restore
you to us in health and safety as well as honor! As to the
honor I can have *no* misgiving. It will be yours as much
if you fail (since you *may* fail in spite of every effort) as if
you succeed; and be assured that, under *any and all circumstances whatever*, such is my unbounded confidence in
you, you will ever possess and be entitled to the enduring
gratitude of your sincere and attached friend,

JANE FRANKLIN.

We were not destined to get to sea that evening. The
'Fox,' hitherto during her brief career, accustomed only to
the restraint imposed upon a gilded pet in summer seas,
seemed to have got an inkling that her duty henceforth was
to combat with difficulties, and, entering fully into the
spirit of the cruise, answered her helm so much more
readily than the pilot expected that she ran aground upon
the bar. She was promptly shored up, and remained in that
position until next morning, when she floated off unhurt at
high water, and commenced her long and lonely voyage.

Scarcely had we left the busy world behind us when we
were actively engaged in making arrangements for present
comfort and future exertion. How busy, how happy, and
how full of hope we all were then!

On the night of the 2d of July we passed through the
Pentland Firth, where the tide rushing impetuously against
a strong wind raised up a tremendous sea, amid which
the little vessel struggled bravely under steam and canvas.
The bleak wild shores of Orkney, the still wilder pilot's
crew, and their hoarse screams and unintelligible dialect,
the shrill cry of innumerable sea-birds, the howling breeze

and angry sea, made us feel as if we had suddenly awoke in Greenland itself. The southern extremity of that ice-locked continent became visible on the 12th. It is quaintly named Cape Farewell; but whether by some sanguine outward-bound adventurer who fancied that in leaving Greenland behind him he had already secured his passage to Cathay; or whether by the wearied homesick mariner, feebly escaping from the grasp of winter in his shattered bark, and firmly purposing to bid a long farewell to this cheerless land, history altogether fails to enlighten us.

From January until July this coast is usually rendered unapproachable by a broad margin of heavy ice, which drifts there from the vicinity of Spitzbergen, and, lapping round the Cape, extends alongshore to the northward about as far as Baal's River, a distance of 250 miles. Although it effectually blockades the ports of South Greenland for the greater part of the summer, and is justly dreaded by the captains of the Greenland traders, it confers important benefits upon the Greenlander by bearing to his shores immense numbers of seals and many bears. The same current which conveys hither all this ice is also freighted with a scarcely less valuable supply of driftwood from the Siberian rivers.

About this time, one of my crew showing symptoms of diseased lungs, I determined to embrace the earliest opportunity of sending him home out of a climate so fatal to those who are thus affected; and having learnt from Mr. Petersen, who had quitted Greenland only in April last, that a vessel would very soon leave Frederickshaab for Copenhagen, I resolved to go to that place in order to catch this homeward-bound ship.

It was necessary to push through the Spitzbergen ice, and we fortunately succeeded in doing so after eighteen hours of buffeting with this formidable enemy; at first we found it tolerably loose, and the wind being strong and favorable, we thumped along pleasantly enough; but as we advanced, the ice became much more closely packed, a thick fog came on, and many hard knocks were exchanged; at length our steam carried us through into the broad belt of clear water between the ice and land, which Petersen assures me always exists here at this season.

The dense fog now prevented further progress, and as evening closed in I gave up all hope of improvement for the night, when suddenly the fog rolled back upon the land, disclosing some islets close to us, then the rugged points of mainland, and at length, lifting altogether, the distant snowy mountain-peaks against a deep blue sky.

The evening became bright and delightful; the whole extent of coast was fringed with innumerable islets, backed by lofty mountains, and, being richly tinted by a glorious western sun, formed an unusually splendid sight. Greenland unveiled to our anxious gaze that memorable evening, all the magnificence of her natural beauty. Was it to welcome us that she thus cast off her dingy outer mantle, and shone forth radiant with smiles?—such winning smiles!

A faint streak of mist, which we could not account for, appeared to float across a low, wide interval in the mountain range; the telescope revealed its true character,—it was a portion of the distant glacier. We found ourselves upon the Tallard Bank, 30 miles north of our port, having been rapidly carried northwards by the Spitzbergen current.

July 20th.—This morning the chief trader of the settlement, or, as he is more usually styled by the English, the Governor, came off to us, and his pilot soon conducted us into the safe little harbor of Frederickshaab. I was much gratified to learn that we were just in time to secure a passage home for our ailing shipmate.

For trading purposes Greenland is monopolized by the Danish Government; its Esquimaux and mixed population amount to about 7000 souls. About 1000 Danes reside constantly there for the purpose of conducting the trade, which consists almost exclusively in the exchange of European goods for oil and the skins of seals, reindeer, and a few other animals.

The Esquimaux are not subject to Danish laws, but although proud of their nominal independence they are sincerely attached to the Danes, and with abundant reason; a Lutheran clergyman, a doctor, and a schoolmaster, whose duty it is to give gratuitous instruction and relief, are paid by the Government, and attached to each district; and when these improvident people are in distress, which not unfrequently happens during the long winters, provisions are issued to them free of cost; spirits are strictly prohibited. All of them have become Christians, and many can read and write.

Have we English done more, or as much, for the aborigines in any of our numerous colonies, and especially for the Esquimaux within our own territories of Labrador and Hudson's Bay?

Greenland is divided into two inspectorates, the northern and southern; the inspector of the latter division, Dr. Rink, had arrived at Frederickshaab upon his summer round of visits only the day previous to ourselves. He came on board to call upon me, and after Divine service I landed, and enjoyed a ramble with him over the moss-clad hills. Our first meeting was in North Greenland, in 1848; we had not seen one another since, so we had much to talk about. Dr. Rink is a gentleman of acknowledged talent, a distinguished traveler, and is thoroughly conversant with the sciences of geology and botany.

Unfortunately for me his excellent work on Greenland has not been translated into English.

We were kindly permitted to purchase eight tons of coals, and such small things as were required; the only fresh supplies to be obtained beside codfish, which was abundant,

consisted of a very few ptarmigan and hares, and a couple
of kids; these last are scarce.   Some goats exist, but for
eight months out of the year they are shut up in a house,
and even now — in midsummer — are only let out in the
daytime.   We also purchased of the Esquimaux some specimens of Esquimaux workmanship, such as models of the
native dresses, kayaks, etc., also birds' skins and eggs.   I
saw fine specimens of a white swan, and of a bird said to
be extremely rare in Greenland — it was a species of grebe,
Podiceps cristatus, I imagine.   Frederickshaab is just now
well supplied with wood : besides an unseaworthy brig, the
wreck of a large timber-ship lay on the beach, and an
abandoned timber-vessel, which was met with between Ice-
land and Greenland in July by Prince Napoleon, drifted
upon the coast 30 miles to the northward in the following
September.

CHAPTER II.

Fiskernaes and Esquimaux — The 'Fox' reaches Disco — Disco Fiord –
Summer scenery — Waigat Strait — Coaling from the mine — Purchas-
ing Esquimaux dogs — Heavy gale off Upernivik — Melville Bay —
The middle ice — The great glacier of Greenland — Reindeer cross
the glacier.

23d *July.*—SAILED the day before yesterday for Godhaab.
The fog was thick, and wind strong and contrary, but the
current being favorable we found ourselves off the small
out-station of Fiskernaes, when early this morning our fore
topmast was carried away; this accident induced me to run
in and anchor for the purpose of repairing the damage.

After passing within the outer islets, the Moravian settlement of Lichtenfels came in view upon the right hand; it
consists of a large, sombre-looking wooden house, over
which is a belfry, a smaller wooden house, and about a
dozen native huts, roofed with sods, and scarcely distinguishable from the ground they stand on, even at a very short
distance. The land immediately behind is a barren rocky
steep, now just sufficiently denuded of snow to look desolate in the extreme. A strong tide was setting out of the
fiord as we approached, and anchored in the rocky little
cove of Fiskernaes; here we were not only sheltered from
the wind, but the steep dark rocks within a ship's length on
each side of us, reflected a strong heat, whilst large mosqui-
toes lost no time in paying us their annoying visits. This
remote spot has been visited by the Arctic voyagers, Captain Inglefield, R.N., and Dr. Kane, U.S.N., and still
more recently by Prince Napoleon. Dr. Kane's account

of his visit is full and very interesting. Cod-fishing was now in full activity, and the few men not so employed had gone up the fiord to hunt reindeer.

The solitary dwelling-house belongs, of course, to the chief trader, and is a model of cleanliness and order; built of wood, it exhibits all the resources of the painter's art; the exterior is a dull red, the window-frames are white, floors yellow, wooden partitions and low ceilings pale blue. The lady of the house had resided here for about eight years, and appeared to us to be, and acknowledged she was, heartily tired of the solitude. She gave me coffee, and some seeds for cultivation at our winter quarters; these were lettuce, spinach, turnips, carraway and peas, the latter being the common kind used on board ship; usually they have only produced leaves on this spot, but once the young peas grew large enough for the table. I expressed a wish to see the interior of an Esquimaux tent. Petersen pulled aside the thin membrane of some animal which hung across the doorway, and served to exclude the wind, but admitted light, for, although past midnight, the sun was up. Some seven or eight individuals lay within, closely packed upon the ground; the heads of old and young, males and females, being just visible above the common covering. Going to bed here, only means lying down with your clothes on, upon a reindeer skin, wherever you can find room, and pulling another fur-robe over you.

Fiskernaes appeared to be a sunny little nook, yet all the people we saw there were suffering from colds and coughs, and many deaths had occurred during the spring. The boys brought us handfuls of rough garnets, some of them as large as walnuts, receiving with evident satisfaction biscuits in exchange.

By next morning we were able to put to sea, and early on the day following arrived off the large settlement of Godhaab; it is in the "Gilbert Sound" of Davis, and appears in many old charts as Baal's River. Almost adjoining Godhaab is the Moravian settlement of New Herrnhut.   Here it was that Hans Egede, the missionary father of Greenland, established himself in 1721, and thus reopened the communication between Europe and Greenland, which had ceased upon the extinction of its early Scandinavian settlers, in the 14th century.

A few years after Egede's successful beginning, the Moravian mission still existing under the name of New Herrnhut was established.   At present the Moravians support four missions in Greenland; they are not subject to the Danish authorities, but are not permitted in any way to trade.

As we were about to enter the harbor, the Danish vessel —the sole object of our visit—came out, so not a moment was lost in sending on board our invalid and our letter-bag, and in landing our coasting pilot.   This man had brought us up from Frederickshaab for the very moderate sum of three pounds; he was an Esquimaux, and, as the brother of poor Hans, Dr. Kane's unhappy dog-driver, was received with favor amongst us, and soon won our esteem by his quiet, obliging disposition, as also by his ability in the discharge of his duty; he was so keensighted, and so vigilant, it was quite a comfort to have him on board during the foggy weather, for he could recognise, on the instant, every rock or point, even when dimly looming through the mist. We were not long in discovering that his absence was a loss to us.

When passing out to the north of the Kookornen Islands, the wind suddenly failed, and at the same time a swell from to seaward reached us; we therefore had considerable difficulty in towing the ship clear of the rocks; for nearly half an hour our position was most critical.

July 31*st.*—Anchored at Godhaven (or Lievely), in Disco, for a few hours.   I presented a letter from the Di-

4

rectors of the Royal Greenland Commerce to the Inspector
of North Greenland, Mr. Olrik, authorising him to furnish
us with any needful supplies.   Our only wants were sledge-
dogs and a native to manage them.   We soon obtained ten
of the former, but were advised to go into Disco Fiord,
where many of the Esquimaux were busy in taking and
drying salmon-trout, and where some would most probably
be obtained.

I was much pleased with Mr. Olrik's kind reception of
me, and soon found him to be not only agreeable but well
informed ; born in Greenland, of Danish parents, he is
thoroughly conversant with the language and habits of the
Esquimaux, and has devoted much of his leisure time in
collecting rare specimens of the animal, vegetable, and
mineral productions of the country.   I came away enriched
by some fossils from the fossil forest of Atanekerdluk, also
with specimens of native coal.

It was here I met with the late commanders of the
whalers ' Gipsy' and ' Undaunted,' of Peterhead, which had
been crushed by the ice in Melville Bay, five or six weeks
previously ; all the other whalers had returned from the
north, along the pack edge, and passed south of Disco.
They said that the ice in Melville Bay was all broken up,
and that they thought we should find but little difficulty at
this late period in passing through it into the North Water.

Leaving Godhaven in the afternoon with a native pilot,
we found ourselves some 10 or 12 miles up Disco Fiord at
an early hour next morning.   After despatching the pilot
to announce our arrival to his countrymen at their fishing
station, 7 or 8 miles further up, the Doctor and I landed
upon the north side to explore.

The scenery is charming, lofty hills of trap rock, with
unusually rich slopes (for the 70th parallel) descending to
the fiord, and strewed with boulders of gneiss and granite.
We found the blue campanula holding a conspicuous place

amongst the wild flowers.   I do not know a more enticing spot in Greenland for a week's shooting, fishing, and yachting than Disco Fiord; hares and ptarmigan may be found along the bases of the hills; ducks are most abundant upon the fiord, and delicious salmon-trout very plentiful in the rivers.   Formerly Disco was famed for the large size and abundance of its reindeer; but for some unexplained reason they now confine themselves to the mainland.

At this season the natives of Godhaab resort here and enjoy the trout fishery,—it is truly their season of harvest: the weather is pleasant, food delicious and abundant, and the labor an agreeable pastime.

Some kayaks soon came off to the ship, bringing salmon-trout, both fresh and smoked.

A young Esquimaux, named Christian, volunteered his services as our dog-driver, and was accepted; he is about twenty-three years of age, unmarried, and an orphan.   The men soon thoroughly washed and cropped him: soap and scissors being novelties to an Esquimaux: they then rigged him in sailor's clothes; he was evidently not at home in them, but was not the less proud of his improved appearance, as reflected in the admiring glances of his countrymen.

We now hastened away to the Waigat Strait to complete our coals.   When passing Godhaven, the pilot was launched off our deck in his little kayak without stopping the ship ! As a kayak is usually about 18 feet long, 8 inches deep, and only 16 or 17 inches wide, it requires great expertness to perform such a feat without the addition of a capsize.

4th August.—Entered the Waigat yesterday morning, slowly steaming through a sea of glass.   Its surface was only rippled by the myriads of eider-ducks which extended over it for several miles: most of them were immature in plumage, and were probably the birds of last year.

After running about twenty-four miles, toward evening we approached a low range of sandstone cliffs on the Disco shore, in which horizontal seams of coal were seen. Here we anchored, and immediately commenced coaling. It was fortunate we did so, for soon it began to blow hard; and ere noon to-day we were obliged, for the safety of the ship, to leave our exposed anchorage, having however secured eight or nine tons of tolerable coal. Formerly these coal seams were worked for the supply of the neighboring settlements, but for several years past it has been found more profitable and convenient to send out coals from Denmark, and thus permit the natives to devote their whole time to the seal-fishery.

The Waigat scenery is unusually grand; the strait varies from 3 to 5 leagues in width; on each side are mountains of 3000 feet in height. The Disco side, upon which we landed, is composed of trap, sandstone appearing only at the beach, and occasionally rising in cliffs to about 100 feet. Upon the moss-clad slopes many fragments of quartz and zeolite were met with. The north end of Disco is almost a precipice to its snow-capped summit, which is 4000 feet high.

5th.—A pleasant fair wind carries us rapidly northward, passing many icebergs. Our rigging is richly garnished with split codfish, which we hoped would dry and keep; but a warm day in Disco Fiord, and much rain with a southerly gale in the Waigat, have destroyed it for our own use. It is however still valuable as food for our dogs. I am very anxious to complete my stock of these our native auxiliaries, as without them we cannot hope to explore all the lands which it is the object of our voyage to search. We could only obtain ten at Godhaven, and require twenty more.

6th.—By Petersen's intimate knowledge of the coast we were enabled to run close into the little settlement of Proven during the night, and obtain a few dogs and dogs' food. This morning we reached the extreme sta-

tion of Upernivik, the last trace of civilization we shall
meet with for some time. It is in lat. 72¾ N. Here Petersen resided for twelve of the eighteen years he has spent in
Greenland, and his unlooked-for re-appearance astonished
and delighted the small community, more especially Governor Fleischer and his household, who received us with a
most hearty welcome.

7th.—Yesterday, when we hove to off Upernivik, the
weather was very bad and rapidly growing worse, therefore
our stay was limited to a couple of hours. The last letters
for home were landed, fourteen dogs and a quantity of
seal's flesh for them embarked, and the ship's head was
turned seaward.

It 'was then blowing a southerly gale, with overcast,
murky sky, and a heavy sea running. When four miles outside the outer island, breakers were suddenly discovered
ahead, only just in time to avoid the ledge of sunken rocks
upon which the sea was beating most violently. Many
such rocks lie at considerable distances beyond the islands
which border this coast, and greatly add to the dangers
of its navigation. Being now fairly at sea, and the ship under
easy sail for the night, I went early to bed in the hope of
sleeping. I had been up all the previous night, naturally
anxious about the ship threading her way through so many
dangers, uncertain about being able to complete the number
of our sledge-dogs, and much occupied in closing my cor-
respondence, to which there would be an end for at least a
year. All this over, the uncertain future loomed ominously
before me. The great responsibilities I had undertaken
seemed now and at once to fall with all their weight upon me.
A mental whirlpool was the consequence, which, backed
by the material storm, and the howling of the wretched
dogs in concert on deck, together with the tumbling about
of every thing below, long kept sleep in abeyance.

One thought and feeling predominated: it was gratitude,

deep and humble, for the success which had hitherto attended us, and for some narrow escapes which I must ever regard as providential.

Yesterday's gale has given place to calm, foggy weather. An occasional iceberg is seen. The officers amuse themselves in trying new guns, and shooting sea-birds for our dogs.

Governor Fliescher told me yesterday that for the last four weeks southerly winds prevailed, and that only a fortnight ago his boat was unable to reach the Loom Cliffs at Cape Shackleton, 50 miles north of Upernivik, in consequence of the ice being pressed in against the land. I fear these same winds have closed together the ice which occupies the middle of Davis' Strait (hence called the middle ice), so that we shall not be able to penetrate it. However, we are standing out to make the attempt.

To the uninitiated it may be as well to observe that each winter the sea called Baffin's Bay freezes over; in spring this vast body of ice breaks up, and drifting southward in a mass—called the main-pack, or the middle ice—obstructs the passage across from east to west.

The "North Passage" is made by sailing round the north end of this pack; the "Middle Passage," by pushing through it; and the "Southern Passage," by passing round its southern extreme; but seasons do occur when none of these routes are practicable.

It is very remarkable that southward of Disco northerly winds have prevailed. They greatly impeded our progress up Davis' Strait, but we cheered ourselves with the hope that they would effectually clear a path for us across the northern part of Baffin's Bay.

8th.—Last night we reached the edge of the middle ice, about 70 miles to the west of Upernivik, and ran southward along its edge all night. This morning, in thick fog, the ship was caught in its margin of loose ice. The fog soon

after cleared off, and we saw the clear sea about two miles
to the eastward, whilst all to the west was impenetrable
closely-packed floe-pieces. After steaming out of our pre-
dicament (a matter which we could not accomplish under
sail) we ran on to the southward until evening, but found
the pack edge still composed of light ice very closely
pressed together.

Having now closely examined it for an extent of 40
miles, I was satisfied that we could not force a passage
through it across Baffin's Bay, as is frequently done in ordinary seasons; therefore, taking advantage of a fair wind,
we steered to the northward, in order to seek an opening in
that direction.

12th.—We are in Melville Bay; made fast this afternoon
to an iceberg, which lies aground in 58 fathoms water,
about two miles from Browne's Islands, and between them
and the great glacier which here takes the place of the
coast-line.

We have got thus far without any difficulty, sailing along
the edge of the middle ice; but here we find it pressing in
against Browne's Islands, and covering the whole bay to
the northward, quite in the steep face of the glacier. This
is evidently the result of long-continued southerly winds;
but as the ice is very much broken up, we may expect it to
move off rapidly before the autumnal northerly winds now
due, and these winds invariably remove the previous season's
ice. All that we know of Melville Bay navigation in August, is derived from the experience of Government and
private searching expeditions during eight or nine seasons.
My own three previous transits across it were made in this
month. The whalers either get through in June or July,
or give up the attempt as being too late for their fishing.
It frequently happens that they get round the south end of
the middle ice, between latitudes 66° and 69° N., and up
the west coast of Baffin's Bay late in the season; but we

have no accounts of these voyages, nor should I be justified, at this late period of the season, in abandoning the prospect before me, in order to attempt a route which, even if successful, would lengthen our voyage to Barrow Strait by 700 or 800 miles. We have already passed what is usually the most difficult and dangerous part of the Melville Bay transit.

There is much to excite intense admiration and wonder around us; one cannot at once appreciate the grandeur of this mighty glacier, extending unbroken for 40 or 50 miles. Its sea-cliffs, about 5 or 6 miles from us, appear comparatively low, yet the icebergs detached from it are of the loftiest description. Here, on the spot, it does not seem incorrect to compare the icebergs to mere chippings off its edge, and the floe-ice to the thinnest shavings.

The far-off outline of glacier, seen against the eastern sky, has a faint tinge of yellow; it is almost horizontal, and of unknown distance and elevation.

There is an unusual dearth of birds and seals; everything around us is painfully still, excepting when an occasional iceberg splits off from the parent glacier; then we hear a rumbling crash like distant thunder, and the wave occasioned by the launch reaches us in six or seven minutes, and makes the ship roll lazily for a similar period. I cannot imagine that within the whole compass of nature's varied aspects, there is presented to the human eye a scene so well adapted for promoting deep and serious reflection, for lifting the thoughts from trivial things of every day life to others of the highest import.

The glacier serves to remind one at once of Time and of Eternity—of time, since we see portions of it break off to drift and melt away; and of eternity, since its downward march is so extremely slow, and its augmentations behind so regular, that no change in its appearance is perceptible from age to age. If even the untaught savages of luxuriant tropical regions regard the earth merely as a temporary abode, surely all who gaze upon this ice-overwhelmed region, this wide expanse of "terrestrial wreck," must be similarly assured that here "we have no abiding place."

During daytime the strong glare is very distressing, hence the subdued light of midnight, when the sun just skims along the northern horizon, is much the most agreeable part of the twenty-four hours; the temperature varies between 30° and 40° of Fahrenheit.

The drift-ice of various descriptions about us is constantly in motion under the influence of mysterious surface and under currents (according to their relative depths of floatation), which whirl them about in every possible direction.

To the S. E. are two small islands, almost enveloped in the glacier, and far within it an occasional mountain-peak protrudes from beneath.

From observing closely the variations in the glacier surface, I think we may safely infer that where it lies unbroken and smooth, the supporting land is level; and where much crevassed, the land beneath is uneven. The crevassed parts are of course impassable, but, by following the windings of the smooth surface, I think the interior could be reached. Some attempts to cross the glacier in South Greenland have failed, yet, by studying its character and attending to this remark, I think places might be found where an attempt would succeed. Mr. Petersen tells me that the Esquimaux of Upernivik are unable to account for occasional disappearances and reappearances of immense herds of reindeer, except by assuming that they migrate at intervals to feeding-grounds beyond the glacier, the surface of which he also says is smooth enough in many places even for dog-sledges to travel upon. As there is much uninhabited land, both to the northward and southward of Upernivik, I do not see the necessity for this supposition. The habits of the Esquimaux confine them almost exclusively to the islands and sea-coasts.

CHAPTER III.

Melville Bay—Bese₁ ₁n Melville Bay—Signs of Winter—The coming
storm—Drifting ᵑn the pack—Canine appetite—Resigned to a winter
in the pack—J rner stolen by sharks—The Arctic shark—White
Whales and Kil.ers.

15th August.—THREE days of the most perfect calm
have sadly taxed our patience.   Lovely bright weather,
but scarcely a living creature seen.   This afternoon the
anxiously-looked-for north wind sprang up, and immediately the light ice began to drift away before it, but it is not
strong enough to influence the icebergs, and they greatly
retard the clearing out of the bay.   We have noticed a constant wind off the glacier, probably the result of its cooling
effect upon the atmosphere ; this wind does not extend
more than 3 or 4 miles out from it.

16th.—One of the loveliest mornings imaginable : the
icebergs sparkled in the sun, and the breeze was just sufficiently strong to ripple the patches of dark blue sea ; beyond this, there was nothing to cheer one in the prospect
from the Crow's-nest at four o'clock ; but little change had
taken place in the ice ; I therefore determined to run back
along the pack-edge to the southwestward, in the hope that
some favorable change might have taken place further off
shore.   The barometer was unusually low, yet no indication
of any change of weather.   A seaman's chest was picked
up ; it contained only a spoon, a fork, and some tin can-
isters, and probably drifted here from the southward, where
the two whale-ships were crushed in June, affording another

proof of the prevalence of southerly winds. As we steamed on, the ice was found to have opened considerably; it fell calm, and mist was observed rolling along the glacier from the southward. By noon a S. E. wind reached us; all sail was set, the leads or lanes of water became wider, and our hopes of speedily crossing Melville Bay rose in proportion as our speed increased. We are pursuing our course without let or hindrance.

17th.—The fog overtook us yesterday evening, and at length, unable to see our way, we made fast at eleven o'clock to the ice. The wind had freshened, it was evidently blowing a gale outside the ice. During the night we drifted rapidly together with the ice, and this morning, on the clearing off of the fog, we steamed and sailed on again, threading our way between the floes, which are larger and much covered with *dry* snow. This evening we again made fast, the floes having closed together, cutting off advance and retreat. A wintry night, much wind and snow.

19th.—Continued strong S. E. winds, pressing the ice closely together, dark sky and snow; everything wears a wintry and threatening aspect; we are closely hemmed in, and have our rudder and screw unshipped. This recommencement of S. E. winds and rapid ebbing of the small remaining portion of summer makes me more anxious about the future than the present. Yesterday the weather improved, and by working for thirteen hours we got the ship out of her small ice-creek into a larger space of water, and in so doing advanced a mile and a half. It is now calm, but the ice still drifts, as we would wish it, to the N.W. Yesterday we were within 12 miles of the position of the 'Enterprise' upon the same day in 1848, and under very similar conditions of weather and ice also.

20th.—No favorable ice-drift: this detention has become most painful. The 'Enterprise' reached the open water upon this day in 1848, within 50 miles of our present posi-

tion; unfortunately our prospects are not so cheering.
There is no relative motion in the floes of ice, except a
gradual closing together, the small spaces and streaks of
water being still further diminished. The temperature has
fallen, and is usually below the freezing-point. I feel most
keenly the difficulty of my position; we cannot afford to
lose many more days. Of all the voyages to Barrow
Strait, there are but two which were delayed beyond this
date, viz., Parry's in 1824, and the 'Prince Albert's' in
1851. Should we not be released, and therefore be compelled
to winter in this pack, notwithstanding all our efforts, I
shall repeat this trial next year, and in the end, with God's
aid, perform my sacred duty.

The men enjoy a game of rounders on the ice every
evening; Petersen and Christian are constantly on the look-
out for seals, as well as Hobson and Young occasionally;
if in good condition and killed instantaneously, the seals
float; several have already been shot; the liver fried with
bacon is excellent.

Birds have become scarce,—the few we see are returning
southward. How anxiously I watch the ice, weather, barometer, and thermometer! Wind from any other quarter
than S. E. would oblige the floe-pieces to arrange themselves, in doing which they would become loose, and then
would be our opportunity to proceed.

24th.—Fine weather with very light northerly winds.
We have drifted 7 miles to the west in the last two days.
The ice is now a close pack, so close that one may walk for
many miles over it in any direction, by merely turning a
little to the right or left to avoid the small water spaces.
My frequent visits to the crow's-nest are not inspiriting:
how absolutely distressing this imprisonment is to me, no
one without similar experience can form any idea. As yet
the crew have but little suspicion how blighted our prospects are.

27*th*.—We daily make attempts to push on, and sometimes get a ship's length, but yesterday evening we made a
mile and a half! the ice then closed against the ship's sides and
lifted her about a foot.　We have had a fresh east wind for
two days, but no corresponding ice-drift to the west; this
is most discouraging, and can only be accounted for by supposing the existence of much ice or grounded icebergs in
that direction.

The dreaded reality of wintering in the pack is gradually
forcing itself upon my mind,—but I must not write on this
subject, it is bad enough to brood over it unceasingly.　We
can see the land all round Melville Bay, from Cape Walker
nearly to Cape York.　Petersen is indefatigable at seal-
shooting, he is so anxious to secure them for our dogs; he
says they must be hit in the head; "if you hit him in the beef
that is not good," meaning that a flesh-wound does not prevent their escaping under the ice.　Petersen and Christian
practice an Esquimaux mode of attracting the seals; they
scrape the ice, thus making a noise like that produced by a
seal in making a hole with its flippers, and then place one
end of a pole in the water and put their mouths close to
the other end, making noises in imitation of the snorts and
grunts of their intended victims; whether the device is successful or not I do not know, but it looks laughable enough.

Christian came back a few days ago, like a true seal-
hunter, carrying his kayak on his head, and dragging a seal
behind him.　Only two years ago Petersen returned across
this bay with Dr. Kane's retreating party; he shot a seal,
which they devoured raw, and which, under Providence,
saved their lives.　Petersen is a good ice-pilot, knows all
these coasts as well or better than any man living, and
from long experience and habits of observation, is almost
unerring in his prognostications of the weather.　Besides his
great value to us as interpreter, few men are better adapted
for Arctic work,—an ardent sportsman, an agreeable com-

panion, never at a loss for occupation or amusement, and
always contented and sanguine. But we have happily
many such dispositions in the 'Fox.'

30th.—The whole distance across Melville Bay is 170
miles : of this we have performed about 120, 40 of which
we have drifted in the last fourteen days. The 'Isabel,'
sailed freely over this spot on the 20th August, 1852; and
the 'North Star' was beset on the 30th July, 1849, to the
southward of Melville Bay, and carried in the ice across it
and some 70 or 80 miles beyond, when she was set free on the
26th September, and went into Winter quarters in Wolstenholme Sound. What a precedent for us !

Yesterday we set to work as usual to warp the ship
along, and moved her ten feet : an insignificant hummock
then blocked up the narrow passage ; as we could not push
it before us, a two-pound blasting charge was exploded,
and the surface ice was shattered, but such an immense
quantity of broken ice came up from beneath, that the difficulty was greatly increased instead of being removed. This
is one of the many instances in which our small vessel
labors under very great disadvantages in ice-navigation—
we have neither sufficient manual power, steam power, nor
impetus to force the floes asunder. I am convinced that a
steamer of moderate size and power, with a crew of forty
or fifty men, would have got through a hundred miles of
such ice in less time than we have been beset.

The temperature fell to 25° last night, and the pools are
strongly frozen over. I now look matters steadily and
calmly in the face ; whilst reasonable ground for hope remained I was anxious in the extreme. The dismal prospect
of a " winter in the pack " had scarcely begun to dawn upon
the crew; however I do not think they will be much upset
by it. They had some exciting foot-races on the ice yesterday evening.

1st Sept.—The indication of an approaching S. E. gale

are at all times sufficiently apparent here, and fortunately
so, as it is the most dangerous wind in Melville Bay.   It
was on the morning of the 30th, before church-time, that
they attracted our attention : the wind was very light, but
barometer low and falling ; very threatening appearances in
the S. E. quarter, dark-blue sky, and grey detached clouds
slowly rising ; when the wind commenced the barometer
began to rise.   This gale lasted forty-eight hours, and
closed up every little space of water ; at first all the ice
drifted before the wind, but latterly remained stationary.
Twenty seals have been shot up to this time.

On comparing Petersen's experience with my own and
that of the 'North Star' in 1849, it seems probable that the
ice along the shores of Melville Bay, at this season, will
drift northward close along the land as far as Cape Parry,
where, meeting with a S. W. current out of Whale or
Smith's Sound, it will be carried away into the middle of
Baffin's Bay, and thence during the winter down Davis'
Strait into the Atlantic.   From Cape Dudley Digges to
Cape Parry, including Wolstenholme Sound, open water
remains until October.   It is strange that we have ceased to
drift lately to the westward.

6th.—During the last week we have only drifted 9 miles
to the west.   Obtained soundings in 88 fathoms ; this is a
discovery, and not an agreeable one.   Of the six or seven
icebergs in sight, the nearest are to the west of us ; they are
very large, and appear to be aground ; we approach them
slowly.   Pleasant weather, but the winds are much too gentle to be of service to us ; although the nights are cold, yet
during the day our men occasionally do their sewing on
deck.   Our companions the seals are larger and fatter than
formerly, therefore they float when shot ; we are disposed
to attribute their improved condition to the better feeding
upon this bank.   The dredge brought up some few shell-
fish, star-fish, stones and much soft mud.

9th.—On this day, in 1824, Sir Edward Parry got out of
the middle ice, and succeeded in reaching Port Bowen. To
continue hoping for release in time to reach Bellot Strait
would be absurd; yet to employ the men we continue our
preparations of tents, sledges, and gear for traveling. Two
days ago the ice became more slack than usual, and a long
lane opened; its western termination could not be seen
from aloft. Every effort was made to get into this water,
and by the aid of steam and blasting powder we advanced
100 yards out of the intervening 170 yards of ice, when
the floes began to close together, a S. E. wind having sprung
up. Had we succeeded in reaching the water, I think we
should have extricated ourselves completely, and perhaps
ere this have reached Barrow Strait, but S. E. and S. W.
gales succeeded, and it now blows a S.S.E. gale, with sleet.

10th.—Young went to the large icebergs to-day; the
nearest of them is 250 feet high, and in 83 fathoms water;
it is therefore probably aground, except at spring tide; the
floe-ice was drifting past it to the westward, and was crushing up against its side to a height of 50 feet.

13th.—Thermometer has fallen to 17° at noon. We have
drifted 18 miles to the W. in the last week; therefore our
neighbors, the icebergs, are not always aground, but even
when afloat drift more slowly than the light ice. There is
a water-sky to the W. and N. W.; it is nearest to us in the
direction of Cape York; *could we only advance 12 or 15
miles in that direction, I am convinced we should be free
to steer for Barrow Strait.* Forty-three seals have been
secured for the dogs; one dog is missing, the remaining
twenty-nine devoured their two days' allowance of seal's
flesh (60 or 65 lbs.) in forty-two seconds! it contained no
bone, and had been cut up into small pieces, and spread out
upon the snow, before they were permitted to rush to dinner; in this way the weak enjoy a fair chance, and there is
no time for fighting. We do not allow them on board.

16*th.*—At length we have drifted past the large icebergs, obtaining soundings in 69 fathoms within a mile of them; they must now be aground, and have frequently been so during the last three weeks; and being directly upon our line of drift, are probably the immediate cause of our still remaining in Melville Bay. The ice is slack everywhere, but the temperature having fallen to 3°, new ice rapidly forms, so that the change comes too late. The western limit of the day — Cape York — is very distinct, and not more than 25 miles from us.

18*th.*—Lanes of water in all directions; but the nearest is half a mile from us. They come too late, as do also the N. W. winds which have now succeeded the fatal south-easters. The temperature fell to 2° below zero last night. We are now at length in the "North Water;" the old ice has spread out in all directions, so that it is only the young ice—formed within the last fortnight—which detains us prisoners here.

The icebergs, the chief cause of our unfortunate detention, and which for more than three weeks were in advance of us to the westward, are now, in the short space of two days, nearly out of sight to the eastward.

The preparations for wintering and sledge-traveling go on with unabated alacrity; the latter will be useful should it become necessary to abandon the ship.

Notwithstanding such a withering blight to my dearest hopes, yet I cannot overlook the many sources of gratification which do exist; we have not only the necessaries, but also a fair portion of the luxuries, of ordinary sea-life; our provisions and clothing are abundant and well suited to the climate. Our whole equipment, though upon so small a scale, is perfect in its way. We all enjoy perfect health, and the men are most cheerful, willing, and quiet.

Our "native auxiliaries," consisting of Christian and his twenty-nine dogs, are capable of performing immense ser-

5

vice ; whilst Mr. Petersen, from his great Arctic experience, is of much use to me, besides being all that I could wish as an interpreter.   Humanly speaking, we are not unreasonable in confidently looking forward to a successful issue of this season's operations, and I greatly fear that poor Lady Franklin's disappointment will consequently be the more severely felt.

We are doomed to pass a long winter of absolute inutility, if not of idleness, in comparative peril and privation ; nevertheless the men seem very happy—thoughtless, of course, as true sailors always are.

We have drifted off the bank into much deeper water, and suppose this is the reason that seals have become more scarce.

22nd.—Constant N. W. winds continue to drift us slowly southward.   Strong indications of water in the N. W., W., and S. E. ; its vicinity may account for a rise in the temperature, without apparent cause, to 27° at noon to-day.

The newly formed ice affords us delightful walking ; the old ice on the contrary is covered with a foot of soft snow. We have no shooting ; scarcely a living creature has been seen for a week.

24th.—Yesterday I thought I saw two of our men walking at a distance, and beyond some unsafe ice, but on inquiry found that all were on board : Petersen and I set off to reconnoitre the strangers ; they proved to be bears, but much too wary to let us come within shot.   It was dark when we returned on board after a brisk walk over the new ice.   The calm air felt agreeably mild.   We were without mittens ; and but that the breath froze upon mustachios and beard, one could have readily imagined the night was comfortably warm.   The thermometer stood at +5°.

To-day when walking in a fresh breeze the wind felt very cold, and kept one on the look-out for frost-bites, although the thermometer was up to 10°.   Games upon the ice and skating are our afternoon amusements, but we also have some few lovers of music, who embrace the opportunity for vigorous execution, without fear of being reminded that others may have ears more sensitive and discriminating than their own.

26th.—The mountain to the North of Melville Bay, known as the 'Snowy Peak,' was visible yesterday, although 90 miles distant; I have calculated its height to be 6000 feet. A raven was shot to-day.

27th.—Our salt meat is usually soaked for some days before being used; for this purpose it is put into a net, and lowered through a hole in the ice; this morning the net had been torn, and only a fragment of it remained. We suppose our twenty-two pounds of salt meat had been devoured by a shark; it would be curious to know how such fare agrees with him, as a full meal of salted provision will kill an Esquimaux dog, which thrives on almost any thing. I used to remonstrate upon the skins of sea-birds being given to our dogs, but was told the feathers were good for them! Here all sea-birds are skinned before being cooked, otherwise our ducks, divers, and looms would be uneatably fishy. A well-baited shark-hook has been substituted for the net of salt meat; I much wish to capture one of the monsters, as wonderful stories are told us of their doings in Greenland: whether they are the white shark or the basking shark of natural history I cannot find out. It is only of late years that the shark fishery has been carried on to any extent in Greenland; they are captured for the sake of their livers, which yield a considerale quantity of oil. It has very recently been ascertained that a valuable substance resembling spermaceti may be expressed from the carcase, and for this purpose powerful screw presses are now employed. In early winter the sharks are caught with hook and line through holes in the ice.

The Esquimaux assert that they are insensible to pain;

and Petersen assures me he has plunged a long knife several times into the head of one whilst it continued to feed upon a white whale entangled in his net !! It is not sufficient to drive them away with sundry thrusts of spears or knives, but they must be towed away to some distance from the nets, otherwise they will return to feed. It must be remembered that the brain of a shark is extremely small in proportion to the size of its huge head. I have seen bullets fired through them with very little apparent effect; but if these creatures *can* feel, the devices practiced upon them by the Esquimaux must be cruel indeed.

It is only in certain localities that sharks are found, and in these places they are often attracted to the nets by the animals entangled in them. The dogs are not suffered to eat either the skin or the head, the former in consequence of its extreme roughness, and the latter because it causes giddiness and makes them sick.

The nets alluded to are set for the white whale or the eal; if for the former, they are attached to the shore and extended off at right angles so as to intercept them in their autumnal southern migration, when they swim close along the rocks to avoid their direst foe, the grampus, or killer, of sailors, the *Delphinus orca* of naturalists. When the white whale is stopped by the net it often appears at first to be unconscious of the fact, and continues to swim against it, affording time for the approach of the boat and deadly harpoon from behind. If entangled in the net a very short time suffices to drown them, as, like all the whale tribe, they are obliged to come to the surface to breathe.

The killer is also a cetacean of considerable size, 15 to 20 feet in length, but of very different habits; it is very swift, is armed with powerful teeth, and is gregarious. When in sufficient numbers they even attack the whale, impeding his progress by fastening on his fins and tail. In summer they appear in the Greenland seas, and the seals instantly seek refuge from them in the various creeks and inner harbors; and the Esquimaux hunter in his frail kayak, when he sees the huge pointed dorsal fin swiftly cleaving the surface of the sea, is scarcely less anxious to shun such dangerous company. With such stories as these Petersen beguiles the time; I never tire of listening to them, and now amuse myself in jotting scraps of them down.

CHAPTER IV.

Snow crystals—Dog will not eat raven—An Arctic school—The dogs
invade us — Bear-hunting by night—Ice-artillery—Arctic palates—
Sudden rise of temperature—Harvey's idea of a sortie.

3d Oct.—SEPTEMBER has passed away and left us as a
legacy to the pack; what a month have we had of anxious
hopes and fears !

Up to the 17th S. E. winds prevailed, forcing the ice into
a compact body, and urging it north-westward; subsequently N. W. winds set in, drifting it southward, and
separating the floe-pieces; but the change of wind being
accompanied by a considerable fall of temperature, they
were either quickly cemented together again, or young ice
formed over the newly opened lanes of water, almost as
rapidly as the surface of the sea became exposed. During
the month the thermometer ranged between $+36°$ and $-2°$
Two more bears and a raven have been seen. A wearied
ptarmigan alighted near the ship, but before it could take
wing again the dogs caught it, and scarcely a feather remained by the time I could rush on deck.

Our beautiful little organ was taken out of its case to-
day, and put up on the lower deck; the men enjoy its
pleasing tones, whilst Christian unceasingly turns the handle
in a state of intense delight; he regards it with such awe
and admiration, and is so entranced, that one cannot help
envying him; of course he never saw one before. The
instrument was presented by the Prince Consort to the
searching vessel bearing his name which was sent out by

Lady Franklin in 1851; it is now about to pass its third winter in the frozen regions.

Two dogs ran off yesterday, in the vain hope, I suppose, of bettering their condition,—we only feed them three times a week at present; they returned this morning.

Seals are daily seen upon the new ice, but in- this doubtful sort of light they are extremely timid, therefore our sportsmen cannot get within shot. The bears scent or hear our dogs, and so keep aloof; even the shark has deserted us, the bait remains intact. The snow crystals of last night are extremely beautiful; the largest kind is an inch in length; its form exactly resembles the end of a pointed feather. Stellar crystals two-tenths of an inch in diameter have also fallen; these have six points, and are the most exquisite things when seen under a microscope. I remember noticing them at Melville Island in March, 1853, when the temperature rose to $+8°$; as these were formed last night between the temperatures of $+6°$ and $+12°$, it would appear that the form is due to a certain fixed temperature. In the sun, or even in moonlight, all these crystals glisten most brilliantly; and as our masts and rigging are abundantly covered with them, the 'Fox' was never so gorgeously arrayed as she now appears.

13th.—One day is very like another; we have to battle stoutly with monotony; and but that each twenty-four hours brings with it necessary though trivial duties, it would be difficult to remember the date. We take our guns and walk long distances, but see nothing. Two of the dogs go hunting on their own account, sometimes remaining absent all night. What they find or do is a mystery. The weather is generally calm and cold — very favorable for freezing purposes at all events — for the ice of only three weeks' growth is two feet thick.

I hardly expect any considerable disruption of the ice before the general break-up in the spring, yet we do not trust any of our provisions upon it, nor is it sufficiently still to set up a magnetic observatory, for which purpose the instruments have been supplied to us.

Petersen still hopes we may escape and get into Upernivik, as the sea is not permanently frozen over there before December. I am surprised to hear that eagles have been seen so far north as Upernivik, although it is but twice in twenty-four years that specimens have been noticed there. In Richardson's 'Fauna Boreali Americana' the extreme northern limit of these birds is given as $66°$; but Upernivik is in $72\frac{3}{4}°$.

A few bear and fox tracks have been seen, but no living creatures for several days, except a flock of ducks hastening southward, and a solitary raven.

It is said that Esquimaux dogs will eat everything except fox and raven. There are exceptions, however; one of ours, old "Harness Jack," devoured a raven with much gusto some days ago. All the other dogs allowed their harness to be taken off when they were brought on board; but old Jack will not permit himself to be unrobed; when attempted, he very plainly threatens to use his teeth. This canine oddity suddenly became immensely popular, by constituting himself protecting head of the establishment when one of his tribe littered; he took up a most uncomfortable position on top of the family cask (our *impromptu* kennel), and prevented the approach of all the other dogs; but for his timely interference on behalf of the poor little puppies, I verily believe they would all have been stolen and devoured! Dogs may do even worse than eat raven.

I have attempted some experiments for the purpose of determining the mean hourly change of oscillation of a pendulum due to the earth's diurnal motion; but as mine was only $11\frac{1}{2}$ feet in length, I failed of any approach to accuracy. The mean of several observations gave $17° 47'$, whereas the change due to our latitude is about $14° 30'$. A single experiment gave 14° 10′ and this was the longest in point of time of any of them, the pendulum having swung for thirty-six minutes.

24th.—Furious N. W. and S. E. gales have alternated of late; the ship is housed over, to keep out the driving snow; so high is the snow carried in the air that a little box perforated with small holes and triced up 50 feet high is soon filled up; this box is supplied morning and evening with a piece of prepared paper to detect the presence and amount of ozone in the atmosphere; it is a peculiar pet of the Doctor's.

At eight o'clock this evening I noticed the falling of a very brilliant meteor; it passed through the constellation of Cassiopœia in a N. N. E. direction before terminating its visible existence, which it did very much like a huge rocket; the flash was so brilliant that a man whose back was turned to it mistook the illumination for lightning.

26th.—Our school opened this evening, under the auspices of Dr. Walker. He reports eight or nine pupils, and is much gratified by their zeal. At present their studies are limited to the three R's—reading, 'riting, and 'rithmetic. They have asked him to read and explain something instructive, so he intends to make them acquainted with the trade-winds and atmosphere. This subject affords an opportunity of explaining the uses of our thermometer, barometer, ozonometer, and electrometer, which they see us take much interest in. It is delightful to find a spirit of inquiry amongst them. Apart from scholastic occupation, I give them healthful exercise in spreading a thick layer of snow over the deck, and encasing the ship all round with a bank of the same material.

28th.—Midnight. This evening, to our great astonishment, there occurred a disruption and movement of the ice within 200 yards of the ship. The night was calm; the reflection of a bright moon, aided by the more than ordinary

brilliancy of the stars upon the snowy expanse, made it
appear to us almost daylight. As I sit now in my cabin I
can distinctly hear the ice crushing; it resembles the continued roar of distant surf, and there are many other occasional sounds; some of them remind one of the low moaning of the wind, others are loud and harsh, as if trains of
heavy wagons with ungreased axles were slowly laboring
along. Upon a less-favored night these sounds might be
appalling ; even as it is, they are sufficiently ominous to invite reflection. Cape York has been in sight for some days
past.

29th.—Another heavenly night, and still greater ice dis-
turbance; some of the crushed-up pieces are nearly four
feet thick. The currents, icebergs, and changes of temperature, may contribute to this ice action; but I think the
tides are the chief cause, and for these reasons: that it
wants but two days to the full moon, and that the ice-
movements are almost confined to the night, and change
their direction morning and evening. Now we know that
the night tides in Greenland greatly exceed the day-tides.
One thing is evident—the weather continues calm, therefore the winds are not concerned in the matter.

2nd Nov.—Having observed some days ago that a few
of the dogs were falling away—from some cause or other
not having put on their winter clothing before the recent
cold weather set in—they were all allowed on board, and
given a good extra meal. Since then we can scarcely
keep them out. One calm night they made a charge, and
boarded the ship so suddenly that several of the men rushed
up very scantily clothed, to see what was the matter. Vigorous measures were adopted to expel the intruders, and
there was desperate chasing round the deck with broom-
sticks, &c. Many of them retreated into holes and corners, and two hours elapsed before they were all driven out;

but though the chase was hot, it was cold enough work for the half-clad men.

Sailors use quaint expressions. The nightly foraging expeditions are called "sorties;" they point out to me the various corners between decks where the "ice corrodes," *i. e.*, the moisture condenses and forms frost; a ramble over the ice is called "a bit of a peruse." I presume this indignity is offered to the word perambulation.

There was a very sudden call "to arms" to-night. Whether sleeping, prosing, or schooling, every one flew out upon the ice on the instant, as if the magazine or the boiler was on the point of explosion. The alarm of "A bear close-to, fighting with the dogs," was the cause. The luckless beast had approached within 25 yards of the ship ere the quartermaster's eye detected his indistinct outline against the snow; so silently had he crept up that he was within 10 yards of some of the dogs. A shout started them up, and they at once flew round the bear and embarrassed his retreat. In crossing some very thin ice he broke through, and there I found him surrounded by yelping dogs.. Poor fellow! Hobson, Young, and Petersen had each lodged a bullet in him; but these only seemed to increase his rage. He succeeded in getting out of the water, when, fearing harm to the numerous by-standers and dogs, or that he might escape, I fired, and luckily the bullet passed through his brain. He proved to be a full-grown male, 7 feet 3 inches in length. As we all aided in the capture, it was decided that the skin should be offered to Lady Franklin.

The carcase will feed our dogs for nearly a month; they were rewarded on the spot with the offal. All of them, however, had not shown equal pluck; some ran off in evident fright, but others showed no symptom of fear, plunging or falling into the water with Bruin. Poor old Sophy was amongst the latter, and received a deep cut in the shoulder from one of his claws. The authorities have prescribed double allowance of food for her, and say she will soon recover.

For the few moments of its duration the chase and death was exciting. And how strange and novel the scene ! A misty moon affording but scanty light—dark figures gliding singly about, not daring to approach each other, for the ice trembled under their feet—the enraged bear, the wolfish howling dogs, and the bright flashes of the deadly rifles.

3rd.—I remained up the greater part of last night taking observations, for the evening mists had passed away, and a lovely moon reigned over a calm enchanting night ; through a powerful telescope she resembled a huge frosted-silver melon, the large crater-like depression answering to that part from which the footstalk had been detached. Not a sound to break the stillness around, excepting when some hungry dog would return to the battlefield to gnaw into the blood-stained ice.

On the 1st the sun paid us his last visit for the year, and now we take all our meals by lamp-light.

5th.—In order to vary our monotonous routine, we determined to celebrate the day ; extra grog was issued to the crew, and also for the first time a proportion of preserved plum-pudding. Lady Franklin most thoughtfully and kindly sent it on board for occasional use. It is excellent.

This evening a well-got-up procession sallied forth, marched round the ship with drum, gong, and discord, and then proceeded to burn the effigy of Guy Fawkes. Their blackened faces, extravagant costumes, flaring torches, and savage yells, frightened away all the dogs ; nor was it until after the fireworks were set off and the traitor consumed that they crept back again. It was school-night, but the men were up for fun, so gave the .Doctor a holiday.

12th.—Yesterday I had the good fortune to shoot two seals ; they were very fat, and their stomachs were filled with shrimps. To-day Young and Petersen shot three more, and many others have been seen. This is cheering, and entices people out for hours daily. There is just enough movement in the ice to keep a few narrow lanes and small pools of water open; the floes or fields of ice are more inclined to spread out from each other than to close. We have latterly been drifting before northerly winds.

16th.—A renewal of ice-crushing within a few hundreds yards of us. I can hear it in my bed. The ordinary sound resembles the roar of distant surf breaking heavily and continuously; but when heavy masses come in collision with much impetus, it fully realizes the justness of Dr. Kane's descriptive epithet, "ice-artillery." Fortunately for us, our poor little 'Fox' is well within the margin of a stout old floe; we are therefore undisturbed spectators of ice-conflicts which would be irresistible to anything of human construction. Immediately about the ship all is still, and as far as appearances go she is precisely as she would be in a secure harbor—housed all over, banked up with snow to her gunwales. In fact, her winter plumage is so complete that the masts alone are visible. The deck and the now useless sky-lights are covered with hard snow. Below hatches we are warm and dry; all are in excellent health and spirits, looking forward to an active campaign next winter. God grant it may be realized!

Yesterday Young shot the fiftieth seal, an event duly celebrated by our drinking *the* bottle of champagne which had been set apart in more hopeful times to be drunk on reaching the North Water—that unhappy failure, the more keenly felt from being being so very unexpected.

Petersen saw and fired a shot into a narwhal, which brought the blubber out. When most Arctic creatures are wounded in the water, blubber more frequently than blood appears, particularly if the wound is superficial—it spreads over the surface of the water like oil. Bills of fare vary much, even in Greenland. I have inquired of Petersen, and

he tells me that the Greenland Esquimaux (there are many
Greenlanders of Danish origin) are not agreed as to which
of their animals affords the most delicious food; some of
them prefer reindeer venison, others think more favorably
of young dog, the flesh of which, he asserts, is "just like
the beef of sheep." He says a Danish captain, who had
acquired the taste, provided some for his guests, and they
praised his *mutton!* after dinner he sent for the skin of the
animal, which was no other than a large red dog! This
occurred in Greenland, where his Danish guests had resided
for many years, far removed from European *mutton.* Baked
puppy is a real delicacy all over Polynesia: at the Sand-
wich Islands I was once invited to a feast, and had to feign
disappointment as well as I could on being told that puppy
was so extremely scarce it could not be procured in time,
and therefore sucking pig was substituted!

19th.—A heavy southerly gale has increased the ice
movements; happily we are undisturbed. As Young was
seated under the lee of a hummock, watching for seals to
pop up to breathe, the strong ice under him suddenly cracked
and separated! He escaped with a ducking, and was just
able to reach his gun from the bank ere it sank through the
mixture of snow and water.

Yesterday we were all out; I saw only one seal, but was
refreshed by the sight of a dozen narwhals. It is a positive
treat to see a living creature of any kind. The only birds
that remain are dovekies, but they are scarce, and, being
white, are very rarely visible.

The dogs are fed every second day, when 2 lbs. of seal's
flesh—previously thawed when possible—is given to each;
the weaker ones get additional food, and they all pick up
whatever scraps are thrown out; this is enough to sustain,
but not to satisfy them, so they are continually on the look-out
for anything eatable. Hobson made one very happy without intending it; he meant only to give him a kick, but his

slipper, being down at heel, flew off, and away went the lucky dog in triumph with the prize, which of course was no more seen.

Two large icebergs drifted in company with us; our relative positions have remained pretty nearly the same for the last month.

23rd.—A heavy gale commenced at N. E. on the 21st, and continued for thirty-six hours unabated in force, but changed in direction to S. S. W. It appears to have been a revolving storm, moving to the N. W. Yesterday as the wind approached S. E., the temperature rose to +32°; the deck sloppy; the lower deck temperature during Divine Service was 75°!! As the wind veered round to S. S. W., the wind moderated, and temperature fell; this evening it is — 7°. How is it that the S. E. wind has brought us such a very high temperature? Even if it traversed an unfrozen sea it could not have derived from thence a higher temperature than 29°. Has it swept across Greenland—that vast superficies partly enveloped in glacier, partly in snow? No, it must have been borne in the higher regions of the atmosphere from the far south, in order to mitigate the severity of the northern climate.

Petersen tells me the same warm S. E. wind suddenly sweeps over Upernivik in midwinter, bringing with it abundance of rain; and that it always shifts to the S. W., and then the temperature rapidly falls: this is precisely the change we have experienced in lat. 75°. I believe a somewhat similar, but less remarkable, change of temperature was noticed in Smith's Sound, lat. 78¾° N.

25th.—Mild " Madeira weather," as Hobson calls it, temperature up to +7°. By my desire Dr. Walker is occupied in making every possible experiment upon the freezing of salt water; the first crop of ice is salt, the second less so, the third produces drinkable water, and the fourth is fresh. Frosty efflorescence appears upon ice formed at low

temperatures in calm weather—it is brine expressed by the
act of freezing.   We need not wonder that dogs, when driven
hard over this ice, which soon cuts their feet, suffer intense
pain, and often fall down in fits ; nor that snow, falling
from young (sea) ice, wholly or partially thaws, even when
the temperature is but little above zero ; when near the
freezing point the young ice thus coated over become sludgy
and unsafe.

29th.—Keen, biting, N. W. winds.   No cracks in the ice,
therefore no seals.   Grey dawn at ten o'clock, and dark at
two.   The moon is everywhere the sailor's friend, she is a
source of comfort to us here.   Nothing to excite conversation, except an occasional inroad of the dogs in search
of food ; this generally occurs at night.   Whenever the
deck-light, which burns under the housing happens to go
out, they scale the steep snow banking and rush round the
deck like wolves.   "Why, bless you, Sir, the werry moment
that there light goes out, and the quartermaster turns his
back, they makes a regular sort*ee*, and in they all comes."
"But *where do* they come in, Harvey?"   "Where, Sir?
why everywheres ; they makes no more to do, but in they
comes, clean over all."   Not long ago old Harvey was
chief quartermaster in a line-of-battle ship, and a regular
magnet to all the younger midshipmen.   He would spin
them yarns by the hour during the night-watches about the
wonders of the sea, and of the Arctic regions in particular—its bears, its icebergs, and still more terrific "auroras,
roaring and flashing about the ship enough to frighten a
fellow !"

30th.—Severe cold has arrived with the full moon ; eight
days ago the thermometer stood at the freezing-point, it is
now 64° below it !   So dark is it now that I was able to
observe an eclipse of Jupiter's first satellite before three
o'clock to-day.   For the last two months we have drifted
reely backwards and forwards before N. W. and S. E. winds ;

each time we have gained a more off-shore position, being gradually separated further and further from the land by fresh growths of ice, which invariably follow up every ice-movement. In this manner we have been thrust out to the S.W. 80 miles from the nearest land, and into that free space which in autumn was open water, and which we then vainly struggled to reach.

That the ice has been most free to move in this direction is additional evidence of the recent proximity of an open sea, and shows that in all probability—I had almost said certainty—we should have sailed, or at least drifted into it, had it not been for those enemies to all progress, the grounded bergs.

6

CHAPTER V.

Burial in the pack—Musk oxen in lat. 80° north—Thrift of the Arctic
fox—The aurora affects the electrometer—An Arctic Christmas—
Sufferings of Dr. Kane's deserters—Ice acted on by wind only—How
the sun ought to be welcomed—Constant action of the ice—Return
of the seals—Revolving storm.

4th Dec.—I HAVE just returned on board from the performance of the most solemn duty a commander can be called upon to fulfil. A funeral at sea is always peculiarly impressive; but this evening at seven o'clock, as we gathered around the sad remains of poor Scott, reposing under an Union Jack, and read the Burial Service by the light of lanterns, the effect could not fail to awaken very serious emotions.

The greater part of the Church Service was read on board, under shelter of the housing; the body was then placed upon a sledge, and drawn by the messmates of the deceased to a short distance from the ship, where a hole through the ice had been cut: it was then "committed to the deep," and the Service completed. What a scene it was! I shall never forget it. The lonely 'Fox,' almost buried in snow, completely isolated from the habitable world, her colors half-mast high, and bell mournfully tolling; our little procession slowly marching over the rough surface of the frozen sea, guided by lanterns and direction-posts, amid the dark and dreary depth of Arctic winter; the deathlike stillness, the intense cold, and threatening aspect of a murky, overcast sky; and all this heightened by one of those strange lunar phenomena which are but seldom seen even here, a complete halo encircling the moon, through which passed a horizontal band of pale light that encompassed the heavens; above the moon appeared the segments of two other halos, and there were also mock moons or paraselenæ to the number of six.   The misty atmosphere lent a very ghastly hue to this singular display, which lasted for rather more than an hour.

Poor Scott fell down a hatchway two days only before his death, which was occasioned by the internal injuries then received; he was a steady, serious man; a widow and family will mourn his loss.   He was our engine-driver; we cannot replace him, therefore the whole duty of working the engines will devolve upon the engineer, Mr. Brand.

11th.—Calm, clear weather, pleasant for exercise, but steadily cold; thermometer varies between −20° and −30°. At noon the blush of dawn tints the southern horizon, to the north the sky remains inky blue, whilst overhead it is bright and clear, the stars shining, and the pole-star near the zenith very distinct.   Although there is a light north wind, thin mackerel-clouds are passing from south to north, and the temperature has risen 10°.

I have been questioning Petersen about the bones of the musk oxen found in Smith's Sound; he says the decayed skulls of about twenty were found, all of them to the north of the 79th parallel.   As they were all without lower jaws, he says they were killed by Esquimaux, who leave upon the spot the skulls of large animals, but the weight of the lower jaw being so trifling it is allowed to remain attached to the flesh and tongue.   The skull of a musk ox with its massive horns cannot weigh less than 30 lbs.

Although it has been abundantly proved by the existence of raised beaches and fossils, that the shores of Smith's Sound have been elevated within a comparatively recent geological period, yet Petersen tells me that there exist numerous ruins of Esquimaux buildings, probably one or two centuries old, all of which are situated upon very low points, only just sufficiently raised above the reach of the sea ; such sites, in fact, as would at present be selected by the natives.   These ruins show that no perceptible change has taken place in the relative level of sea and land since they were originally constructed.   At Petersen's Greenland home, Upernivik, the land has sunk, as is plainly shown by similar ruins over which the tides now flow.

Any thing which illustrates the habits of animals in such extremely high latitudes I think is most interesting ; their instincts must be quickened in proportion as the difficulty of subsisting increases.   Foxes, white and blue, are very numerous ; all the birds are merely summer visitors, therefore the hare is the only creature remaining upon which foxes can prey ; but the hares are comparatively scarce : how then do the foxes live for eight months of each year ? Petersen thinks they store up provisions during the summer in various holes and crevices, and thus manage to eke out an existence during the dark winter season ; he once saw a fox carry off eggs in his mouth from an eider-duck's nest, one at a time, until the whole were removed ; and in winter he has observed a fox scratch a hole down through very deep snow, to a cache of eggs beneath.

The men are exercised at building snow huts ; for winter or early spring traveling, this knowledge is almost indispensable..   Upon a calm day the temperature of the external air being −33°, within a snow hut the thermometer stood 17° higher, this important difference being due to the transmission of heat through the ice from the sea beneath.

Evaporation goes on through ice from the water underneath it.   The interior of each snow hut is coated with crystals, and the ice upon which the huts are built is four feet thick, but when no longer in contact with water I cannot discover any evaporation from ice.   For instance, a canvas screen on deck which became wet by the sudden thaw last month still remains frozen stiff.

14th.—Of late there has been much damp upon the lower deck. This has now been remedied by enclosing the hatchway within a commodious snow-porch, which serves as a condenser for the steam and vapor from the inhabited deck below.

19th.—Light N. W. winds, with occasional mists; the temperature is comparatively mild: –12° to –25°.

It is now the time of spring-tides; they cause numerous cracks in the ice; but why so, at such a great distance from the land, I cannot explain. The three nearest points of land are respectively 110, 140, and 180 miles distant from us.

Much aurora during the last two days. Yesterday morning it was visible until eclipsed by the day-dawn at 10 o'clock. Although we could no longer see it, I do not think it ceased: very thin clouds occupied its place, through which, as through the aurora, stars appeared scarcely dimmed in lustre. I do not imagine that aurora is ever visible in a *perfectly* clear atmosphere. I often observe it just silvering or rendering luminous the upper edge of low fog or cloud banks, and with a few vertical rays feebly vibrating.

Last evening Dr. Walker called me to witness his success with the electrometer. The electric current was so very weak that the gold-leaves diverged at regular intervals of four or five seconds. Some hours afterward it was strong enough to *keep* them diverged.

21st.—Midwinter day. Out of the Arctic regions it is better known as the *shortest* day. At noon we could just read type similar to the leading article of the 'Times." Few people could read more than two or three lines without their eyes aching.

27th.—Our Christmas was a very cheerful, merry one.

The men were supplied with several additional articles, such as hams, plum-puddings, preserved gooseberries and apples, nuts, sweetmeats, and Burton ale. After Divine Service they decorated the lower deck with flags, and made an immense display of food. The officers came down with me to see their preparations. We were really astonished! The mess-tables were laid out like the counters in a confectioner's shop, with apple and gooseberry tarts, plum and sponge-cakes in pyramids, besides various other unknown puffs, cakes, and loaves of all sizes and shapes. We bake all our own bread, and excellent it is. In the background were nicely-browned hams, meat-pies, cheeses, and other substantial articles. Rum and water in wine-glasses, and plum-cake, were handed to us: we wished them a happy Christmas, and complimented them on their taste and spirit in getting up such a display. Our silken sledge-banners had been borrowed for the occasion, and were regarded with deference and peculiar pride.

In the evening the officers were enticed down amongst the men again, and at a late hour I was requested, as a great favor, to come down and see how much they were enjoying themselves. I found them in the highest good humor with themselves and all the world. They were perfectly sober, and singing songs, each in his turn. I expressed great satisfaction at having seen them enjoying themselves so much and so rationally. I could therefore the better describe it to Lady Franklin, who was so deeply interested in every thing relating to them. I drank their healths, and hoped our position next year would be more suitable for our purpose. We all joined in drinking the healths of Lady Franklin and Miss Cracroft, and amid the acclamations which followed I returned to my cabin, immensely gratified by such an exhibition of genuine good feeling, such veneration for Lady Franklin, and such loyalty to the cause of the expedition. It was very pleasant also that

they had taken the most cheering view of our future prospects.   I verily believe I was the happiest individual on
board, that happy evening.

Our Christmas-box has come in the shape of northerly
winds, which bid fair to drift us southward toward those
latitudes wherein we hope for liberation next spring from
this icy bondage.

28th.—We have been in expectation of a gale all day.
This evening there is still a doubtful sort of truce amongst
the elements.   Barometer down to 28.83; thermometer up
to +5°, although the wind has been strong and steady from
the N. for twenty-four hours, low scud flying from the E.,
snow constantly falling.   An hour ago the wind suddenly
changed to S. S. E.; the snowing has ceased; thermometer
falls and barometer rises.

2nd Jan. 1858.   New-Year's day was a second edition
of Christmas, and quite as pleasantly spent.   We dwelt
much upon the anticipations of the future, being a more
agreeable theme than the failure of the past.   I confess to a hearty welcome for the new year—anxious, of
course, that we may escape uninjured, and sufficiently early
to pursue the object of our voyage.

Exactly at midnight, on the 31st December, the arrival
of the new year was announced to me by our band—two
flutes and an accordion—striking up at my door.   There
was also a procession, or perhaps I should say a continuation of the band; these performers were grotesquely attired,
and armed with frying pans, gridirons, kettles, pots, and
pans, with which to join in and add to the effect of the *other*
music!

We have a very level hard walk alongside the ship; it is
narrowed to two or three yards in width by a snow-bank
four feet high.   In the face of this bank some twenty-five
holes have been excavated for the dogs and in them they

spend most of their time. It looks very formidable in the moonlight, being a good imitation of a casemated battery.

After our rubber of whist on New Year's night, Petersen related to us some of his dreadful sufferings when with the party of deserters from Dr. Kane. They spent the months of October and November in Booth Sound, lat. 77°; all that time upon the verge of starvation, unable to advance or retreat. For these two months they had no other fuel than their small cedar boat, the smoke of which was not endurable in their wretched hut, and without light, for the sun left them in October, unless we except one inch-and-a-half of taper daily, which they made out of a lump of bees'-wax that accidentally found its way into their boat before leaving the ship. In December they regained their vessel. I am surprised that no account of the extreme hardships of this party—so far exceeding that of their shipmates on board—has ever appeared; and I regret it, as I believe they owed their lives to the experience and fidelity of their interpreter Petersen.* At first the Esquimaux assisted them; latterly they were quite unable to do so, and became anxious to get rid of their visitors. Observing how weakened they had become, the Esquimaux endeavored to separate them from their guns and from each other, and even used threatening language.

During December we drifted 67 miles, directly down Baffin's Bay toward the Atlantic, and are now in lat. 74°. Although it is quite impossible to discriminate between the several influences which probably govern our movements, or to ascertain how much is due to each of them—such as the relative positions of ice, land, and open water, winds, currents and earth's rotation—yet it appears in the present instance that the wind is almost the sole agent in hastening this vast *continent* of ice toward the latitudes of its dissolution. We move before the wind in proportion to its strength : we remain stationary in calm weather. Neither

* For a thrilling account of the sufferings of this party, see "Godfrey's Narrative of the Kane Arctic Exploring Expedition."

surface nor submarine current has been detected ; the large
icebergs obey the same influences as the surface ice.   We
have noticed a slight set to the westward—it is not likely
to be produced by current, and may be the result of the
earth's motion from west to east.

6th.—Many lanes of water.   A seal has been seen, the
only one for six weeks.   Of the old ice which so closely
hemmed us in up to the middle of September, there is
hardly any within several miles of us except the large floe-
piece we are frozen to.   Every crack or lane which opens
is quickly covered with young ice, so that it cannot close
again ; and in this manner the old ice has been spread out.
I rejoice in its dispersion.

To-day I put a tumblerful of our strong ale (Alsopp's)
on deck to freeze : this was soon effected, the temperature
being −35°.   After bringing it below, and when its temperature had risen to 17°, it was almost all thawed—at 22° it
was completely so : it looked muddy, but settled after
standing for a couple of hours, when I drank it off, in
every way satisfied with my experiment and my beer ; it
seemed none the worse for its freezing, but rather flat from
its long exposure in a tumbler.

17th.—Northerly winds blow almost constantly.   We
have drifted 60 miles since the 1st, and are only 115 miles
from Upernivik,—once more upon confines of the habitable
world ! good light for three hours daily ; all this is cheering.   We continue our snow-hut practice, and can build
one in three-quarters of an hour.

28th.—The upper, edge of the sun appeared above the
horizon to-day, after an absence of eighty-nine days ; it was
a gladdening sight.   I sent for the ship's steward, and asked
what was the custom on such occasions ?   "To hoist the
colors, and serve out an extra half-gill, sir," was the ready
reply : accordingly, the Harwich lion soon fluttered in a

breeze cool enough to stiffen the limbs of ordinary lions, and in the evening the grog was issued.

30th.—Our messmate Pussy is unwell, and won't eat; in vain has Hobson tempted her with raw seal's flesh, preserved salmon, preserved milk, etc.; at length castor-oil was forcibly administered. Puss is a great favorite. Our finest dog, Sultan, is also sick, and his coat is in bad order; blubber has been prescribed for him;—and poor old Mary has fits, not uncommon after the long winter. Petersen immediately ordered her to be bled by slitting her ear; but Christian, in his fright and haste, cropped the tip of it off. These comprise our only medical cases. A dovekie, in its white winter plumage, and two seals have been seen lately.

15th Feb.—The returning daylight cheers us up wonderfully—not that we were suffering, either mentally or bodily, but the change is most agreeable; we can take much longer walks than were possible during the dark period. The men have been supplied with muskets, and go out sporting as ardently as schoolboys. I took a long walk towards one of our iceberg companions, but could not quite reach it, as weak ice intervened, each step producing an undulation. Finding the point of my knife went through it with but very slight resistance, I gave up the attempt and turned back. The ship's masts were scarcely visible in the distance; almost the whole of the intervening ice was of this winter's growth, and in many places much crushed up.

Daylight reveals to us evidences of vast ice movements having taken place during the dark months when we fancied all was still and quiet; and we now see how greatly we have been favored, what innumerable chances of destruction we have unconsciously escaped! A few days ago the ice suddenly cracked within ten yards of the ship, and gave her such a smart shock that every one rushed on deck with astonishing alacrity. One of these sudden disruptions occurred between me and the ship when I was returning from

the iceberg; the sun was just setting as I found myself cut
off. Had I been on the other side I would have loitered to
enjoy a refreshing gaze upon this dark streak of water; but
after a smart run of about a mile along its edge, and finding
no place to cross, visions of a patrol on the floe for the
long night of fifteen hours began to obtrude themselves!
At length I reached a place where the jagged edges of the
floes met, so crossed and got safely on board. Nothing
was seen during this walk of nearly 25 miles except one
seal. Recent gales have drifted us rapidly southward;
cracks and lanes are very numerous.

On the 1st a blue (or sooty) fox was shot. Although
130 geographical miles from the nearest land he was very
fat, hence we argue dovekies were much more numerous
during winter than we supposed. We have often noticed
the tracks of foxes following up those of the bears, probably for discarded scraps of the seals upon which they prey.
Hobson's favorite dog "Chummie" has returned, after an absence of six days, decidedly hungry, but he can hardly have
been without food all that time; some fox may have lured
him off. He evinced great delight in getting back, devoted
his first attentions to a hearty meal, then rubbed himself up
against his own particular associates, after which he sought
out and attacked the weakest of his enemies, and, soothed
by their howlings, coiled himself up for a long sleep.

1st *March.*—February has been a remarkably mild,
cloudy, windy month: the winter temperature may be said
to have passed away by the 10th, the average temperature
for the first ten days being –25°, whilst for the remainder
of the month it was –11°. Had one fallen asleep for a
month at least, he could not reasonably have expected to
find a greater change on awaking. Our drift has been also
great,—166 miles. We are south of the 70th parallel, and
may soon be expelled from our icy home.

On the 24th there was a fearful gale of wind. Had not

our housing been very well secured, it must have been blown away. We are preparing for sea, removing the snow from off the deck and round the ship; our skylights have been dug out (in winter they are always covered with a thick layer of snow), and the flood of light which beams down through them is quite charming. How intolerably sooty and smoke-dried everything looks.

On the 27th the first seal of this year was shot; it came in good time, for the fifty-one seals shot in autumn were finished only two days before: our English supply of dogs' food therefore remains almost untouched. Snow was observed to melt against the ship's side exposed to the sun, the thermometer in the shade standing at $-22°$! A very fine dog has died from eating a quantity of salt fish, which he managed to get at, although it was supposed to be quite out of his reach.

One of the two large icebergs which commenced this voyage with us last October, in $75\frac{1}{2}°$ N., has drifted out of sight to the S.E., the other one is far off in the N.W. I attribute these increased distances solely to the spreading abroad of the intervening ice.

When we were far north, and probably drifting more slowly than the ice in the stream of Lancaster Sound to the westward of us, the ship's head turned very gradually from right to left, from N.N.W. to W.; when about the parallel of $72°$ N., we supposed ourselves to be drifting faster than the western ice; in this, as in the previous case, comparing our drift with that of Lieutenant De Haven, the ship's head slowly shifted back to the right as far as W.N.W.; latterly it has not changed at all: we are in a narrower part of Davis' Strait, where the winds probably blow with equal force from shore to shore and drift the whole pack at a uniform rate.

5th.—On the 2nd four fat seals and some dovekies were shot; the largest seal weighed 170 lbs., the smallest 150

lbs.; they were males of the species Phoca hespida, or
Phoca fœtida, the latter epithet being by far the most appropriate at this season; the disagreeable odor resembles
garlic, and taints the whole animal so strongly that even
Esquimaux are nearly overpowered by it: this is almost
the only description of seal we have obtained, but the
females are at all seasons free from fetor. Several long
lanes of water extend at right angles to the straits.

The Doctor has taken a photograph of the ship by the
albumen process on glass; the temperature at the time was
below zero. Upon the 3rd and 4th a well-remarked revolving storm passed nearly over us to the W. N. W.; its extreme diameter was 30 hours, that of the strength of the
gale 18 hours; its centre probably passed about one-tenth
of its diameter to the S. W. The barometer was rather
high, having risen just before the wind commenced at N. E.;
but it now fell half an inch in ten hours, and continued to
fall until the wind shifted—almost suddenly—through S. E.
to S. S. W.; immediately the barometer got up rapidly.
As the barometer fell, the temperature rose from zero to
+18°, and fell again after the change of wind. This
violent storm brought with it a smart hail-shower.

The depression of the ice about the bows, in consequence
of a vast accumulation of snow-drift upon it, brought the
ship down by the head considerably; to-day this ice suddenly detached itself, and the fore part of the vessel sprang
up; she still remains frozen and held down abaft. The
snow-banking looks very woe-begone after this *ice-quake;*
it inclines out from the ship, and in many places has been
prostrated by the shock.

Early on the morning of the 7th the high land of Disco
was seen; its distance was upwards of 90 miles.

CHAPTER VI.

A bear-fight—An ice-nip—Strong gales, rapid drift—The 'Fox' breaks
out of the pack—Hanging on to floe-edge—The Arctic bear—An ice
tournament—The 'Fox' in peril—A storm in the pack—Escape from
the pack.

9th March.—A BEAR was seen this morning; but as he
was going away from us, the dogs were brought out in the
hope that they might keep him at bay until the sportsmen
came up.   It was very pretty to see them take up the scent,
the moment they caught sight of him they set off at full
speed.   Bruin had seen them first, and increased his pace
to a clumsy gallop, yet the dogs were soon around him; he
seemed to care but little about them, steadily making off
and following the trending of a recently frozen crack in
search of clear water, evidently aware that his persecutors
would not follow him there.

After five hours all returned on board again; out of the
ten dogs four were wounded by his claws,—skin deep only,
but one of the wounds was seven inches inches in length,
as if made with a sharp knife! this was sewed up, the
others were merely trimmed, and nature, I am informed,
will do all the rest.   It is really wonderful what cures
nature and instinct effect: notwithstanding the extreme
cold, no external dressings are applied, because the animal
must not be prevented from licking its wound.   Petersen
says this bear must be very thin, else he could not run so
fast.   I think it very probable that he has been hunted

before, and that fear lent him wings. A black whale has been seen.

11th.—Two small seals free from taint were shot yesterday, so we had fried liver and steaks for breakfast this morning; both were good, but the steaks were preferred; they were very dark and very tender, had been cut thin, deprived of all fat, and washed in two or three waters to get rid of the blubber.

16th.—Several long lanes of water have again opened, but now all of them extend parallel to the direction of the straits; one lane passed within 120 yards of the ship; its extremes are not visible even from aloft; the ice upon its east side has a more rapid southerly motion than that upon its west side.

18th.—Last night the ice closed, shutting up our lane, but its opposite sides continued for several hours to move past each other, rubbing off all projections, crushing and forcing out of water masses four feet thick : although 120 yards distant, this pressure shook the ship and cracked the intervening ice.

I went out with a lantern to see the nip,—it certainly was awe-inspiring; no one in his senses could avoid reflecting upon the inevitable fate of a ship if exposed to such fearful pressure. It is now spring tides.

19th.—All yesterday the lane remained open; in the evening it closed with but slight pressure ; yet as the opposing fields of ice continued to move in opposite directions, all jagged points were brushed off, and the debris thus formed between their edges presented a heaving surface of ice-masses,—an ice river. On the separation of the floes, mass after mass forced itself up to the surface, until at length all the submerged ice had risen, except such as had been forced quite under their edges. One seldom meets with a cleanly fractured floe-edge, they are usually fringed with crushed-up ice or newly formed sludge.

23rd.—Seals and dovekies are now common; the latter have already made considerable advances toward their summer plumage.

Yesterday there was a very heavy S. E. gale; it blew so furiously, and the snow-drift was so dense, that we could neither hear nor see what was going on twenty yards off; at night the ship, becoming suddenly detached from the ice, heeled over to the storm; until the cause was ascertained we thought the ice had broken up and pressed against the ship. It was not so; but when the weather moderated we found that there had been heavy pressure upon the edge of the floes,—so much, indeed, that the lane of water was now within 70 yards of the 'Fox;' and that ice $4\frac{1}{2}$ feet thick had been crushed during the storm for a distance of about 50 yards.

25th.—Strong N. W. winds lately, the ship rocking to the breeze, and rubbing her poor sides against the ice, producing a creaking sound which is far from pleasant. More ice squeezing, and a further inroad upon our barrier; it has yielded slightly, nipping the ship, inclining her to port, and lifting her stern about a foot. Occasional groanings within, and surgings of the ice without.

Our boats, provisions, sledges, knapsacks, and equipment, are ready for a hasty departure,—beyond this we can do nothing; as long as our friendly barrier lasts we need not fear, but who can tell the moment it may be demolished, and the ship exposed to destruction? I am scribbling within a foot of the sternpost—in fact, there is a notch in my table to receive it; and I sympathize with its constant groanings; the ice allows it no rest.

27th.—Strong N. W. gale with a return of cold weather. We have drifted 39 miles in the last forty-eight hours! The lane is open; the whole pack appears to have plenty of room to drift, and, I am happy to add, is taking advantage of it,—so much so that the smaller pieces floating freely

in the lane can hardly go at the same pace.   Our remaining
winter companion, the iceberg, was in sight a few days ago,
far away to the N. W.; it may be still visible from aloft,
but these March gales cut so keenly, that the crow's-nest is
but seldom visited.

31st.—Another N. W. gale; it is also spring tides, and
this conjunction makes one fearful of ice movement and
pressure; but it seems as if the pack had more room to
move in, as it does not close much.   Seals are often shot,
bear tracks are common, and narwhals are frequently seen
migrating northward.   The bears must prefer the night-
time for wandering about, else we could not help seeing
them; we often find their tracks within a few hundred yards
of the ship.

Although the last, yet this is the coldest day of the
month—the thermometer down to –27°.   The mean temperature for March has been unusually high, –3°; whilst
Lieutenant De Haven's was –17°.   Notwithstanding that
heavy S. E. gales have three times driven us backward, yet
we have advanced 100 miles further down Davis' Straits.

6th April.—To-day we enjoy fine weather, the more so
since it comes after a tremendous northerly gale of forty-
eight hourss' duration.   Two days ago the friendly old floe,
so long our bulwark of defence, was cracked; the lane of
water thus formed soon widened to 60 yards, passed within
30 yards of the 'Fox,' and cut off three of our boats.
Yesterday morning another crack detached the remaining
30 yards from us, and as it widened the ship swung across
the opening; as quickly as we could effect it the ship was
again placed alongside the ice and within a projecting
point; had it closed only a few feet whilst she lay across
the lane, the consequences must have been very serious.
Even to effect this slight change of position we were fully
occupied for four hours; for the gale blew furiously, and
thermometer stood at 12° below zero, and the cold was very

7

much felt; our hawsers were frozen so stiff as to be quite
unmanageable, and we were obliged to use the chain cables
to warp the ship into safety.

Throughout yesterday the wind continued extremely
strong and keen,—fortunately the ice remained perfectly
still : our funnels refused to draw up the smoke ; so that
between the suffocation, the cold, and anxiety lest the ice
should move, our Easter Monday was sufficiently miserable.
The half of our poor dogs were cut off from the ship by
the lane, and continued to howl dismally until late, when
the new ice over the lane was strong enough to bear them,
and they came across to us.

To-day we have recovered the boats, shot four seals, seen
two whales, and much water to the eastward ; we are in
latitude 67° 18′ N., and highly delighted with the rapidity
of our southern drift.

10*th.*—Yesterday evening the setting sun rendered visible
the western land, probably Cape Dyer. We have drifted
70 miles in the last week, and are only 18 miles from De
Haven's position of escape ; but as we are two months
earlier, we must expect to be carried farther south.

12*th.*—This morning we drifted ingloriously out of the
Arctic regions, and with what very different feelings from
those with which we crossed the Arctic circle eight months
ago ! However, we have not done with it yet ; directly the
ice lets us go, we will (D.V.) re-enter the frigid zone, and
"try again," with, I trust, better success.

A gull and a few terns appeared to-day ; these are the
first of our summer visitors. The temperature improves ;
yesterday at one o'clock it was +19° in the shade, +15°
in the crow's nest 70 feet high, and +51° against a black
surface exposed to the sun.

16*th.*—Last night a bear came to the ship, was wounded
but escaped ; to-day the tracks were followed up for three
miles, the bear found, and again wounded—finally the un-

lucky beast was shot in the water seven miles from the
the ship ; it was lost in consequence of the rapid drifting
of the ice, which ran over the floating carcase.

To-night a dense fog-bank rests upon the water to the
southward ; its upper edge is illuminated by aurora, showing a faint tremulous light.

17*th*.—Another northerly gale ; holding fast to the ice
with three hawsers ; snow-drift limits the view to a couple
of miles, so all to the eastward appears water, and to the
westward ice.

Last night the ice opened considerably : to secure the
ship occupied us for six hours ; several of the dogs were
again cut off; as the ice they were on was rapidly drifting
away, I sent a boat to recover them ; it was a difficult and
hazardous business, but at length the boat and dogs returned in safety, to my great relief, for it was both dark and
late.

18*th*.—Yesterday morning when I wrote up my journal,
I was hoping to hold on quietly to the floe-edge until the
wind moderated, when with clear weather we could take
advantage of the openings and make some progress towards
the clear sea. We were unable to hold on, for the floe-
edge broke away, setting us adrift ; some time was occupied
in fetching off the boats and dogs,—five of the latter unfortunately would not allow themselves to be caught. As speedily as possible the rudder was shipped and sail set, and before three o'clock the ship was running fast to the eastward !
During the night the ice closed, and at daylight scarcely
any water was visible ; with the exception of a couple of
icebergs, all the ice in sight was not more than two days
old ; it mainly owes its origin and rapid growth to the
immense quantities of snow blown off the pack.

It still blows hard, and the thermometer stands at 11°.
A sudden opening of the ice this forenoon allowed us to

run a few miles southward, and then it closed again; we are now surrounded by young ice.

20th.—We have been carried rapidly past the position where the Arctic discovery ship 'Resolute' was picked up.

Yesterday three bears, a fulmar petrel, and a snow-bunting were seen; to-day a fine bear came within 150 yards, and was shot by our sportsmen; as they were standing round it afterwards upon the ice, a small seal, the only one seen for several days, popped up its head as if to exult over its fallen enemy—it was of course instantly shot; we have learnt to esteem seal's liver for breakfast very highly.

It seems hardly right to call polar bears *land* animals; they abound here,—110 geographical miles from the nearest land,—upon very loose broken-up ice, which is steadily drifting into the Atlantic at the rate of 12 or 14 miles daily; to remain upon it would insure their destruction if were they not nearly amphibious; they hunt by scent, and are constantly running across and against the wind, which prevails from the northward, so that the same instinct which directs their search for prey, also serves the important purpose of guiding them in the direction of the land and more solid ice.

I remarked that the upper part of both Bruin's forepaws were rubbed quite bare; Petersen explains that to surprise the seal a bear crouches down with his forepaws doubled underneath, and pushes himself noiselessly forward with his hinder legs until within a few yards, when he springs upon the unsuspecting victim, whether in the water or upon the ice. The Greenlanders are fond of bear's flesh, but never eat either the heart or liver, and say that these parts cause sickness. No instance is known of Greenland bears attacking men, except when wounded or provoked; they never disturb the Esquimaux graves, although they seldom fail to

THE GREENLANDER'S SUPPER APPROPRIATED BY A BEAR.

rob a cache of seal's flesh, which is a similar construction of loose stones above ground.

A native of Upernivik, one dark winter's day, was out visiting his seal-nets. He found a seal entangled, and, whilst kneeling down over it upon the ice to get it clear, he received a slap on the back—from his companion as he supposed; but a second and heavier blow made him look smartly round. He was horror-stricken to see a peculiarly grim old bear instead of his comrade! without deigning further notice of the man, Bruin tore the seal out of the net and commenced his supper. He was not interrupted; nor did the man wait to see the meal finished.

I had long ago resolved, if we escaped before the 15th, or the 20th April at the latest, to go to Newfoundland to refresh the crew and to refit, even if no damage from the ice should be sustained. In order to do so it would have been necessary for us to visit a Greenland port for a supply of water. We could not have calculated upon much assistance from our engines upon such a voyage, Mr. Brand alone being capable of working the engines, so that ten or twelve hours daily is all the steaming that could have been expected.

But we are still ice-locked, so I purpose going to Holsteinborg in preference to a more southern port, as there we may expect to get reindeer and a small supply of stores suitable to our wants. The whalers sometimes reach Disco in March, Upernivik in May, and the North Water early in June. Unless we should be at once set free, we would not have time to spare for a Newfoundland voyage.

.24th.—Another anxious week has passed. Latterly we have experienced southwesterly currents similar to those which Parry describes when beset here in June, 1819. To-day we have had a strong S. E. breeze, with snow and dark weather. The wind had greatly moderated when the swell reached us about eight o'clock this evening. It is now ten o'clock; the long ocean swell already lifts its crest five feet above the hollow of the sea, causing its thick covering of icy fragments to dash against each other and against us with unpleasant violence. It is however very beautiful to look upon, the dear old familiar ocean-swell! it has long been a stranger to us, and is welcome in our solitude. If the 'Fox' was as solid as her neighbors, I am quite sure she would enter into this ice-tournament with all their apparent heartiness, instead of audibly making known her sufferings to us. Every considerable surface of ice has been broken into many smaller ones; with feelings of exultation I watched the process from aloft. A floe-piece near us, of 100 yards in diameter, was speedily cracked so as to resemble a sort of labyrinth, or, still more, a field-spider's web. In the course of half an hour the family resemblance was totally lost; they had so battered each other, and struggled out of their original regularity. The rolling sea can no longer be checked; "the pack has taken upon itself the functions of an ocean," as Dr. Kane graphically expresses it.

26th.—At sea! How am I to describe the events of the last two days? It has pleased God to accord to us a deliverance in which His merciful protection contrasts—how strongly!—with our own utter helplessness; as if the successive mercies vouchsafed to us during our long, long winter and mysterious ice-drift had been concentrated and repeated in a single act. Thus forcibly does His great goodness come home to the mind!

I am in no humor for writing, being still tired, seedy, and perhaps a little seasick; at least I have a headache, caused by the rolling of the ship and rattling noise of everything.

On Saturday night, the 24th, I went on deck to spend the greater part of it in watching, and to determine what to do. The swell greatly increased; it had evidently been approaching for hours before it reached us, since it rose in proportion as the ice was broken up into smaller pieces.

In a short time but few of them were equal in size to the
ship's deck ; most of them not half so large.   I knew that
near the pack-edge the sea would be very heavy and dangerous ; but the wind was now fair, and having auxiliary
steam-power, I resolved to push out of the ice if possible.

Shortly after midnight the ship was under sail, slowly
boring her way to the eastward ; at two o'clock on Sunday
morning commenced steaming, the wind having failed.   By
eight o'clock we had advanced considerably to the eastward, and the swell had become dangerously high, the
waves rising ten feet above the trough of the sea.   The
shocks of the ice against the ship were alarmingly heavy ;
it became necessary to steer exactly head-on to swell.   We
slowly passed a small iceberg 60 or 70 feet high ; the swell
forced it crashing through the pack, leaving a small water-
space in its wake, but sufficient to allow the seas to break
against its cliffs, and throw the spray in heavy showers
quite over its summit.

The day wore on without change, except that the snow
and mists cleared off.   Gradually the swell increased, and
rolled along more swiftly, becoming in fact a very heavy
regular sea, rather than a swell.   The ice often lay so
closely packed that we could hardly force ahead, although
the fair wind had again freshened up.   Much heavy hum-
mocky ice and large berg-pieces lay dispersed through the
pack ; a single thump from any of them would have been
instant destruction.   By five o'clock the ice became more
loose, and clear spaces of water could be seen ahead.   We
went faster, received fewer though still more severe shocks,
until at length we had room to steer clear of the heaviest
pieces ; and at eight o'clock we emerged from the villanous
"pack," and were running fast through straggling pieces
into a clear sea.   The engines were stopped, and Mr. Brand
permitted to rest after eighteen hours' duty, for we now
have no one else capable of driving the engines.

Throughout the day I trembled for the safety of the rudder, and screw; deprived of the one or the other, even for half an hour, I think our fate would have been sealed; to have steered in any other direction than *against* the swell would have exposed, and probably sacrificed both.

Our bow is very strongly fortified, well plated externally with iron, and so very sharp that the ice-masses, repeatedly hurled against the ship by the swell as she rose to meet it, were thus robbed of their destructive force; they struck us obliquely, yet caused the vessel to shake violently, the bells to ring, and almost knocked us off our legs. On many occasions the engines were stopped dead by ice choking the screw; once it was some minutes before it could be got to revolve again. Anxious moments those!

After yesterday's experience I can understand how men's hair has turned gray in a few hours. Had self-reliance been my only support and hope, it is not impossible that I might have illustrated the fact. Under the circumstances I did my best to insure our safety, looked as stoical as possible, and inwardly trusted that God would favor our exertions. What a release ours has been, not only from eight months' imprisonment, but from the perils of that one day! Had our little vessel been destroyed after the ice broke up, there remained no hope for us. But we have been brought safely through, and are all truly grateful, I hope, and believe.

I grieve to think of poor Lady Franklin and our friends at home. Severely as we have felt the failure of our first season's operations, yet the ordeal is now over with us: not so with her and them,—they have still to experience that bitter disappointment.

Our distance within the pack-edge, where we first made sail yesterday, was 22 miles. Before we got clear of the ice the height of the waves was 13½ feet; after passing through the last of it there was no increase, but the sea was more confused; in fact, within the ice all minor disturbances were quelled or merged into one regular fast-following swell. The ship and her machinery behaved most admirably in the struggle; should I ever have to pass through such an ice-covered, heaving ocean again, let me secure a passage in the ' Fox.'

During our 242 days in the packed-ice of Baffin's Bay and Davis' Straits we were drifted 1194 geographical or 1385 statute miles; it is the longest drift I know of, and our winter, as a whole, may be considered as having been mild, but very windy.

We are steering now for Holsteinborg, where I intend to refit and refresh the crew; it is reputed to be the best place for reindeer upon the coast.

CHAPTER VII.

Wednesday night, April 28th.—Safely anchored at
Holsteinborg, and moored to the rocks ; a charming change,
after our position only a few days back. We have been
visited by the Danish residents—the chief trader or governor, the priest, and two others : their latest European intelligence is not more recent than our own, but the Danish
ship is hourly expected ; she usually leaves Copenhagen
about the middle of March.

The winter here has been just the reverse of our own experience ; it has been severe in point of temperature, but
with very little wind ; the land lies buried in snow, and as
yet there is no thaw ; it is too early for the codfishery, and
not a single reindeer has been killed throughout the winter !
Eider-ducks, looms and dovekies are abundant, as well as
hares and ptarmigan.

29th.—A bright and lovely day. Our poor, half-famished
dogs have been landed near the carcases of four whales, so
they must be supremely happy. I visited the Governor to-
day, and found his little wooden house as scrupulously
clean and neat as the houses of the Danish residents in
Greenland invariably are. The only ornaments about the
room were portraits of his unfortunate wife and two children : they embarked at Copenhagen last year to rejoin him,

and the ill-fated vessel has never since been heard of. Poor
Governor Elberg is in ill health, and talks of returning
home—by *home* he means Denmark, the land of his birth,
and where once he had a home.

30*th*.—This is a grand Danish holiday : the inhabitants
are all dressed in their Sunday clothes—at least, all who
have got a change of garments—and there is both morning
and evening service in the small wooden church. As the
Governor could not be persuaded to unlock the door of the
dance-house, our men returned on board early ; yesterday
evening they were all on shore, and, with the Esquimaux,
were squeezed into this one large room : to be squeezed in a
crowd of human beings is positive enjoyment after a winter's isolation such as ours has been. Old Harvey consti-
tuted himself master of the ceremonies, and with his flute
led the orchestra ; it consisted of one other flute and a fiddle ;
he managed to perch himself above all the rest, at one end
of the room, and played with such vigor that our bluejack-
ets and the Esquimaux ladies danced away most furiously
for hours. These ladies can dance in the least possible
space, their costume being particularly well adapted for the
purpose, partaking as it does much more of the "Bloomer"
than the "crinoline."

Christian looks immensely happy : his countrymen regard
him as a man whose fortune is made, and the women gaze
with admiration upon his neat sailor's dress, and his good-
natured, full, round face, and huge fat shining cheeks ; Mr.
Petersen is in great request to interpret between the English, Danes, and Esquimaux.

7*th May*.—I intended sailing for Disco this morning, but
wind and weather were adverse. We have obtained but
little here except water, a tolerable supply of rock cod,
some ptarmigan, hares, wildfowl, and a few items of stores.
The Governor *now* thinks the Danish ship must have been
instructed to visit Godhaab before coming here. We have

left letters to go home in her, and they ought to be in England by the end of June.

I visited to-day a small lake at the foot of Mount Cunningham; it is said to occupy the centre of an extinct volcano : but I saw nothing to bear out the assertion. This is the only part of Greenland where earthquakes are felt. The Governor told me of an unusually severe shock which occurred a winter or two ago. He was sitting in his room reading at the time, when he heard a loud noise like the discharge of a cannon; immediately afterwards a tremulous motion was felt, some glasses upon the table began to dance about, and papers lying on the window-sill fell down : after a few seconds it ceased. He thinks the motion originated at the lake, as it was not felt by some people beyond it, and that it passed from N. E. to S. W.

This mountain scenery is really charming; but a little more animal life—reindeer, for instance—would make it far more pleasing in our eyes. The last twelvemonth's produce of this district amounts only to 500 reindeer skins instead of 3000, as in ordinary years. The clergyman of Holsteinborg was born in this colony, and has succeeded his father in the priestly office; his wife is the only European female in the colony. Being told that fuel was extremely scarce in the Danish houses, and that "the priest's wife was blue with the cold," I sent on shore a present of some coals.

On Sunday afternoon, hearing the church bell ringing I went on shore. It proved to be only a christening. The little dusky infant received a long string of European names. There was a small description of barrel organ, to the sound of which the congregation joined in, keeping a loud monotonous chant. Most of the young people had hymn-books in their hands, printed in the Esquimaux language.

Ravens seem very abundant, also large grey falcons : perhaps the dead whales may have attracted an unusual number.

Poor Christian has not only fallen desperately in love, but has engaged himself to the object of his affections, a pretty Esquimaux girl. He asked me to-day to give her a passage up to Godhavn, as he wished to leave her in charge of his mother until his return there with us next year, when his engagement for the voyage would be fulfilled. Having heard a rumor of a young woman awaiting his return to Godhavn, I taxed him with it, but he replied with great simplicity that "he had never promised her, and would not marry her, as his friends objected to the match!" What are the good Greenlanders coming to? I recommended that he should leave his betrothed in her own home, with her mother and family. His asking a passage for her, in order to leave her with his mother, is strong proof of the sincerity of his engagement, not only to his lady love, but to the 'Fox' also.

I have written to the Admiralty to account for my prolonged absence from England; and to Dr. Rink to acquaint him with the cause of my second visit to his inspectorate.

Governor Elberg has promised to get me some fossil fish, to be found only in North Strom Fiord : they are interesting, as being of unknown geological date.

10th.—On the morning of the 8th we left Holsteinborg with a pleasant land wind and bright weather. When 15 miles off shore we were stopped by ice formed during the last two nights, the thermometer having fallen to 12°; out in the offing the weather was gloomy and cold, and strong northerly winds were blowing. On closing the land again, we regained the offshore wind and bright weather.

Keeping close along shore, and threading our way through a vast deal of "pack" and numerous icebergs, we gained sight of Disco about noon to-day, and by the evening were within an hour's sail of Godhavn, when we were again stopped by a broad belt of ice stretching along the coast; this was a bitter disappointment, more particularly as a gale of wind with heavy sea was fast rising, and snow beginning to fall thickly; there was nothing for it, however, but to stand off under easy sail for the night.

12th.—At anchor at the Whalefish Islands. On the evening of the 10th we stood off from the inhospitable barrier of ice, prepared to meet the storm; snow fell so thickly that we could hardily see the icebergs in time to avoid them. We supposed ourselves to be well to leeward of the Whalefish Islands, but were deceived by the tides; suddenly a small, low islet was seen on the lee bow; not being able to pass to windward, we were obliged to wear ship, and, in doing so, passed within the ship's length of destruction—for we were certainly within that distance of the rocks! The islet was covered with snow, and but for some very few dark points showing through, it could not be distinguished from ice. On the 11th the weather improved, and in the evening we came to our present anchorage. From a hill we can watch an opportunity to enter Godhavn. Notwithstanding the blowing weather, some natives came about five miles off to us; the water washed over their little *kayaks*, and kept the occupants' sealskin dresses streaming with wet up to their shoulders; this part of their dress seems rather part of the kayak, as it is attached to it round the hole in which the *kayaker* sits, so that no water can enter. It is wonderful to see how closely a man can assimilate his habits to those of a fish.

The Danish cooper in charge of this out-station tells us there are thirteen English whalers already out, and some of them have been up to the north end of Disco; two vessels are in sight. The world, it appears, is at peace. Petersen was at one time in charge of this station; he is now seeking out his old acquaintances.

14th.—Summer has suddenly burst upon us—thermometer up to 40°; moreover, we are enjoying English newspapers, and have dined off roast beef and vegetables!

Two days ago I sent a note off to a whaler by a kayak, requesting her captain to lend me some newspapers; the note reached Captain J. Walker, of the 'Jane,' and yesterday his ship, accompanied by the 'Heroine,' Captain J. Simpson, approached us, and they both came in to call upon me, each of them bringing the very acceptable present of some newspapers, besides a quarter of beef, with vegetables. Nothing could exceed their sincere good feeling and kindness; they offered to supply me with any thing their ships could afford. The account they gave of last season is as follows: the whalers reached Devil's Point, near Melville Bay, as early as the 21st of May: southerly winds set in, and blew incessantly for six weeks, during all which time they were closely beset, and the ships 'Gipsey' and 'Undaunted' were crushed. When able to move, the fleet returned southward along the "pack-edge," which was everywhere found to be impenetrable; they sailed southward of Disco, and about the middle of July the earliest ships rounded the southern extremity of middle ice in lat. $62\frac{1}{2}$°, and found no difficulty in their further passage to Pond's Bay. Captain Walker says ships could not have reached Lancaster Sound, as there was much ice north of Pond's Bay which he thought extended quite across to Melville Bay.

The position of the ice last season was considered to be most unusual; the long prevalence of southerly winds appeared to have separated the tail of the pack from the main body, the former lying against the west land about Cape Searle, whilst the latter was forced northward and pressed closely into Melville Bay; the ships sailed freely between these two great divisions, and found the west water unusually extensive.

Had I been able to collect a sufficient number of sledge-dogs at Godhavn last year, it was my intention to have sailed across to the west side if possible, instead of pursuing the usual route through Melville Bay; but the opinions of the captains of the lost whalers were in favor of a "Melville Bay" passage, and the necessity for obtaining dogs left me no choice as to whether I should proceed west, or north to Proven and Upernivik; I have already recorded what were my opinions *at the time*, so need only observe *now* that, although I failed, I believe my decision was justified by all former experience, even independently of the circumstances which obliged me to adopt it.   Nevertheless it is mortifying to find that ships had reached as far as Pond's Bay, and with but little difficulty.   Sir Edward Parry, upon his third voyage, did not reach the west water until very late in the season, although some of the whalers met with better success by following up another route.

There is nothing more uncertain than ice-navigation, dependent as it is upon winds, temperatures, and currents; one can calculate upon "the chances," and how nearly we succeeded we have already seen.   In the preceding year (1856) some of the whalers got through Melville Bay as early as the 15th June, only a few days after the commencement of the summer's thaw.   Captain Walker tells me there are many years in which the whalers can pass up the western shore late in the season, but not always so far as Pond's Bay; of Melville Bay after the 10th or 15th July they know nothing, but the voyages of discovery afford us ample details; whilst of the southern route almost nothing has been made publicly known.

There are many intelligent whaling captains who possess much valuable knowledge of these lands and seas, and even in the terra incognita of Frobisher's Straits, whalers have wintered, whilst our charts scarcely afford even a vague idea of the configuration of these extensive islands.   The so-called "Home Bay" has been penetrated for fifty miles, and is supposed to be a strait leading to Fox's Furthest. Scott's Inlet is also said to be a strait leading into a western arm of the same sea. A surveying vessel would bo usefully employed for a couple of summers in tracing the general outline of these possessions of Her Majesty, more particularly as they are rather thickly inhabited by Esquimaux most eager to barter their produce for rifles, saws, files, knives, needles, and such like articles. Good coal has been found upon Durbin Island (near Cape Searle), in a convenient little cove upon its southern side; and as the old sailing whalers are fast being replaced by steamers, this place may become of great importance to them.

We are refitting, shooting, and devouring quantities of excellent mussels; eider ducks are very abundant, but extremely shy. Poor Puss has been killed; tempted on deck by the unusually warm weather, she was pounced upon by the dogs.

17*th.*—Yesterday our attempt to enter the port of Godhaven failed, it is still filled with ice. This evening Young and I examined a narrow rocky cove—Upernivik Bay of the natives; finding it suitable for our purpose, the ship was brought in and moored to the rocks. We were received. with much kindness by our friends Mr. and Mrs. Olrik, and were presented with a file of late English papers. A considerable supply of beer was ordered to be brewed for us.

I found Mrs. Olrik without a fire in her sitting room; it was unnecessary; the windows looked to the south, and the sun shone brightly in upon a profusion of geraniums and European flowers, at once reminding one of home, and refreshing the senses by their perfume and beauty.; the merry voices of the children were also a most pleasing novelty. Mr. Olrik says the past winter has not been in any way remarkable, except for the prevalence of strong winds; April. and the early part of May have been unusually cold.

24*th.*—We did honor to Her Majesty's birth-day. by dressing the 'Fox' in all her flags, and regaling her crew with plum-pudding and grog. The ice having moved off,.

8

we have come into the harbor of Godhavn, as being more
convenient and safe.   The day has been a busy one : we
have completed our small purchases and closed our letters ;
I have added another Esquimaux lad to our crew, taking
with him his rifle, kayak, and sledge.   This evening there
has been a brisk interchange of presents between us and our
Danish friends.   I have been given an eider-down coverlet
by the Governor, Mr. Andersen ; and, by Mrs. Olrik, some
delicious preserve of Greenland cranberries, a tin of preserved ptarmigan, and a jar of pickled whale-skin ; my
table is decked with European flowers, including roses, mig-
nonnette, and violets.

With good reason shall we remember Godhavn ; we
have certainly been treated as especial favorites.

26th.—Left Godhavn early yesterday morning, and anchored this afternoon in our old position off the Coal Cliffs
in the Waigat ; a party of seal-hunters from Atanekerdluk
came off to us, and their hunting having terminated successfully, they will assist us in coaling.   From these men I obtained much information about this part of the coast ; within
a range of twenty miles upon the Disco shore there are four
distinct coaling places ; but at this early season two of them
are deeply covered with snow.   There is also very good
coal at the S. E. end of Hare Island, where it can be easily
obtained.   The ice in this strait broke up as long ago as
the 3d April ; it has all drifted out to the northward, only
a few icebergs now remain.

28th.—Again hastening northward ; the business of coaling was very speedily and satisfactorily completed, but the
quality of the coals is very inferior.   Upon the green
slopes our sportsmen found nothing but a few ptarmigan
and a hare.

Shortly after running close past the deserted settlement
of Noursak, we arrived off a small bay, and were startled
by finding the water had suddenly changed from transparent

blue to a thick muddy color, but there was no change in its depth; we were crossing the stream of "Makkaks Elvin," or Clay River, which empties itself into the bay after running through a broad and extensive valley, said to abound with reindeer; this river has its origin in lakes and glaciers in the interior, and the discoloration of the water is probably the chief cause of success in white-whale fishing, which is carried on here in the autumn, as those timid animals will not permit boats to approach them in clear water.

This evening we are crossing Omenak's Fiord, and the land-wind, which here and all along the coast northwards blows from the N. E., has come off to us.

31st.—Lying fast to an iceberg off Upernivik.

The whalers are all within a dozen miles of us, unable to penetrate further north. The season appears forward, and the ice much decayed; but southerly winds prevail, retarding its disruption and removal. Captain Parker, of the 'Emma,' tells me he does not expect to make a north passage this year, and as his experience extends over a period of at least thirty years, I give his reason; it is simply this, —that as during the months of February, March, and April northerly winds prevailed to an unusual degree, therefore southerly winds may now be expected to continue; if he prove a prophet, it will be to our serious hindrance at this critical season. Governor Fliescher says the winter has been mild; there has been but little wind, and that chiefly from the southward.

4th June.—We have received much kindness from our friends Captains Parker and J. Simpson, as well as from others of the whaling fleet; the former has generously supplied us with many things we were rather short of, not only in ship's stores, but provisions and coals, and in return I have of course furnished him with a receipt for his owners. Captain Simpson has most handsomely presented the 'Fox' with a sail and yards, which, after some slight alterations, will enable us to add a main topsail to our spread of canvas. For the two days we lay at the iceberg, alongside of the 'Emma,' I made furious attacks upon Captain Parker's beefsteaks and porter; we amply availed ourselves of his hearty welcome. By the arrival of the fine steam whaler, 'Tay,' from Scotland, we have received papers up to 17th April.

This morning we slowly steamed away from Upernivik, threading our way betwixt islands, and ice, for about 30 miles, and now await further ice movement before it will be possible to proceed.

These are called the Woman Islands, so named by the celebrated Arctic explorer John Davis, who visited them in Queen Elizabeth's reign; he found here only a few old women, their frightened lords and more active juniors having effected their escape.

Upon one of these islands a stone was picked up some 30 years ago, bearing a Runic inscription; it was sent home to Copenhagen as a most interesting relic of the early Scandinavian voyagers; but nothing was on it except the names of those men "who cleared this place" (or formed a settlement), and the date, 1135. In all probability their sojourn was extremely short, perhaps only for a single summer. The Esquimaux did not make their appearance for nearly two centuries later.

After Egede's settlement at Godhaab in 1721, the Danish trading establishments gradually extended along the coast, and Upernivik was one of them; but it appears to have been soon abandoned. During Napoleon's wars all the Danish posts were withdrawn, as the British fleet effectually cut off communication with Europe; but after peace was restored in 1815, the trading posts were again resorted to, and a new settlement formed near the ruins of the old one at Upernivik; it enjoys pre-eminence as the most northern abode of civilized man.

CHAPTER VIII.

Fox' nearly wrecked—Afloat, and push ahead—Arctic hairbreadth es-
capes—Nearly caught in the pack—Shooting little auks—The Arctic
Highlanders—Cape York—Crimson snow—Struggling to the westward
—Reach the West-land—Off the entrance of Lancaster Sound.

June 8th.—YESTERDAY morning we passed close outside
Buchan Island; it is small but lofty, its north side is almost precipitous, yet notwithstanding this strong indication
of deep water, a reef of rocks lies about a mile off it. I
happened to be aloft with the look-out-man at half-past
eight o'clock as we were steaming through a narrow lead in
the ice, when I saw a rock close ahead; it was capped with
ice, therefore was hardly distinguishable from the floating
masses around; the engines were stopped and reversed, but
there was neither time nor room to avoid the reef, which
now extended on each side of us, and upon which the ship's
bow stuck fast whilst her stern remained in 36 feet water;
the tide had just commenced to fall, and all our efforts to
haul off from the rocks were ineffectual. The floes lay
within 30 yards of us upon each side. I feared their drifting down upon the ship and turning her over; but fortunately it was perfectly calm, and as the tide fell, points of
the reef held them fast. The ship continued to fall over to
starboard; at dead low water her inclination was 35°, the
water covered the starboard gunwale from the mainmast aft,
and reached almost up to the after hatchway; at this time
the slightest shake must have caused her to fall over upon
her side, when she would have instantly filled and sunk.

The dogs, after repeated ineffectual attempts to lie upon
the deck, quietly coiled themselves up upon such parts of
the lee gunwale as remained above water and went to sleep.

To me the moments seem lengthened out beyond anything
I could have imagined; but at length the water began to
rise, and the ship to resume her upright position. Boats,
anchors, hawsers, etc., were got on board again with the
utmost alacrity, and the ship floated off unhurt after having
been eleven hours upon the reef.   We had grounded during
the day tide and were floated off by the night tide, which upon
this coast occasions a much greater rise and fall,—so far we
were favored, but the poor little ' Fox' had a very narrow
escape; as for ourselves, there was not the slightest cause
for apprehension, three steam whalers being within signal
distance.

To-day we are steaming along after the three vessels
which passed us last evening and disappeared round Cape
Shackleton during the night.   The contrast between our
prospects yesterday and to-day fills one with delight,—to
be afloat and advancing unobstructedly once more is indeed
charming.

11*th*.—On the afternoon of the 8th we joined the steamers
' Tay,' Captain Deuchars; ' Chase,' Captain Gravill, sen.;
and ' Diana,' Gravill, jun. After repeated ice-detentions,
we have reached Duck Island.   Captain Deuchars says
there is every prospect of an early north passage; we have
had several conversations about the Pond's Bay natives,
and their reports of ships, wrecks, and Europeans.   There
appears to be not only great difficulty, but also uncertainty,
in arriving at their meaning; to form an idea of the time
elapsed since an event, or the distance to the spot where it
occurred, is a still harder task. I look forward to our
visit at Pond's Bay with greatly increased interest.

In August, 1855, when Captain Deuchars was crossing
through the middle ice, in latitude 70°, he found part of a

THE 'FOX' ON A ROCK NEAR BUCHAN ISLAND.

steamer's topmast imbedded in heavy ice; he also saw the moulded form of a ship's side, and thinks the latter must have sunk; the portion of the topmast visible was sawed off and taken to England. It is most probable that the vessel was either H. M. S. 'Intrepid' or 'Pioneer,' as two months later, and 250 miles further south, the 'Resolute' was picked up. About two or three years ago, Captain Deuchars lost his ship 'Princess Charlotte,' in Melville Bay. It was a beautiful morning; they had almost reached the North Water, and were anticipating a very successful voyage; the steward had just reported breakfast ready, when Captain Deuchars, seeing the floes closing together ahead of the ship, remained on deck to see her pass safely between them, but they closed too quickly; the vessel was *almost* through, when the points of ice caught her sides abreast of the mizenmast, and, passing through, held the wreck up for a few minutes, barely long enough for the crew to escape and save their boats! Poor Deuchars thus suddenly lost his breakfast and his ship; within *ten minutes* her royal yards disappeared beneath the surface. How closely danger besets the Arctic cruiser, yet how insidiously; everything looks so bright, so calm, so still, that it requires positive experience to convince one that ice only a very few inches, perhaps only three or four inches, *above water*, perfectly level, and moving extremely slow, could possibly endanger a strong vessel! The 'Princess Charlotte' was a very fine, strong ship, and her captain one of the most experienced Arctic seamen. He now commands the finest whaler in the fleet.

14*th*.—We have only advanced a few miles to the northward. The steamer 'Innuit' has joined our small steam squadron. Captain Sutter left Scotland only a month ago; he has very kindly and promptly sent us a present of newspapers and potatoes. Captain Deuchars has also been good enough to supply us with some potatoes and porter, perhaps the most serviceable present he could have made us after our long subsistence upon salt and preserved meats.

18*th.*—Once more alone in Melville Bay. The 'Innuit' and 'Chase' steamed much too fast for us, and the last of the four vessels, the 'Tay,' parted from us in a thick fog yesterday. We have come close along the edge of the fixed ice, passing about six miles outside of the Sabine Islands, and are advancing as opportunities offer. This morning the man who was stationed to watch a nip about a quarter of a mile ahead of the ship, came running back, pursued by three bears—a mother with her half-grown cubs. I suppose they followed him chiefly because he ran from them; and at all events they were very close up before he reached the ship. Another bear was seen about the same time, but none of them came within shot. Rotchies (or little auks) are very abundant. Seals are occasionally shot. I ate some boiled seal to-day, and found it good: this is the first time I have eaten positive *blubber;* all scruples respecting it henceforth vanish.

25*th.*—The land-ice broke away inshore of the 'Fox' on the 19th or 20th, and we found ourselves drifting southward amongst extensive fields of ice. Sad experience has already shown us how absolutely powerless our small craft is under such circumstances. But after many attempts we regained the edge of the fast ice this morning, and steamed merrily along it towards Bushnan Island. When within a few miles a nip brought us to a standstill: here five or six icebergs lie encompassed by land-ice, and apparently aground; one of them juts out and has caught the point of an immense field of ice. There is some slight movement in the latter, but not enough to let us pass through.

Twelve or eighteen miles to the south there is a cluster of bergs, in all probability aground upon our "70 fathom bank" of last September. The ice-field appears to rest against them, as both to the east and west there is much clear water. Exactly at this spot Captain Penny was similarly detained by a nip in August, 1850. Although progress is denied to us at present, yet it is an unspeakable relief to have got out of the drifting ice.

I have passed very many anxious days in Melville Bay, but hardly any of them weighed so heavily upon me as yesterday. There was the broad, clear *land-water* within a third of a mile of me, clear weather, and a fair breeze blowing. The intervening nip worked sufficiently with wind and tide to keep one in suspense; it *nearly* opened at high water, but closed again with the ebb tide. I thought of the week already spent in struggling amongst drifting floes, and was haunted by visions of everything horrible— gales, ice-crushing, etc. Nor was it consoling to reflect that all the sailing ships as well as the steamers might have actually slipped past us. In fact, I must acknowledge that anxiety and weariness had worked me up into a state of burning impatience and of bitter chagrin at being so repeatedly baffled in all my efforts by the varying yet continual perplexities of our position. The only difference in favor of our prospects over those of the past year consisted in our having arrived here two months earlier; but the importance of this difference is incalculable.

The opportunities afforded by the delays to which we have been subjected were turned, however, to some account. Nearly one thousand rotches were shot; they are excellent eating; their average weight is four ounces and a half, but when prepared for the table they probably do not yield more than three ounces each. A young bear imprudently swam up to the ship, and was shot,—his skin fell to the sportsman, and carcase to the dogs. Several others have been seen : we watched one fellow surprise a seal upon the ice, and carry it about in his mouth as a cat does a mouse.

27*th*.—Lying fast to the ice off the Crimson Cliffs of

Sir John Ross. Yesterday we succeeded in passing through the nip, and by evening reached Cape York. Seeing natives running out upon the land-ice, the ship was made fast for an hour in order to communicate with them. A party of eight men came on board: they immediately recognised Petersen, for they lived at Etah in Smith's Sound when he was there in the American expedition. They asked for Dr. Kane, and told us Hans was married and lived in Whale Sound. They all said he was most anxious to return to Greenland, but had neither sledge-dogs nor kayak; hunger had compelled him to eat the sealskin which covered the framework of the latter. Petersen gave them messages for Hans from his Greenland friends, and advice that he should fix his residence here, where he might see the whalers and perhaps be taken back to Greenland. The natives did not seem to be badly off for anything except dogs, some distemper having carried off most of these indispensable animals. I was therefore unable to procure any from them. These people spent the winter here; they seemed healthy, well-clad, and happy little fellows. One of them is brother-in-law to Erasmus York, who voluntarily came to England in the 'Assistance' in 1851. This man is an *angekok*, or magician; he has a still flatter face than the rest of his countrymen, but appears more thoughtful and intelligent.

Petersen pointed out to me a stout old fellow, with a tolerable sprinkling of beard and moustache. This worthy perpetrated the only murder which has taken place for several years in the tribe: he disliked his victim and stood in need of his dogs, therefore he killed the owner and appropriated his property! Such motives and passions usually govern the "unsophisticated children of nature;" yet, as savages, the Esquimaux may be considered exceedingly harmless.

Of late years these Arctic Highlanders have become alarmed by the rapid diminution of their numbers through famine and disease, and have been less violent towards each other in their feuds and quarrels.

The appearance of these men as they danced and rolled about in frantic delight at our approach, was wild and strange, and their costume uniform and picturesque. Their long, coarse, black hair hung loosely over the seal-skin frock which in its turn overlapped their loose shaggy bear-skin breeches, and these again came down over the tops of their seal-skin boots. Most of them carried a spear formed out of the horn of a narwhal.

Having distributed presents of knives and needles, and explained to them that we did so because they had behaved well to the white people, (as we learned from Dr. Kane's narrative of their treatment of him and his crew), we pursued our voyage, not doubting but that we should soon reach the *North Water*, an extensive sea through which we could sail uninterruptedly to Pond's Bay.

During the night we advanced through loose ice; but fog and a rising S. E. gale delayed us, and to-day the pack has pressed in against the land, so that our wings are most unexpectedly clipped. A walrus was shot through the head by a Minie bullet; none other will penetrate such a massive skull : unfortunately for my collection of specimens, and for the dogs, the animal sank.

2d July.—For five days we have been almost beset amongst loose ice and grounded bergs; the winds were generally from the S. E. and accompanied by fog. To avoid being squeezed we had constantly to shift our position; once we were caught and rather severely nipped; the ship was heeled over about ten degrees and lifted a couple of feet : the ice was three feet thick, but broke readily under her weight. Unfortunately there was not time to unship the rudder, so it suffered very severely. Upon a previous occasion the screw-shaft was bent and a portion of the screw broken off.

Landed to obtain a good view of the sea in the offing; from the hills we could see nothing but pack to seaward. There was no land-ice; we stepped out of the boat upon a narrow icefoot which fringed the coast; immediately above it we trod over a velvet sward of soft bright green moss; the turf beneath was of considerable depth. Here and there under this noble range of cliffs, which are composed of primary rocks, there exists much vegetation for so high a latitude. From the fact of thick layers of turf descending quite down to the sea, it is evident that the land has been gradually sinking. Steep slopes of rocky *debris*, which screen the bases of the most precipitous cliffs, form secure nurseries for the little auk; these localities were literally alive with them; they popped in and out of every crevice, or sat in groups of dozens upon every large rock. I have nowhere seen such countless myriads of birds. The *rotchie*, or little auk, lays its single egg upon the bare rock, far within a crevice beyond the reach of fox, owl, or burgomaster gull. We shot a couple of hundred during our short stay on shore, and, by removing the stones, gathered several dozen of their eggs.

The huge predatory gulls, long ago named "Burgomasters" by Dutch seamen (because they lord it over their neighbors, and appropriate everything good to themselves), have established themselves in the cliffs, where their nests are generally inaccessible: we were a month too late for their eggs; the young birds were as large as spring chickens. Of course we obtained specimens of the red snow, but had to seek rather diligently for it; its color was a dirty red, very like the stain of port wine: very few patches of it were found.

Last night a westerly wind blew freshly and dispersed the ice outside of us, so much so that this evening we have got out into almost clear water. Farewell Greenland!—hurrah for the west!

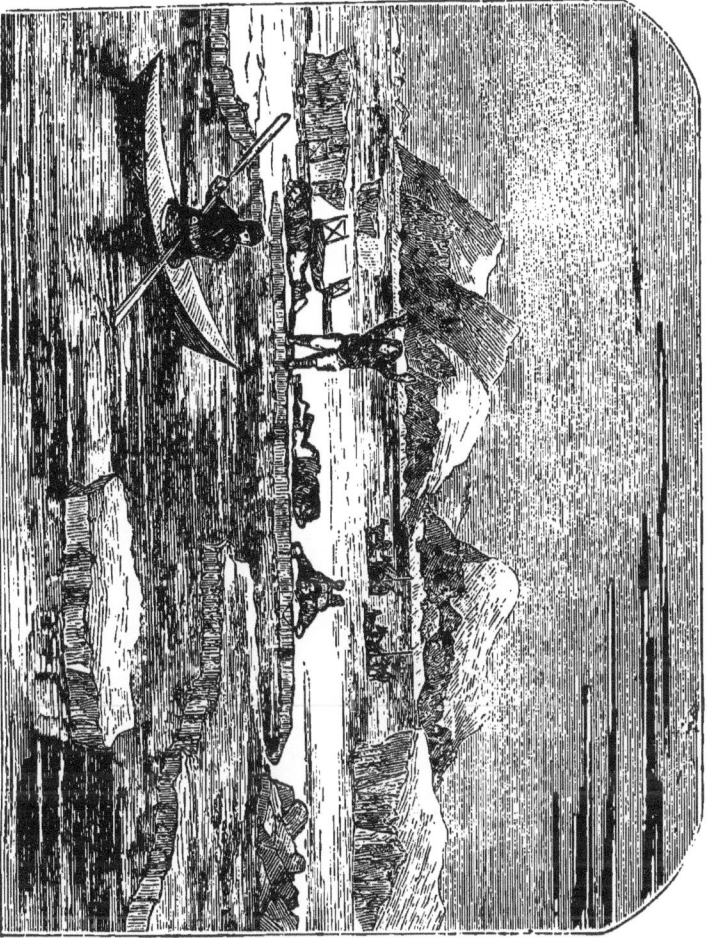

ESQUIMAUX IMITATING ANIMALS TO INDUCE EUROPEANS TO APPROACH.

5th.—After getting free from the ice off the Crimson
Cliffs, we soon lost sight of the last fragment, and steered
for Pond's Bay.   And now we all set to work in zealous
haste to write our last letters for England, by the whalers,
which we hoped soon to meet there.

After running 60 miles the ice reappeared, and we sailed
through a vast deal of it, but it became more closely packed,
and a thick fog detained us for a day.

When the weather became clear, the main pack was seen
to the W., S., and S. E.; in the hope of rounding its northern
extreme we ran along it to the N. W. To-day it has led us
to the N. and N. E., so that this evening Wolstenholme
Sound is in sight. To the N. the pack appears impenetrable, and there is a strong ice-blink over it. All the ice we
have lately sailed through is loose, and much decayed; it
seems but recently to have broken away from the land, is
not water-washed, neither has it been exposed to a swell,
the fractured edges remaining sharp.

6th.—Midnight. Last evening I persevered to the N.
until every hope of progress in that direction vanished.
To the W. the pack appeared tolerably loose; the wind was
fresh at E. S. E., so I determined once more to push into
it, and endeavor to battle our way through; I hoped it
would prove to be merely a belt of 30 or 40 miles in width.
We found the ice to lie for the most part in streams at
right angles to the wind, and therefore much more open
than it had appeared: there was seldom any difficulty in
winding through it from one water-space to another.   The
wind greatly increased, bringing much rain, but fortunately
no fog;—the dread of this hung over me like a night-
mare,—our progress depended upon the vigilance of the
look-out kept in the crow's-nest. By noon we had made
good 60 miles. Throughout the day the wind has gradually moderated; the rain gave place to snow, which in its
turn was succeeded by mist. The evening was fine eventu-

ally and clear; but still we find the ice is all around. Just before midnight the termination of our lead was discovered, whilst the ice through which we had passed was closing together, and a dense fog came rolling down. Under these circumstances the ship was made fast as near to the nip as safety permitted, to await some favorable change.

10th.—All the 7th we remained in our small basin, there being no outlet from it, and but little water anywhere visible. To pass away the dull hours and get rid of unwelcome reflections upon the similarity of our present position and that in August last, I commenced an attack upon all the feathered denizens of the pack—they seemed so provokingly contented with it—but they soon became wary, and deserted our vicinity, so I shot only a dozen fulmar petrels, three ivory gulls, two looms,* and a *Lestris parasiticus;* some of them were useful as specimens, and such as were not destined for our table were given to the dogs. Although Cobourg Island was 45 miles distant from us, its lofty rounded outlines were very distinct, and much covered with snow. On the 8th we squeezed through nips for 4 or 5 miles, and on the 9th, reaching a large space of water, steamed towards Cobourg Island until again stopped by the pack at an early hour this morning, when within 5 or 6 leagues of it.

This evening we are endeavoring to steam in toward the West-land, and fancy we can trace with the crow's-nest telescope a practicable route through the intervening ice-mazes to a faint streak of water along the shore. This sort of navigation is not only anxious, but wearying. To me it seems as if several months instead of only eight days has elapsed since we left Cape York. We are constantly wondering what our whaling friends are about, and where they are ?

---

* These birds are called willocks at home; they are the " Uria Brunnichii" of naturalists.

14*th*.—The faint streak of water seen on the night of the
10th proved to be an extensive sheet to leeward of Cobourg
Island. We reached it next morning. Jones' Sound appeared open, and a slight swell reached us from it, but all
along the shore there was close pack. Although but little
water was visible to the southward, we persevered in that
direction, and, as the ice was rapidly moving off shore
under the combined influence of wind and tide, we were
only occasionally detained.

Two hundred and forty-two years ago—to a day, I believe—William Baffin sailed without hindrance along this
coast and discovered Lancaster Sound. What a very different season he must have experienced!

Passing near Cape Horsburgh we approached De Ros
Islet at midnight. The air being very calm, and still, the
shouting of some natives was heard, although we could
scarcely distinguish them upon the land-ice. The ship was
made fast, and the shouting party, consisting of three men,
three women, and two children, eagerly came on board.
Only four individuals remained on shore.

The old chief Kal-lek is remarkable amongst Esquimaux
for having a bald head. He inquired by name for his friend
Captain Inglefield. These three families have spent the last
two years upon this coast, between Cape Horsburgh and
Croker Bay. Their knowledge does not extend further in
either direction. They are natives of more southern lands,
and crossed the ice in Lancaster Sound with dog-sledges.
Since the visit of the 'Phœnix' in '54 they have seen no
ships, nor have any wrecks drifted upon their shores. They
seemed very fat and healthy, but complained that all the
reindeer had gone away, and asked if *we* could tell where
they went to? Our presents of wood, knives, and needles
were eagerly received. They assured us that Lancaster
Sound was still frozen over, and that all the sea was covered
with pack. After half an hour's delay we steamed onward,

and on reaching a larger space of water our hopes (somewhat depressed by the native intelligence) began to revive.
But we soon found that our clear water terminated near
Cape Warrender. Lancaster Sound, although not frozen
over, was crammed full of floes and icebergs. The wind
increased to a strong gale from the east, and pressed in
more ice. At length the ship was with difficulty made fast
to a strip of land-ice a few miles westward of Point Osborn.
Gradually the gale subsided, but not until the pack was
close in against the land. The tides kept sweeping it to
and fro to our great discomfort. The land is composed of
gneiss, and the gravelly shore is low. A few ducks only
have been shot, and traces of reindeer and hares seen. Our
Melville Bay friends, the rotchies, are very rare visitors upon
this side of Baffin's Bay.

Part of a ship's timber has been found upon the beach;
it measures 7 inches by 8 inches, is of American oak, and,
although sound, has long been exposed to the weather.

CHAPTER IX.

Off Cape Warrender—Sight the whalers again—Enter Pond's Bay—Communicate with Esquimaux—Ascend Pond's Inlet—Esquimaux information—Arctic summer abode—An Arctic village—No intelligence of
Franklin's ships—Arctic trading—Geographical information of natives
—Information of Rae's visit—Improvidence of Esquimaux—Travels
of Esquimaux.

16th July.—To borrow a whaling phrase, we are "dodg-
ing about in a hole of water" off Cape Warrender. I
recognize the little bay just to the west of the cape where
Parry landed in September, 1824.   The "immense mass of
snow and ice containing strata of muddy-looking soil" is
there still, and, I should think, had considerably increased.
Here his party shot three reindeer out of a small herd.
We have narrowly scanned the steep hill-sides with our
glasses, but without discovering any such inducement to
land.
-No cairns are visible upon Cape Warrender ; the natives
have probably removed them.   Dense pack prevents us from
approaching Port Dundas or crossing to the southern shore.
We all find these vexatious delays are by no means conducive to sleep.   The mind is busy with a sort of magic-lantern
representation of the past, the present, and the future, and
resists for weary hours the necessary repose.

17th.—Last night's calm has allowed the pack to expand
so much, that to-day we have steamed through it until
within three miles of the noble cliffs of Cape Hay ; and
now we are drifting eastward with the ice precisely as did
the 'Enterprise' and 'Investigator,' in September, '49.

9

Upon that occasion we were set free off Pond's Bay. There is a very extensive *loomery* at Cape Hay; we regret the circumstances which prevent our levying a tax upon it. Here, if anywhere, I expected to find a clear sea, but east winds have prevailed for twenty days out of the last twenty-five, and this accounts for the present state of the sea; the next succession of west winds will probably effect a prodigious clearance of ice.

21st.—The 'Tay' was seen to-day in loose ice, and much further off the land. She gradually steamed through it to the southward, and by night was almost out of sight. Her appearance surprised us, as we supposed she must have reached Pond's Bay long ago. Ten hours' struggling with steam and sails at the most favorable intervals has only advanced us five miles. The weather is remarkably warm, bright, and pleasant. A very large bear came within 150 yards, and was shot by Petersen, the Minie bullet passing through his body. This beast measured 8 ft. 3 in. in length; his fat carcase was hoisted on board with great satisfaction, as our dogs' food was nearly expended.

24th.—Last night the ice became slack enough to afford some prospect of release, so we charged the nips vigorously, and steamed away through devious openings toward Cape Fanshawe. For several hours but little progress was made, but this morning the ice became more open; clear water was seen ahead, and reached by noon. Although it is calm I prefer waiting for a breeze to expending more coals. We are only ten miles from Possession Bay. The air is so very clear that the land appears quite close to us. All that is not mountainous is well cleared of snow. There is immense refraction. Only a single iceberg in sight. The sea-water is light green, as remarked by Parry in 1819.

26th.—A vessel was seen yesterday morning; the day continuing calm, we steamed through some loose ice, and joined her off Cape Walter Bathurst in the evening. It proved to be the 'Diana;' she parted from us on the 16th of June in Melville Bay, has everywhere been obstructed by the pack, as we have been, and only reached Cape Warrender three days before us.   From thence to Possession Bay she met with *no obstruction*.   The subsequent east winds brought in all the ice which has so much retarded us.

The 'Diana' has already captured twelve whales.   Taking the hint from Capt. Gravill, we have made fast to a loose floe, and are drifting very nearly a mile an hour to the southward along the edge of a very formidable land-ice, which i seven or eight miles broad.   All to seaward of us is packe ice.   The old whaling seamen of the 'Diana' are astonisheu at the unusual and unaccountable abundance of ice which everywhere fills up Baffin's Bay.   All the 'Diana's' steaming coals, her spare spars, wood, and even a boat, have been burnt in the protracted struggle through the middle ice.

27th.—After putting our letter-bag on board the 'Diana' this morning, we steamed on for Pond's Bay, and at noon made fast near Button Point to the land-ice, which still extends across it.

For four hours Petersen and I have been bargaining with an old woman and a boy, not for the sake of their sealskins, but in order to keep them in good humor whilst we extracted information from them. 'They said they knew nothing of ships or white people ever having been within this inlet, nor of any wrecked ships.   They knew of the depôt of provisions left at Navy Board Inlet by the 'North Star,' but had none of them.   The woman has traced on paper the shores of the inlet as far as her knowledge extends, and has given me the name of every point.   She says the ice will break up with the first fresh wind.   These two individuals are alone here.   They remained on purpose to barter with the whalers, and cannot now rejoin their friends, who are only 25 miles up the inlet, because the ice is unsafe to travel over, and the land precipitous and impracticable.

This afternoon the 'Tay' stood in toward us, and Capt. Deuchars kindly sent his boat on board with an offer to take charge of our letters. The 'Tay' reached this coast only a few days ago, having met with the same difficulties which we experienced. The 'Innuit' was last seen nearly a month ago beset off Jones' Sound. The remaining steamer, the 'Chase,' has not been seen or heard of.

29th.—The old woman's denial of all knowledge of the wrecks or cast-away men was very unsatisfactory. I determined to visit her countrymen at their summer village of Kaparöktolik, which she described as being only a short day's journey up the inlet.

Petersen and one man accompanied me. We started yesterday morning with a sledge and a Halkett boat. Although the ice over which we purposed traveling broke away from the land soon after setting out, yet we managed to get half way to the village before encamping. This morning we learnt the truth of the old woman's account. A range of precipitous cliffs rising from the sea cut us off by land from Kaparöktolik, so we were obliged to return to the ship. Our walk afforded the opportunity of examining some native encampment and caches. We found innumerable scraps of seal-skins, bird-skins, walrus and other bones, whalebone, blubber, and a small sledge. The latter was very old, and composed of pieces of wood and of large bones ingeniously secured together with strips of whalebone. Five preserved-meat tins were found; some of them retaining their original coating of red paint. Doubtless these were part of the spoils from Navy Board Inlet depôt. The total absence of fresh wood or iron was strongly in favor of the old woman's veracity. Since yesterday, ice, about 16 miles in extent, has broken up in the inlet, and is drifting out into Baffin's Bay.

During my absence our shooting parties have twice visited a *loomery* upon Cape Graham Moore, and each-

time have brought on board 300 looms. Very few birds
and no other animals were seen during our walk over the
rich mossy slopes to-day. I saw a pair of Canadian brown
cranes, the first of the species I have ever seen so far north,
though Sir Robert M'Clure found them, I know, on Bank's
Land.

The lands enjoying a southern aspect, even to the summits of hills 700 or 800 feet in height, were tinged with
green; but these hills were protected by a still loftier range
to the north. Upon many well-sheltered slopes we found
much rich grass. All the little plants were in full flower;
some of them familiar to us at home, such as the buttercup,
sorrel, and dandelion. I have never found the latter to the
north of 69° before.

The old woman is much less excited to-day; she says
there was a wreck upon the coast when she was a little
girl; it lies a day and a half's journey, about 45 miles, to
the north; and came there without masts and very much
crushed; the little which now remains is almost buried in
the sand. A piece of this wreck was found near her *abode*,
—she has neither hut nor tent, but a sort of lair constructed
of a few stones and a seal-skin spread over them, so that
she can crawl underneath. This fragment is part of a floor
timber, English oak, $7\frac{1}{2}$ inches thick; it has been brought
on board.

30th.—A gale of wind and deluge of rain has detained
the ship until this evening; we are now steaming up the
inlet, having the old lady and the boy on board as our
pilots; they are delighted at the prospect of rejoining their
friends, from whom they were effectually cut off until the
return of winter should freeze a safe pathway for them;
they had, however, abundance of looms stored up *en câche*
for their subsistence. She has drawn me another chart,
much more neatly than the former, but so like it as to prove
that her geographical knowledge, and not her powers of in-

vention, have been taxed. She is a widow; her daughter is married, and lives at a place called Igloolik, which is six or seven days' journey from here,—three days up the inlet, then about three days overland to the southward, and then a day over the ice.

Thinking it not quite impossible that this Igloolik might be the place where Parry wintered in 1822–3, I told Petersen to ask whether ships had ever been there? She answered, "Yes, a ship stopped there all one winter; but it is a long time ago." All she could distinctly recollect having been told about it was, that one of the crew died, and was buried there, and his name was Al-lah or El-leh. On referring to Parry's 'Narrative,' I found that the ice-mate, Mr. Elder, died at Igloolik! This is a very remarkable confirmation of the locality,—for there are several places called Igloolik. She also told us it was an island, and near a strait between two seas. The Esquimaux take considerable pains to learn, and remember names; this woman knows the names of several of the whaling captains, and the old chief at De Ros Islet remembered Captain Inglefield's name, and tried hard to pronounce mine.

She now told us of another wreck upon the coast, but many days' journey to the south of Pond's Bay; it came there before her first child was born. Her age is not less than forty-five.

August 4th.—Our Esquimaux friends have departed from us with every demonstration of friendship, to return to their village. We have had free communication with them for four days—not only through Mr. Petersen, but also through our two Greenlanders; the result is, that they have no knowledge whatever of either of the missing or the abandoned searching ships. Neither wrecked people nor wrecked ships have reached their shores. They seemed to be much in want of wood; most of what they have consists of staves of casks, probably from the Navy Board Inlet depôt.

In their bartering with us, saws were most eagerly sought for in exchange for narwhal's horns; they are used by them in cutting up the long strips of the bones of whales with which they shoe the runners of their sledges, also the ivory and bone used to protect the more exposed parts of their kayaks and the edges of their paddles from the ice.

Files were also in great demand, and I found were required to convert pieces of iron-hoop into arrow and spear heads. If any suspicion existed of their having a secret supply of wood, such as a wreck or even a boat would afford, it was removed by their refusing to barter the most trifling things for axes or hatchets.

But I must relate the events of the last few days as they occurred. When 17 miles within the inlet we reached the unbroken ice and made the ship fast. Here the *strait* —originally named Pond's *Bay*, and more recently Eclipse *Sound*—appears to be most contracted, its width not exceeding 7 or 8 miles. Both its shores are very bold and lofty, often forming noble precipices. The prevailing rock is grey gneiss, generally dipping at an angle of 35° to the west.

Early on the 1st of August I set out for the native village with Hobson, Petersen, two men, and the two natives from Button Point. Eight miles of wet and weary ice-travelling, which occupied as many hours, terminated our journey; the surface of the ice was everywhere deeply channelled and abundantly flooded by the summer's thaw; we were almost constantly launching our small boat over the slippery ridges which separated pools or channellings through which it was generally necessary to wade.

After toiling round the base of a precipice, we came rather suddenly in view of a small semicircular bay; the cliffs on either side were 800 or 900 feet high, remarkably forbidding and desolate; the mouth of a valley or wide mountain gorge opens out into its head. Here, in the depth of

the bay, upon a low flat strip of land, stood seven tents,—
the summer village of Kaparōk-to-lik. I never saw a locality more characteristic of the Esquimaux than that which
they have here selected for their abode; it is widely picturesque in the true Arctic application of the term.

Although August had arrived, and the summer had been
a warm one, the bay was still frozen over; and if there was
an ice-covered *sea* in front, there was also abundance of
ice-covered *land* in the rear—a glacier occupied the whole
valley behind and to within 300 yards of the chosen spot!

The glacier's height appeared to be from 150 to 200
feet; its sea-face extending across the valley,—a probable
width of 300 or 400 yards,—was quite perpendicular, and
fully 100 feet high. All last winter's snow had thawed
away from off it and exposed a surface of mud and stones,
fissured by innumerable small rivulets, which threw themselves over the glacier cliffs in pretty cascades, or shot far
out in strong jets from their deeply serried channels in its
face; whilst other streamlets near the base burst out
through subglacial tunnels of their own forming.

What a strange people to confine themselves to such a
mere strip of beach! Upon each side they have towering
rocky hills rising so abruptly from the sea, that to pass
along their bases or ascend over their summits, is equally
impossible; whilst a threatening glacier immediataly behind, bears onward a sufficient amount of rock and earth
from the mountains whence it issues, to convince even the
unreflecting savage of its progressive motion.

The land is devoid of game, although lemmings and ermines are tolerably numerous; it only supplies the moss
which the natives burn with blubber in their lamps, and the
dry grass which they put in their boots; even the soft
stone, *lapis ollaris*, out of which their lamps and cooking
vessels are made and the iron pyrites with which they strike
fire, are obtained by barter from the people inhabiting the

THE VILLAGE AND 'R OF KAPEROKTOLIK, GREENLAND.

land to the West of Navy Board Inlet. But the sea compensates for every deficiency. The assembled population amounted to only 25 souls: 9 men, the rest women and children.

All of them evinced extreme delight at seeing us; as we approached the huts the women and children held up their arms in the air and shouted "Pilletay" (give me), incessantly; the men were more quiet and dignified, yet lost no opportunity, either when we declined to barter, or when they had performed any little service, to repeat "Pilletay" in a beseeching tone of voice.

We walked everywhere about the tents and entered some of them, carefully examining every chip or piece of metal; our visit was quite unexpected. They had only two sledges; both were made of $2\frac{1}{2}$ inch oak-planks, devoid of bolt-holes or treenails, and having but very few nail-holes. These sledges had evidently been constructed for several years, the parts not exposed to friction were covered with green fungus: one of them measured 14 feet long, the other about 9 feet; we were told the wood came from a wreck to the southward of Pond's Bay. Most of the sledge crossbars were ordinary staves of casks. Amongst the poles and large bones which supported the tents we noticed a painted fir oar. Some pieces of iron-hoop and a few preserved-meat tins—one of which was stamped "Goldner,"—completed their stock of European ·les.

·tersen questioned all the men *separately* as to their ledge of ships or wrecks; but their accounts only served to confirm the old woman's story. None of them had ever heard of ships or wrecks any where to the westward. Both individually and collectively we got them to draw charts of the various coasts known to them, and to mark upon them the positions of the wrecks. The two chiefs, Nöo-luk and A-wäh-lah, soon made themselves known to me, and, when we desired to go to sleep, sent away the people who were eagerly pressing round our tent. All these natives were better-looking, cleaner, and more robust than I expected to find them.

A-wăh-lah has been to Igloolik; one of his wives, for each chief has *two*, has a brother living there. I spread a large roll of paper upon a rock, and got him to draw the route overland, and also round by the coast to it; this novel proceeding attracted the whole population about us; A-wăh-lah constantly referred to others when his memory failed him; at length it was completed to the satisfaction of all parties. When I gave him the knife I had promised as his reward, and added another for his wives, he sprang up on the rock, flourished the knives in his hands, shouted, and danced with extravagant demonstrations of joy. He is a very fine specimen of his race, powerful, impulsive, full of energy and animal spirits, and moreover an admirable mimic. The men were all about the same height, 5 feet 5 inches; they eagerly answered our questions, and imparted to us all the geographical knowledge, although at first they hesitated when we asked them about Navy Board Inlet, in consequence of the depot placed there having been plundered; but we soon found that they were easily tired under cross-examination, and often said they knew no more; it was necessary to humor them.

According to their account the depot was discovered and robbed by people living further west. This is probably true, as so few relics were to be seen here, which would not be the case if such active fellows as A-wah-lah and Noo-luk had received the first intimation of its proximity. These people of Kaparöktolik are the only inhabitants of the land lying eastward of Navy Board Inlet, and live entirely upon its *southern* shore. In a similar manner, it is only the *southern* coast of the land to the west of Navy Board Inlet that is inhabited. After distributing presents

to all the women and children, and making a few trifling purchases from the men, we returned next day to the ship.

During my absence more ice had broken away, involving
the ship and almost forcing her on shore. It required every
exertion to save her. For two hours she continued in
imminent danger, and was only saved by the warping and
ice-blasting, by which at last she got clear of the drifting
masses, *four minutes* only before these were crushed up
against the rocks !

Four Esquimaux came off to the ship in their kayaks,
bringing whalebone, narwhals' horns, etc., to barter. Next
to handsaws and files, they attached the greatest value to
knives and large needles. These men remained on board
for nearly two days, and drew several charts for us. Noo-
luk explained that seven or eight days' journey to the
southward there are *two* wrecks a short day's journey apart.
The southern is in an inlet or strait which contains several
islands, but here his knowledge of the coast terminates.
The man A-ra-neet said he visited these wrecks five winters
ago. All of them agreed that it is a very long time since
the wrecks arrived upon the coast; and Noo-luk, who appears to be about forty-five years of age, showed us how
tall he was at that time.

In the 'Narrative of Parry's Second Voyage,' at p. 437,
mention is made of the arrival at Igloolik of a sledge constructed of ship-timber and staves of casks; also of two
ships that had been driven on shore, and the crews of which
went away in boats. In August, 1821, nearly two years
previous to the arrival of this report through the Esquimaux to Igloolik, the whalers 'Dexterity' and 'Aurora'
were wrecked upon the west coast of Davis' Strait, in lat.
72°, 70 or 80 miles southward of Pond's Bay. The old
man, Ow-wang-noot, drew the coast-line northward from
Cape Graham Moore to Navy Board Inlet, and pointed out
the position of the northern wreck a few miles east of Cape

Hay. Had it been conspicuous we must have seen it when we slowly drifted along that coast.

These people usually winter in snow-huts at Green Point, a mile or two within the northern entrance of Pond's Bay. They hunt the seal and narwhal, but when the sea becomes too open they retire to Kaparōktolik ; and when the remaining ice breaks up — usually about the middle of August—a further migration takes place across the inlet to the S. W., where reindeer abound, and large salmon are numerous in the rivers. Every winter they communicate with the Igloolik people. Two winters ago (1856–7) some people who lived far beyond Igloolik, in a country called A-ka-nee (probably the Ak-koo-lee of Parry), brought from there the information of white people having come in two boats, and passed a winter in snow-huts at a place called by the following names :—A-mec-Ice-oke, A-wee-lik, Net-tec-lik.

Our friends pointed to our whale-boats and said the boats of the white people were like it, but larger. These whites had tents inside their snow-huts; they killed and eat reindeer and narwhal, and smoked pipes; they bought dresses from the natives; none died; in summer they all went away, taking with them two natives, a father and his son. We could not ascertain the name of the white chief, nor the interval of time since they wintered amongst the Esquimaux, as our friends could not recollect these particulars.*

The name of the locality, A-wee-lik (spelt as written down at the moment), may be considered identical with "Ay-wee-lik," the name of the land about Repulse Bay in the chart of the Esquimaux woman, Iligliuk (Parry's 'Second Voyage,' p. 197).

---

* Dr. Rae wintered at Repulse Bay in *stone* huts in 1846–7. Again wintered there in *snow* huts in 1853–4.

We were of course greatly surprised to find that Dr. Rae's visit to Repulse Bay was known to this distant tribe; and also disappointed to find they had heard nothing of Franklin's Back-River parties through the same channel of communication.   They were anxiously and repeated questioned, but evidently had not heard of any other white people to the westward, nor of their having perished there.

Ow-wang-noot lived at Igloolik in his early days, and made a chart of the lands adjacent, but said he was so young at the time that "it seemed like a dream to him." He was acquainted with Ee-noo-loo-apik, the Esquimaux who once accompanied Captain Penny to Aberdeen, and told us he had died, lately I think, at a place to the southward called Kri-merk-su-malek, but that his sister still lives at Igloolik.

Although they told us the Iglooklik people were worse off for wood than they were themselves, yet it was evident that here also, it is very scarce.   We could not spare them light poles or oars such as they were most desirous to obtain for harpoon and lance staves and tent-poles; and they would willingly have bartered their kyaks to us for rifles (having already obtained some from the whaling-ships), but that they had no other way of getting back to their homes, nor wood to make the light framework of others.

They collect whalebone and narwhal's horns in sufficient quantity to carry on a small barter with the whalers.   A-wäh-lah showed us about thirty horns in his tent, and said he had many more at other stations.   A few years ago, when first this bartering sprang up, an Esquimaux took such a fancy to a fiddle that he offered a large quantity of whalebone in exchange for it.   The bargain was soon made, and subsequently this whalebone was sold for upwards of a hundred pounds!   Each successive year, when the same ship returns to Pond's Bay, this native comes on board to visit his friends, and goes on shore with many presents in remembrance of the memorable transaction. It is much better for him thus to receive annual gifts than to have received a large quantity at first, as the improvidence of these men surpasses belief.

Of the "rod of iron about four feet long, supposed to have been at one time galvanized," which was brought home in 1856 by Captain Patterson, and forwarded to the Admiralty, I could obtain no information. The natives were shown galvanized iron, and said they had never seen any before; if their countrymen had any, it must have come from the whalers; none like it was found in the wrecks. Rod-iron is very valuable to the Esquimaux for spears and lances, and narwhals' horns very tempting to the seamen, not only as valuable curiosities, but the ivory is worth half a crown a pound; and I have but little doubt that many of the things said to have been stolen by the natives were fraudulently bartered away by the sailors. That there was no galvanized iron on board any of the Government searching ships, nor in the missing expedition which sailed from England as far back as 1845, I am almost certain. But is it *certain* that this rod was galvanized? The natives gave Captain Patterson to understand that they got it from the wreck to the north.

In July, 1854, Captain Deuchars was at Pond's Bay, and many natives visited his ship, coming over the ice on twelve or fourteen sledges made of ship's planking. Now at this time Sir Edward Belcher's ships were still frozen up in Barrow Strait. My own impression is that the natives whom Captain Deuchars communicated with in 1854 were visitors at Pond's Bay—certainly from the *southward*—and probably attracted by the barter recently grown up at that whaling rendezvous. Having discovered the use of the saws obtained by barter from our whalers, they had successfully applied them to the stout planking of the old wrecks, which they could not have stripped off with any tools previously in their possession.

That the various tribes, or rather groups of families, occasionally visit each other, sometimes for change of hunting-grounds, but more frequently for barter, is well known. Captain Parker told me that a native, whom he had met one summer at Durbin Island, came on board his ship at Pond's Bay the following year. The distance between the two places, as travelled by this man in a single winter, is scarcely short of 500 miles; and the information given us of Rae's wintering at Repulse Bay, information which must have travelled here in two winters, shows that these natives communicate at still greater distances.

Did other wrecks exist nearer at hand, our Pond's Bay friends would be much better supplied with wood. If the Esquimaux knew of any within 300, 400, or even 500 miles, the Pond's Bay natives would at least have heard of them, and could have had no reason for concealing it from us. I only regret that we had not the good fortune to see more than a few natives, and but two sledges of ship's planking; otherwise our own information might have been more copious, and the origin of the fresh supply of planking decisively ascertained.

CHAPTER X.

6th Aug.—CONTINUED calms have delayed us. This evening we steamed from Pond's Bay northward, although our coals have been sadly reduced by the almost constant necessity for steam-power since leaving the Waigat. The three steam-whalers have gone southward; none others have arrived. They appear to us to be leaving the whales behind them; we saw many whilst up the strait, and at the edge of the remaining ice. The natives said they would remain as long as the ice remained, but when it all broke up they would return into Baffin's Bay and go southward; and that these animals arrive in early spring, and do not pass through the strait into any other sea beyond.

Monday evening, 9th.—On the night of the 6th a pleasant, fair breeze sprang up, and enabled us to dispense with the engine. An immense bear was shot; he measured 8 feet 7 inches in length, and is destined for the museum of the Royal Dublin Society. On the 7th the wind gradually freshened and frustrated my intention of examining the wreck spoken of near Cape Hay; at night it increased to a very heavy gale. Although past Navy Board Inlet, very little ice had yet been met with. The weather, and fear of ice to leeward, obliged us to heave the vessel to,

MOONLIGHT IN THE ARCTIC REGIONS.
Drawn by Captain May.

under main trysail and fore staysail.   The squalls were extremely violent and seas unusually high.

All Sunday, the 8th, the gale continued, although not with such extreme force ; the deep rolling of the ship, and moaning of the half-drowned dogs amidst the pelting sleet and rain, was anything but agreeable.   Notwithstanding that I had been up all the previous night, I felt too anxious to sleep ; the wind blew directly up Barrow Strait, drifting us about two miles an hour.   Occasionally she drifted to leeward of masses of ice, reminding us that if any of the dense pack which covered this sea only three weeks ago remained to leeward of us, we must be rapidly setting down upon its weather edge.   The only expedient in such a case is to endeavor to run into it—once well within its outer margin a ship is comparatively safe—the danger lies in the attempt to penetrate ; to escape out of the pack afterwards is also a doubtful matter.

In the evening we were glad to see the land, and find ourselves off the north shore near Cape Bullen, for the violent motion of the ship and very weak horizontal magnetic force had rendered our compasses useless.   This morning, the 9th, the gale broke, and the sea began to subside rapidly ; by noon it was almost calm, but a thick gloom prevailed, ominous, it might be, of more mischief. All along the land there is ice, but, broken up into harmless atoms.   We have carried away a maingaff and a jibstay, but have come remarkably well through such a gale with such trifling damage.

11th.—Before noon to-day we anchored inside Cape Riley, and immediately commenced preparations for embarking coals.   I visited Beechey Island house, and found the door open ; it must have been blown in by an easterly gale long ago, for much ice had accumulated immediately inside it.   Most of the biscuit in bags was damaged, but every thing else was in perfect order.   Upon the north and west

10

sides of the house, where a wall had been constructed, there
was a vast accumulation of ice, in which the lower tier of
casks between the two were imbedded, and its surface
thawed into pools.   Neither casks nor walls should have
been allowed to stand near the house.   The southern and
eastern sides were clear and perfectly dry.   The 'Mary'
decked boat, and two 30-feet lifeboats, were in excellent
order, and their paint appeared fresh, but oars and bare
wood were bleached white.

The gutta-percha boat was useless when left here, and
remains in the same state.   Two small sledge travelling
boats were damaged; one of them had been blown over
and over along the beach until finally arrested by the
other.   The bears and foxes do not appear to have touched
any thing.   I have taken on board all letters left here for
Franklin's or Collinson's expeditions, and also a 20-feet
sledge-boat for our own travelling purposes.

Last night we steamed very close round Cape Hurd in
a dense fog, and crept along the land as our only guide:
we were thus led into Rigby Bay, and discovered a shoal
off its entrance by grounding upon it.   After a quarter of
an hour we floated off unhurt.

In lowering a boat to pursue a bear, Robert Hampton
fell overboard; fortunately he could swim, and was very
soon picked up, but the intense cold of the water had almost
paralyzed his limbs.   The bear was shot and taken on
board.

Sunday 15th, 9 P. M.—Our coaling was completed yesterday, and the ship brought over and anchored off the
house in Erebus and Terror Bay.   A small proportion of
provisions and winter clothing has been embarked to complete our deficiencies; the ice has been scraped out of the
house and its roof thoroughly repaired, a record deposited,
and door securely closed.

I found lying at Godhavn a marble tablet which had

been sent out by Lady Franklin, in the American expedition of 1855 under Captain Hartstein, for the purpose
of being erected at Beechey Island. Circumstances prevented the Americans executing this kindly service, and it
fell to my lot to convey it to the site originally intended.
The tablet was constructed in New York, under the direction of Mr. Grinnell, at the request of Lady Franklin, in
order that the only opportunity which then offered of sending it to the Arctic regions might not be lost. I placed
the monument upon the raised flagged square in the centre
of which stands the cenotaph recording the names of those
who perished in the Government expedition under Sir Edward Belcher. Here also is placed a small tablet to the
memory of Lieutenant Bellot. I could not have selected
for Lady Franklin's memorial a more appropriate or conspicuous site. The inscription runs as follows:

TO THE MEMORY OF
FRANKLIN,
CROZIER, FITZJAMES,

AND ALL THEIR
GALLANT BROTHER OFFICERS AND FAITHFUL
COMPANIONS WHO HAVE SUFFERED AND PERISHED
IN THE CAUSE OF SCIENCE AND
THE SERVICE OF THEIR COUNTRY.

THIS TABLET

IS ERECTED NEAR THE SPOT WHERE
THEY PASSED THEIR FIRST ARCTIC
WINTER, AND WHENCE THEY ISSUED
FORTH TO CONQUER DIFFICULTIES OR

TO DIE.

IT COMMEMORATES THE GRIEF OF THEIR
ADMIRING COUNTRYMEN AND FRIENDS,
AND THE ANGUISH, SUBDUED BY FAITH,
OF HER WHO HAS LOST, IN THE HEROIC
LEADER OF THE EXPEDITION, THE MOST
DEVOTED AND AFFECTIONATE OF
HUSBANDS.

———o———

"AND SO HE BRINGETH THEM UNTO THE
HAVEN WHERE THEY WOULD BE."

1855.

This stone has been entrusted to be affixed in its place by the Officers and Crew of
the American Expedition, commanded by Lt. H. J. Hartstein, in search of Dr.
Kane and his Companions.

This Tablet having been left at Disco by the
American Expedition, which was unable to
reach Beechey Island, in 1855, was put on
board the Discovery Yacht Fox, and is now
set up here by Captain M'Clintock, R. N.,
commanding the final expedition of search
for ascertaining the fate of Sir John Franklin
and his companions, 1858.

We are now ready to proceed upon our voyage from Beechey Island, and there is no ice in sight; but having worked almost unceasingly since our arrival up to the present hour, the men require a night's rest. Nearly forty tons of fuel have been embarked.

The total absence of ice in Barrow Strait is astonishing. No less so are the changes and chances of this singular navigation. Twelve days later than this in 1850, when I belonged to Her Majesty's ship 'Assistance,' with considerable difficulty we came within sight of Beechey Island; a cairn on its summit attracted notice; Captain Ommanney managed to land, and discovered the *first traces* of the missing expedition. Next day the United States schooner 'Rescue' arrived; the day after, Captain Penny joined us, and subsequently Captain Austin, Sir John Ross, and Captain Forsyth,—in all, ten vessels were assembled here. *This day* six years, when in command of the 'Intrepid,' we sailed from here for Melville Island in company with the 'Resolute.' Again I was here at this time in 1854,—still frozen up,—in the 'North Star,' and doubts were entertained of the possibility of *escape*.

To come down to a later period, it was this day fortnight only that I set out for the native village in Pond's Inlet, under the guidance of an old woman; the trip was interesting, but we failed to obtain the slightest clue to the "whereabouts" of the missing ships; moreover, our own little vessel had a most providential escape from being crushed against the cliffs; and this day week was spent in contending with a furious gale, during which the ship had nearly been driven to leeward and dashed to pieces by the sea-beaten pack. Yet these are only preliminaries,—we are only *now* about to commence the interesting part of our voyage. It is to be hoped the poor 'Fox' has many more lives to spare.

Monday night, 16th Aug.—Sailed from Beechey Island

this morning, and in the evening landed at Cape Hotham.
A small depot of provisions and three boats were left there
by former expeditions. Of the depot all has been destroyed
with the exception of two casks landed in 1850. The boats
were sound, but several of their oars, which had been secured upright, were found broken down by bears—those
inquisitive animals having a decided antipathy to anything
stuck up—stuck up things in general being, in this country,
unnatural. Fragments of the depot and the broken oars
were tossed about in every direction. Numerous records
were found; to the most recent a few lines were added,
stating that we had removed the two whale-boats—one to
be left at Port Leopold, the other to replace our own
crushed by the ice.

17th.—Last night battling against a strong foul wind
with *sea*, in rain and fog. To-day much loose ice is seen
southward of Griffith's Island. The weather improved this
afternoon, and we shot gallantly past Limestone Island, and
are now steering down Peel Strait; all of us in a wild state
of excitement—a mingling of anxious hopes and fears!

18th.—For 25 miles last evening we ran unobstructedly
down Peel Strait, but then came in sight of unbroken ice
extending across it from shore to shore! It was much decayed, and of one year's growth only; yet as the strait continues to contract for 60 miles further, and it appeared to
me to afford so little hope of becoming navigable in the
short remainder of the season, I immediately turned about
for Bellot Strait, as affording a better prospect of a passage
into the western sea discovered by Sir James Ross from
Four River Point in 1849. Our disappointment at the
interruption of our progress was as sudden as it was severe.
We did not linger in hope of a change, but steered out
again into the broad waters of Barrow Strait. However,
should Bellot Strait prove hopeless, I intend to return

hither to make one more effort before the close of the
season.

We are now approaching Port Leopold, where it is necessary to stop for a few hours to examine the state of the
steam launch, provisions and stores, left there in 1849, as
adverse circumstances may oblige me to fall back upon it as
a point of support.

19th.—At anchor in Port Leopold ; it is perfectly clear
of ice ; we arrived in the night. How astonishingly bare
the land looks ; it is more barren than Beechey Island,
whilst the rock contains far fewer fossils ! On this day nine
years ago the harbor and sea continued covered with ice,
and the ships ('Enterprise' and 'Investigator') were unable
to escape. At some period since then the ice has been
pressed in upon the low shingle point ; it has forced the
launch up before it, and left her broadside on to the beach,
with both bows stove in, and in want of considerable re-
pairs, but the means are all at hand for executing them.
We tried to haul her further up, but she was firmly imbedded and frozen into the ground. Many things appear
to have been covered with the loose shingle, bags of coal
and coke just appearing through it scarcely above high-
water mark. Amongst the missing articles is the steam-
engine.

Although the flagstaff upon the summit of North East
Cape is still standing, the one erected upon this point and
almost the whole of the framing of the house lies prostrate.
The provisions appeared to be sound, but were not generally examined. The whale-boat we removed from Cape
Hotham was landed here, and a record of our proceedings
added to the many which have accumulated here during
the last ten years. Some coke and a few things useful to
us and merely decaying here were taken on board, and by
evening we were again speeding onward with augmented
resources, and the confidence inspired by a secure depôt in

our rear; buoyed up moreover by the joyful anticipation of
soon reaching the goal of our long-deferred hopes.

20*th.*—Noon. Exactly off Fury Point. There is one
large iceberg far off in the S. E. ; no other ice in sight ! I
would have landed at Fury Beach to examine the remaining supplies there, but a snow shower prevented our distin-
guishing anything, and a strong tide carried us past before
we were aware of it.

We *feel* that the crisis of our voyage is near at hand.
Does Bellot Strait really exist ? if so, is it free from ice ?

A depôt of provisions is being got ready to be landed,
should it be practicable for us to push through and proceed
to the southward.

21*st.*—On approaching Brentford Bay last evening packed
ice was seen streaming out of it, also much ice in the S. E.
The northern point of entrance was landed upon by Sir
John Ross in 1829, and named Possession Point; we
rounded it closely, and could distinguish a few stones piled
up upon a large rock near its highest part—this is his
cairn. As we passed westward between the point and
Browne's Island, through a channel a mile in width, a close
pack was discovered a few miles ahead ; and it being past
ten o'clock, and almost dark, the ship was anchored in a
convenient bay three or four miles within Possession Point.
Here our depôt is to be landed, therefore we shall name this
for the present *Depôt Bay;* a very narrow isthmus between
its head and Hazard Inlet unites the low limestone peninsula, of which Possession Point is the extreme, to the mainland.

To-day an unsparing use of steam and canvas forced the
ship eight miles further west; we were then about half-way
through Bellot Strait ! Its western capes are lofty bluffs,
such as may be distinguished fifty miles distant in clear
weather; between them there was a clear broad channel,
but five or six miles of close heavy pack intervened—tho

sole obstacle to our progress. Of course this pack will
speedily disperse ;—it is no wonder that we should feel
elated at such a glorious prospect, and content to bide our
time in the security of Depôt Bay. A feeling of tranquillity
—of earnest, hearty satisfaction—has come over us. There
is no appearance amongst us of anything boastful ; we
have all experienced too keenly the vicissitudes of Arctic
voyaging to admit of such a feeling.

At the turn of tide we perceived that we were being
carried, together with the pack, back to the eastward;
every moment our velocity was increased, and presently we
were dismayed at seeing grounded ice near us, but were
very quickly swept past it at the rate of nearly six miles an
hour, though within 200 yards of the rocks, and of instant
destruction ! As soon as we possibly could we got clear
of the packed ice, and left it to be wildly hurled about by
various whirlpools and rushes of the tide, until finally
carried out into Brentford Bay.   The ice-masses were large,
and dashed violently against each other, and the rocks lay
at some distance off the southern shore ; we had a fortunate
escape from such dangerous company. After anchoring
again in Depôt Bay, a large stock of provisions and a
record of our proceedings were landed, as there seems every
probability of advancing into the western sea in a very few
days.

The appearance of Bellot Strait is precisely that of a
Greenland fiord ; it is about 20 miles long and scarcely a
mile wide in the narrowest part, and there, within a quarter
of a mile of the north shore the depth was ascertained to be
400 feet.   Its granitic shores are bold and lofty, with a very
respectable sprinkling of vegetation for lat. 72°.   Some of
the hill-ranges rise to about 1500 or 1600 feet above the
sea.

The low land eastward of Depot Bay is composed of limestone, destitute alike of fossils and vegetation.   The granite

commences upon the west shore of Depot bay, and is at once bold and rugged. Many seals have been seen; a young bear was shot, and Walker took a photograph of him as he lay upon our deck, the dogs creeping near to lick up the blood.

The great rapidity of the tides in Bellot Strait fully accounts for the spaces of open water seen by Mr. Kennedy* when he travelled through, early in April. The strait runs very nearly east and west, but its eastern entrance is well masked by Long Island; when half-way through, both seas are visible. As in Greenland, the night tides are much higher than the day tides; last night it was high water at about half-past eleven; as nearly as we can estimate, the tide runs through to the west, from two hours before high water until four hours after it; that is, the flood-tide comes from the west! Such is also the case in Hecla and Fury Strait; in both places the tide from the west is much the strongest. I am not sufficiently informed to discuss this subject, but infer the existence of a channel between Victoria and Prince of Wales' Land. The rise and fall is much less upon the western side of the Isthmus of Boothia than upon the east, and it likewise decreases, we know, in Barrow Strait, as we advance westward.

23rd.—Yesterday Bellot Strait was again examined, but the five miles of close pack occupied precisely the same position as if heaped together by contending tides; considerable augmentations were moreover seen drifting in from the western sea. Finding nothing could be effected in Bellot Strait, we sought in vain for the more southern channel which should exist to form Levesque Island: we did, however, find a beautiful harbor, and are now securely anchored in its north-west arm; I have named it after the gentleman whose former island I have thus reluctantly converted into

---

* Mr. Kennedy discovered this important passage when in command of the 'Prince Albert,' in 1851.

the northern extreme of the Boothian Peninsula, and consequently of the American continent.   The south-western
angle of Brentford Bay is still covered with unbroken ice.

This evening we all landed to explore our new ground.
Young and Petersen shot some brent geese; Walker saw
two deer, but he was botanizing, and had no gun; others
were seen by some of the men, and followed, but without
success.

I enjoyed a delightfully refreshing ramble, a mile or two
inland, through a gently ascending valley, then two miles
along the narrow margin of a pretty little lake between
mountains, beyond which lay a much larger one, four or five
miles in diameter; this farther lake was only partially di-
vested of its winter ice.   Here the scenery was not only
grand, but beautiful; there was enough of vegetation to
tint the craggy hill-sides and to make the sheltered hollows
absolutely green; deer-tracks and the footprints of wild
fowl were everywhere numerous along the water-side.   I
saw two decayed skulls of musk oxen, and circles of stones
by the little lake, doubtless at some remote period the
summer residence of wandering Esquimaux; hence I infer
that fish abound in the lake, and that this valley is a
favorite deer-pass.

But the contemplation of these objects, although agreeable, was not the object of my solitary ramble; I came on
shore to cogitate undisturbed in a leisurely and philosophic
manner.   We hoped very soon to enter an unknown sea;
discoveries were to be made, contingencies provided for,
and plans prepared to meet them.

Yesterday Petersen shot an immense bearded seal; it
sank, but floated up in an hour afterwards.   This animal
measured 8 feet long and weighed about 500 lbs.   We prefer its flesh to that of the small seals, and its blubber will
afford a valuable addition to our stock of lamp oil for the
coming winter.

25th.—In Depot Bay. We remained but twenty-four hours in Levesque Harbor ; a change of wind led us to hope for a removal of the ice in Bellot Strait, therefore I determined to make another attempt.

When off the table-land, where the depth is not more than from 6 to 10 fathoms, and the tides run strongest, the ship hardly moved over the ground, although going 6½ knots through the water ! Thus delayed, darkness overtook us, and we anchored at midnight in a small indentation of the north shore, christened by the men *Fox's Hole,* rather more than half-way through.

For several hours we had been coquetting with huge rampant ice-masses that wildly surged about in the tide-way, or we dashed through boiling eddies, and sometimes almost grazed the tall cliffs ; we were therefore naturally glad of a couple or three hours' rest, even in such a very unsafe position. At early dawn we again proceeded west, but for three miles only ; the pack again stopped us, and we could perceive that the western sea was covered with ice ; the east wind, which could alone remove it, now gave place to a hard-hearted westerly one.

All the strait to the eastward of us, and the eastern sea, as far as could be seen from the hill-tops, is perfectly free from ice. whereas in the direction we wish to proceed there is nothing but packed-ice, or water which cannot be reached. Bitterly disappointed we are, of course ; yet there is reasonable ground for hope ; grim winter will not ratify the obstinate proceedings of the western ice for nearly four weeks.

Last evening's *amusement* was most exciting, nor was it without its peculiar perils. With cunning and activity worthy of her name, our little craft warily avoided a tilting-match with the stout blue masses which whirled about, as if with wilful impetuosity, through the narrow channel ; some of them were so large as to ground even in 6 or 7 fathoms water. Many were drawn into the eddies, and, acquiring considerable velocity in a contrary direction, suddenly broke bounds, charging out into the stream, and entering into mighty conflict with their fellows. After such a frolic the masses would revolve peaceably or unite with the pack, and await quietly their certain dissolution; may the day of that wished-for dissolution be near at hand! Nothing but strong hope of success induced me to encounter such dangerous opposition. I not only hoped, but almost felt, that we deserved to succeed.

Two plans were now occupying my thoughts, both of them resulting from the conviction that we should probably be compelled to winter to the eastward of Bellot Strait: the most important of these plans is that of finding some series of valleys, chain of lakes, or continuous low land, practicable as an overland sledge-route to the western coast, along which we may transport depôts of provisions this autumn; for it is certain that the strong tides will prevent Bellot Strait from being frozen over till winter is far advanced, and its surface will afford us no means of passing westward with our sledges.

The other plan, and that which we are now about to execute, is to land a small depôt of provisions 60 or 70 miles to the southward, and down Prince Regent's Inlet, in order to facilitate communication with the Esquimaux either this autumn or in early spring.

This precautionary step became so necessary in the event of the west coast presenting unusual difficulties, that I determined to carry it at once into execution. Quitting the "Fox's Hole," and resting for one night in Depôt Bay, we sailed thence on the 26th; a fine breeze carried us rapidly southward along the coast of Regent Inlet; there was but little obstruction; occasionally it was necessary to pass through a stream of loose ice; but we saw little of any kind, compared to the experiences of Sir John Ross in 1829.

About dusk (nine o'clock) much loose ice to the south-ward prevented our making any attempt at further pro-gress; we therefore anchored off the coast—in Stillwell Bay, I think—about 45 miles from the Depôt Bay. Here the depôt, consisting of 120 rations, was landed. I observe that it has only been on penetrating into Brentford Bay that we have found the primary rocks washed by the sea; the coast-line both north and south, as far as, and beyond our present position, is a low shore of pale limestone, desti-tute of fossils; we can, however, see granitic hill-ranges far in the interior.

On the 27th we commenced beating back to the north-ward, tacking between the land and the ice which lay about 15 miles off shore. Towards night the wind greatly in-creased, and the ship, under reefed sail, plunged violently into the short, swift, high seas; we also felt quite as uneasy and restless as the ship, in our great anxiety to get back and ascertain what changes were likely to be effected by the gale.

28*th*.—To-night the weather is more pleasant; the keen and contrary wind has given place to a gentle, fair breeze, the swell has almost subsided, no ice has been seen to-day, and the night is dark and unusually mild. I can hardly fancy that the sea which gently rocks us is not the ocean, and the soft air the breath of our own temperate region! The delusion is charming!

30*th*.—Yesterday after anchoring in Depôt Bay I walked over to Possession Point, to visit Ross's cairn. I found a few stones piled up on two large boulders, and under each a halfpenny, one of which I pocketed. Upon the ground lay the fragments of a bottle which once contained the re-cord, and near it a staff about 4 feet long. Having calcu-lated upon finding the bottle sound, I was obliged to make an impromptu record-case of its long neck, into which I thrust my brief document, and consigned it to the safe custody of a small heap of stones, the staff being erected over it.

It was dark before I got on board again. The strait had been reconnoitered from the hills, and was reported to be perfectly clear of ice ! This morning we made a fourth attempt to pass through ; but Bellot Strait was by no means clear ; the same obstruction existed which defeated our last attempt, and in precisely the same place. Returning eastward, we entered a narrow arm of the sea, nearly a couple of miles to the west of Depôt Bay, and anchored in a small creek perfectly sheltered and land-locked, at the foot of a sugarloaf hill.*   The temperature is falling ; last night it stood at 24°.

---

* Subsequently named Mount Walker.

CHAPTER XI.

MOST anxious to know the real state of the ice in the
western sea — upon which our hopes so entirely depend — I
intend starting this evening by boat, as far through Bellot
Strait as the ice will permit, then land and ascend the western coast-hills.

1st Sept.—My boat party consisted of four men and the
doctor, who came with me for the novelty of the cruise,
bringing his camera to fasten upon anything picturesque.
We landed near Half-way Island, and pitched our tent for
the night. Early next morning I commenced the rather
formidable undertaking of ascending the hills, for it is not
possible to pass under the cliffs, and at last I gained the
summit of the loftiest, overlooking Cape Bird at a distance
of 3 or 4 miles, and affording a splendid view to the westward, as well as glimpses between the hills of the blue
eastern sea. Long and anxiously did I survey the western
sea, ice, and lands, and could not but feel that in all probability we should not be permitted to pass beyond our present
position.

To the northward Four River Point — Sir James Ross'
farthest in 1849 — was at once recognized ; rather more
than nine years ago I stood upon it with him, and gazed

M'CLINTOCK IN HIS BOAT SAILING THROUGH BELLOT STRAIT.
Drawn by Captain May.

almost as anxiously in this direction! My present view
confirmed the impression then received, of a wide channel
leading southward. The outline of the western land is very
distant; it is of considerable but uniform elevation, and
slopes gradually down to the strait, which is between 30
and 40 miles wide. This western land appears to be limestone, and without off-lying islands. Our side of the strait
or sea, on the contrary, is primary rock, and fringed with
islets and rocks; its southern extreme bears S. S. W., and
is probably 30 miles distant.

Now for the ice. Although broken up, it lies against
this shore in immense fields : there is but little water or
room for ice-movement. Along the west shore I can distinguish long faint streaks of water. There is no appearance of disruption about Four River Point or in the contracted part of Peel Strait — we have nothing to hope for
in that quarter; neither is there any evidence of current or
pressure; the ice appears much decayed; but, as I am
surveying it from a height of about 1600 feet, I may be
deceived.

The strong contrast between the eastern and western seas
and lands is very unfavorable to the latter.

Apart from the ice, I was fortunate, however, in discovering a long narrow lake, occupying a valley which lies between a small inlet near Cape Bird and Hazard Inlet — in
fact, a sort of echo of Bellot Strait — and I look upon it
as our sledge-route for the autumn, since it appears probable we shall winter in our present position.

This is a *wondrous rough* country to scramble over; one
never ceases to wonder how such huge blocks of rock can
have got into such strange positions. I noticed two masses
in particular, each of them perched upon three small stones.
The rock is gneiss; there is also much granite. Even
upon the hill-tops pieces of limestone are occasionally met
with.

11

My walk occupied eleven hours, and, although I everywhere saw traces of animals, the only living thing seen was a grey falcon. During my absence from the tent the men rambled all over the hills, but saw no game; our encampment was therefore shifted to a better position near the eastern termination of the table-land. This morning we explored the neighboring valleys; saw three deer, and shot one, returning on board the 'Fox' in time for dinner.

Many deer had been seen not far from the ship, and Hobson had shot a bearded seal. I have organized another boat party; Young will start with it to-morrow morning to seek a sledge route from the southern angle of Brentford Bay to the western sea.

5th.—Young returned this morning; he reports the south-west angle of the bay not to run in so far as we expected, and to be environed by very high land, impracticable for sledges.

Our Esquimaux, Samuel, shot a fawn to-day.

Strong northerly winds have latterly prevailed; Bellot Strait is quite clear of ice; to-morrow morning, therefore, we shall make our *fifth* attempt to get the 'Fox' through.

6th.—Steamed through the clear waters of Bellot Strait this morning, and made fast to the ice across its western outlet at a distance of two miles from the shore, and close to a small islet which we have already dubbed *Pemmican Rock*, having landed upon it a large supply of that substantial traveller's fare, with other provisions for our future sledging-parties. This ice is in large stout fields, of more than one winter's growth, apparently immovable in consequence of the numerous islets and rocks which rise through and hold it fast. If the weather permits, we shall remain here. for a few days and watch the effects of winds and tides upon it; that the ship will get 'any further seems improbable.

10th.—I have explored a small inlet near Cape Bird, which we have named *False Strait*, from its striking re-

semblance to the true one, and find it is only separated
from the long lake by half a mile of low land; the lake we
have ascertained to be about 12 miles long, and from it
valleys extend eastward and southward, so that we are sure
of a good sledge-route,—an important matter, as the hills
rise to 1600 feet above the sea.

Cape Bird is 500 feet high; from its summit we carefully
observe the ice. This granite coast presents a jagged
appearance; it is deeply indented and studded with islets.
The ice in the Western Sea (or Peel's Strait) is much more
broken up than it was upon the 31st ultimo; there is no
longer any fixed ice except within the grasp of the islets.
Birds and animals have become very scarce; three seals
have been shot, and a bear seen.   To-morrow we shall return to our harbor, and endeavor to procure a few more
reindeer before they migrate southward.

12th.—Yesterday we anchored within the entrance of our
creek, being a more convenient position than up at its head.
We are already in our wintering position, and, being without occupation, one day seems most remarkably like another! Although the fondly cherished hope of pushing
further in our ship can no longer be entertained, yet as long
as the season continues navigable it is our duty to be in
readiness to avail ourselves of any opportunity, however
improbable, of being able to do so.

Once firmly frozen in, our autumn travelling will commence, and afford welcome occupation. Almost all on
board have guns; ammunition is supplied, and a sailor
with a musket is a very contented and zealous sportsman,
if not always a successful one; it is a powerful incentive
to exercise.   To-day the ramblers saw only two hares, an
ermine, and an owl.   Some peregrine falcons have lately
been shot; Petersen declares they are "*the best beef in
the country, and the young birds tender and white as
chicken.*"

A few days ago a large cask of biscuit was opened, and a living mouse discovered therein! it was small, but mature in years. The cask, a strong watertight one, was packed on shore at Aberdeen, in June, 1857, and remained ever afterwards unopened: there was no hole by which the mouse could have got in or out, besides it is the only one ever seen on board. Ship's biscuit is certainly *dry feeding*, but who dares assert, after the experience of our mouse, that it is not wonderfully nutritious?

15th.—Two nights ago a comet was observed just beneath the constellation of the Great Bear; a series of measurements were commenced for determining its path. Yesterday I walked through the most promising valleys for eight hours, but did not see a living creature; yet there is very fair show of vegetation, much more than at Melville Island, where the game is abundant. To the east there is not a speck of ice, excepting only a huge iceberg, probably the same we saw off Fury Point, a very unusual visitor from Baffin's Bay, whence it must have been driven by those long-continued east winds (of painful memory) in June and July.

Hobson and two men encamped out for three days in order to scour the country; they have only seen one hare and one lemming! Walker geologizes; amongst other things he finds much iron pyrites. The dredge has been used, but with very little success. The thermometer ranges between 20° and 30°. Fresh water pools are frozen over, sea-ice forms in every sheltered angle of the creeks. There is no snow upon the land, and this is one cause of the difficulty of finding game.

I have determined upon naming this beautiful little anchorage *Port Kennedy,* after my predecessor, the discoverer of Bellot Strait, of which it is decidedly *the* port. This is not a compliment to him, but an agreeable duty to me, and nowhere could Mr. Kennedy's name be more appropriately affixed then in close proximity with his interesting discovery. And now having made this acknowledgment, I may venture to confer our little vessel's name upon the islets which protect its entrance.

The island upon which Mr. Kennedy and Lieutenant Bellot encamped was Long Island, about three miles further to the south-east.

17*th.*—Of late we have been preparing provisions and equipments for our travelling parties. My scheme of sledge search comprehends three separate routes and parties of four men ; to each party a dog-sledge and driver will be attached; Hobson, Young, and I will lead them.

My journey will be to the Great Fish River, examining the shores of King William's land in going and returning; Petersen will be with me.

Hobson will explore the western coast of Boothia as far as the magnetic pole, this autumn, I hope, and from Gateshead Island westward next spring.

Young will trace the shore of Prince of Wales' Land from Lieutenant Browne's farthest, to the south-westward to Osborn's farthest, if possible, and also examine between Four River Point and Cape Bird.

Our probable absence will be sixty or seventy days, commencing from about the 20th of March.

In this way I trust we shall complete the Franklin search and the geographical discovery of Arctic America, both left unfinished by the former expeditions; and in so doing we can hardly fail to obtain some trace, some relic, or, it may be, important records of those whose mysterious fate it is the great object of our labors to discover. But previous to setting forth upon these important journeys, I must communicate with the Boothians, if possible, either upon the west or east coast, in November or February. Sir John Ross' 'Narrative' informs us that they sometimes winter as far north upon the east coast as the Agnew River;

and we know that upon the west, at the magnetic pole, their
abandoned snow huts were occupied in June by Sir James
Ross.

19*th.*—Yesterday we steamed once more through Bellot
Strait, and took up our former position at the ice-edge,
off its western entrance; the ice, hemmed in by islets, has
not moved.

From the summit of Cape Bird I had a very extensive
view this morning: there is now much water in the offing
only separated from us by the belt of islet-girt ice *scarcely
four miles in width!* My conviction is that a strong east
wind would remove this remaining barrier; it is not yet too
late. The water runs parallel to this coast, and is four or
five miles broad; beyond it there is ice, but it appears to
be all broken up.

Yesterday Young went upon a dog-sledge to the nearest
south-western island, distant 7 or 8 miles. He reports the
intervening ice cracked and weak in some places, but practicable for loaded sledges; the far side of the island is
washed by a clear sea, and a bear which he shot plunged
into it, and, drifting away, was lost. Young is in favor of
carrying out the depot of provisions to or beyond this island
by boat; but as the temperature fell to 18° last night, and
new ice forms wherever it is calm, I prefer the safer, although more laborious mode of sledging; accordingly to-day
our dogs carried out two sledge-loads of the provisions intended for the use of our parties hereafter.

22*nd.*—All the provisions have now been carried out to
the nearest island, which I shall temporarily name *Separation,** as there our spring parties will divide; and a portion intended for Hobson's party and my own has been carried on to the next island 7 or 8 miles further. Our tra-

---

* Subsequently named after my excellent friend A. Arcedeckne, Esq.,
Commodore of the Royal London Yacht Club.

velling boat and a small reserve depot have been placed
upon Pemmican Rock, so already something has been done.
Animal life is very scarce; a few seals, an occasional gull,
and three brown falcons, are the only creatures we have seen
for several days past.   Last evening at eight o'clock a very
vivid flash of lightning was observed; its appearance in
these latitudes is very rare; once only have I seen it before
—in September, 1850.

25th.—Saturday night.   Furious gales from N. and S.
W., but our barrier of coast-ice remains undiminished.
This morning Hobson set off upon a journey of 14 or
15 days' duration, with seven men and fourteen dogs; he
is to advance the depots along shore to the south, and if
successful will reach latitude 71°.

The temperature is mild (+17°), but it is snowy and disagreeable weather; there is already enough snow upon the
old ice to make walking laborious, and the land has also
assumed its wintry complexion.

28th.—The ship was kept available for prosecuting her
voyage up to the *latest hour;* it was only yesterday that we
left the western. ice, and in consequence of the vast accumulation of yong ice in Bellot Strait we have had considerable difficulty in reaching the *entrance* of Port Kennedy:
all within was so firmly frozen over that after three hours'
steaming and working we only penetrated 100 yards; however, we are in excellent position, although our wintering
place will be farther out by a quarter of a mile than I intended.

To-day we are unbending sails and laying up the engines
—uncertainty no longer exists—here we are compelled to
remain; and if we have not been as successful in our voyage as a month ago we had good reason to expect, we
may still hope that fortune will smile upon our more humble, yet more arduous, pedestrian explorations—" Hope on,
hope ever."   In the meantime the sudden transition, from

mental and physical wear and tear, to the security and quiet
of winter quarters, is an immense relief.

2nd Oct.—M. Petersen has shot two very fine bucks ; one
is a magnificent fellow, weighing 354 lbs. (minus the
paunch).   Several deer have been seen ; they come from
the N. along the slopes of the eastern hills.   An ermine
came on board a few nights ago and kept the dogs in a violent state of excitement, being much too wary to come out
from under the boat to be caught by them ; at length one
of the men secured it.   This beautiful little animal does
not appear to be full grown ; its extreme length is 13
inches.   Two others came off to the ship, and to our great
amusement eluded the men who gave chase, by darting into
the soft snow—which is now a foot deep—and reappearing
several yards off.

The weather is too mild to satisfy us ; we wish for severe
frost to seal us up securely, and make the ice strong enough
to bear the sledge-loads of provisions, etc., which are to be
landed for the purpose of making more room in the ship.

6th.—A herd of a dozen reindeer crossed the harbor to-
day.   Last night Hobson and his companions returned, all
well.   They were stopped by the sea washing against the
cliffs in latitude $71\frac{1}{2}°$, and to that point they have advanced
the depots.   Although the weather has been stormy here, they
have been able to travel every day.   They found the coast
still fringed with islets, and deeply indented ; upon every
point, moss-grown circles of stones indicated the abodes of
Esquimaux in times long since gone by.

One night they muzzled a dog, as she was in the habit of
gnawing her harness : in this defenceless state, unable even
to bark and arouse the men, her *amiable* sisterhood attacked
her so fiercely that she died next day.

In honor of so important and successful a commencement
of our travelling, as that accomplished by Hobson, we had
a feast of good venison, plum pudding and grog.   It is

quite evident that no more travelling can be accomplished
until the ice forms a pathway alongshore; in this, as in
some other respects, we anxiously await the advance of the
season.   The weather is mild; Bellot Strait is almost
covered with ice, which drifts freely with every tide.   Reindeer are seen almost daily; they too are awaiting the
freezing over of the sea to continue their southern travels.
Our harbor-ice is weak, and covered a foot deep with a
sludgy compound of snow and water.

8th.—Yesterday an ermine was caught in a trap; hitherto these most active little skirmishers have successfully robbed our fox-traps of their baits as fast as they could be renewed.   To-day Petersen shot another reindeer; it weighs
130 lbs.; many others were seen, also a wolf.   Sometimes
a few ptarmigan are met with, but hares very rarely.

12th. — Fine weather generally prevails.   We have
landed about 100 casks, all our boats, and much lumber,
so we shall have abundance of room on board.   I enjoyed
a long and exhilarating ramble upon snow-shoes to-day;
without them I could not have gone over half the distance
—the snow lies so deep and soft—but I only saw one reindeer.

14th.—One of our magnetic observatories has been built;
it stands upon the ice, 210 yards S. (magnetic) from the
ship, and is built of ice sawed into blocks—there not being
any suitable snow; it is just large enough to hold the declinometer for hourly observations, to be noted throughout
the winter.   The housings have been put over the ship
already, as Hobson will leave us again in a few days to advance his depot and my own to the vicinity of the magnetic
pole, if possible.   I would also send Young upon a similar
duty, but the western sea cannot have frozen over yet.

19th.—All the 17th a N. W. gale blew with fearful violence; yesterday it abated, but not sufficiently to allow our
party to start.   This morning Hobson got away with his

nine men and ten dogs; his absence may be from eighteen
to twenty days. Autumn travelling is most disagreeable;
there is so much wind and snow, the latter being soft, deep
and often wet; the sun is almost always obscured by mist,
and is powerless for warmth or drying purposes, and the
temperature is very variable. Moreover there are now only
eight hours of misty daylight. To-day the morning was
fine, and temperature $+8^{\circ}$. Having completed the preliminary observations of the times of horizontal and vertical
vibrations, also of the magnetic intensity, I set up to-day
the declinometer, and commenced the hourly series of observations on the diurnal variation. I trust it may continue unbroken until we all set out upon our spring travels
in March. A hare has been shot, but no other animals
seen.

29th.—It generally blows a gale of wind here; the only
advantage in return for so much discomfort is that the snow
is the more quickly packed hard. As we have only three
working men and an Esquimaux left on board for ship's duties, I was assisted a few days ago by the doctor, the engineer, and the interpreter, in building another observatory,
intended for certain monthly magnetic observations. This
edifice is constructed of snow. Whenever we have a calm
night we can hear the crushing sound of the drift-ice in Bellot Strait, which continues open to within 500 yards of the
Fox Islands, and emits dark chilling clouds of hateful, pes-
tilent, abominable mist.

The last two days have been very fine and calm : the men
visited their fox and ermine traps, which are secreted
amongst the rocks in a most mysterious manner—one ermine
only has been taken. Seven or eight reindeer, and some
ptarmigan were seen; two of the latter and a hare were
shot. We have commenced brewing sugar beer.

2nd Nov.—Very dull times. No amount of ingenuity
could make a diary worth the paper it is written on. An

occasional raven flies past, a couple more ptarmigan have been shot; another N. W. gale is blowing, with temperature down to −12°.

6th.—Saturday Night. The N. W. gale blew without intermission for seventy hours, the temperature being about −15° : we hoped that our absent shipmates might be housed safely in snow huts. This afternoon all doubts respecting them were dispelled by their arrival in good health, but they evidently have suffered from cold and exposure during their absence of nineteen days. For the first six days they journeyed outward successfully; on that night they encamped upon the ice; it was at spring-tide; a N. E. gale sprang up, and blowing off shore detached the ice and drifted them off! The sea froze over on the cessation of the gale, and two days afterwards they fortunately regained the land near the position from which they were blown off; they have indeed experienced much unusual danger and suffering from cold.

As soon as they discovered that the ice was drifting off shore with them, they packed their sledges, harnessed their dogs, and passed the night in anxious watching for some chance to escape. When the ice got a little distance off shore, it broke up under the influence of the wind and sea, until the piece they were upon was scarce 20 yards in diameter; this drifted across the mouth of a wide inlet* until brought up against the opposite shore. The gale was quickly followed by an intense frost, which in a single night formed ice sufficiently strong to bear them in safety to the land, although it bent fearfully beneath their weight.

The depots were eventually established in latitude 71°;

---

* Named after Lord Wrottesley, in remembrance of the support given by him to the expedition, his advocacy of it in the House of Lords, and of the facilities granted me by the Royal Society—of which he was President—for the pursuit of scientific observations.

beyond this Lieutenant Hobson did not attempt to advance, not only because their remaining provisions would not have warranted a longer absence, but because the open sea was seen to beat against the next headland. They have lived in tents only, and have not experienced the heavy gales so frequent here, and which are probably due mainly to our position in Bellot Strait, which performs the part of a funnel for both winds and tides between the two seas.

That the western sea should still remain open argues a vast space southward for the escape of the ice, and prevents our western party from carrying across their depot: the attempt to do so would be extremely hazardous. We must only be stirring earlier in the spring. I am truly thankful for the safe return of our travelers—all this toil and exposure of ten persons and ten dogs has only advanced the depots 30 miles further—*i. e.* from 60 to 90 miles distant from the ship.

Hardly a particle of snow remains upon the harbor-ice, the recent gales having swept it away; and the porch of my snow-hut has been fretted away to a mere cob-web by the attrition of the snow-drift: the doctor and I rebuilt it to-day. Three reindeer and a wolf have been seen.

CHAPTER XII.

Death of our engineer—Scarcity of game—The cold unusually trying—
Jolly, under adverse circumstances—Petersen's information—Return
of the sun of 1859—Early spring sledge parties—Unusual severity of
the winter—Severe hardships of early sledging—The western shores of
Boothia—Meet the Esquimaux—Intelligence of Franklin's ships—Return to the 'Fox'—Allen Young returns.

Nov. 7th.—Sunday evening.—BRIEF as is the interval
since my last entry, yet how awful, and, to one of our small
company, how fatal it has been! Yesterday Mr. Brand was
out shooting as usual, and in robust health; in the evening
Hobson sat with him for a little time. Mr. Brand turned
the conversation upon our position and employments last
year; he called to remembrance poor Robert Scott, then in
sound health, and the fact of his having carried our "Guy
Fawkes" round the ship on the preceding day twelvemonth,
and added mournfully, "Poor fellow! no one knows whose
turn it may be to go next." He finished his evening pipe,
and shut his cabin door shortly after nine o'clock. This
morning, at seven o'clock, his servant found him lying upon
the deck, a corpse, having been several hours dead. Apoplexy appears to have been the cause. He was a steady,
serious man, under forty years of age, and leaves a widow
and three or four children; what their circumstances are I
am not aware.

10th.—This morning, the remains of Mr. Brand, inclosed
in a neat coffin, were buried in a grave on shore. A suitable
headboard and inscription will be placed over it. From all
that I have gathered, it appears that his mind had been

somewhat gloomy for the last few days, dwelling much upon
poor Scott's sudden death.   Whether he really saw three
reindeer on Saturday, watched their movements, and fired
his Minie rifle at them when 700 yards distant, or whether
it was the creation of a disordered brain, none can tell.
On his first return on board he said he had seen deer *tracks*
only.

We are now without either engineer or engine-driver : we
have only two stokers, and they know nothing about the
machinery.   Our numbers are reduced to twenty-four, including our interpreter and two Greenland Esquimaux.

15*th.*—We have enjoyed ten days of moderate winds and
calms, but the temperature has fallen as low as –31°.   This
causes frost-cracks in the ice *across* the harbor; they will
freeze over, and others will form, and gape, and freeze at
intervals, so that by next spring we shall probably be moved
several inches, perhaps feet, off shore.

Mists have obscured the sun of late, and now it does not
rise at all.   We are indifferent; its departure has become
to us a matter of course.   The usual winter covering of
snow has been spread upon deck rather more than a foot
thick.   Its utility in preventing the escape of heat became
at once strikingly apparent.   Nothing has been seen but a
few ptarmigan and one reindeer, which trotted off towards
the ship.   Our bullets missed him, and the dogs unfortunately caught sight and chased him away.   I do not think
any dogs could overtake a reindeer in this rough country ;
the rocks would speedily lame them, and the snow, in many
places, is quite deep enough to fatigue them greatly, whereas
it offers but slight impediment to the deer, furnished as he
is with long legs and spreading hoofs.

29*th.*—Animals have become very scarce.   A few ptarmigan and willow-grouse have been seen, and three shot.
Two days ago I saw two reindeer.   The eastern sea is frozen
over, and our old acquaintance the iceberg in Prince Re·

gent's Inlet is still visible on a clear day. We brew sugar-
beer, and we set nets for seals, but catch none. The nets
have been made and set in favorable positions under the ice
by the Greenlanders, so we suppose the seals also have migrated elsewhere; if so, the Esquimaux could not winter
here. We have no regular school this winter, but five of
the men study navigation every evening under the guidance
of Young. Hobson and I are doing all we can to make
the ship dry, warm, and comfortable : our large snow porches
over the hatchways are a great improvement.

5th Dec.—Cold, windy weather, with chilling mists from
the open water in Bellot Strait. We can seldom leave the
shelter of the ship for a walk on shore, and, when we do,
rarely see even a ptarmigan.

12th.—Very cold weather : thermometer down to –41°,
and the breeze comes to us loaded with mist from the open
water, causing the air to feel colder than it otherwise would.
Bellot Strait has become a nuisance, not only from this
cause, but from the strong winds—purely local—which seldom cease to blow through it.

The seal nets have produced nothing ; and as there are
no seals, we no longer wonder at not seeing bears. Three
foxes have been trapped and a hare seen. Our canine force
numbers twenty-four serviceable dogs and six puppies; but
these, I fear, will not be strong enough for sledging by
March. The monotony of our lives is vastly increased by
want of occupation, and confinement, by severe gales, to the
ship for five days out of every seven. The general health
is good, but there is a natural craving for fresh meat and
fresh vegetables—in a great measure, perhaps, because they
cannot be obtained; but a well-filled letter-bag would be
more welcome than anything I know of.

26th.—Upon four days only during the last fourteen has
the weather permitted us to walk. I allude to the wind as
the obstacle to our exercise ; for temperature, when the air

is still, is no bar to any reasonable amount of it. Three or four coveys of ptarmigan have been seen, and of these I shot one brace. The cold increases : thermometer has fallen to $-47\frac{1}{2}°$, although blowing a moderate gale at the time, and the atmosphere dense with mist.

Our Christmas has been spent with a degree of loyalty to the good old English custom at once spirited and refreshing. All the good things which could possibly be collected together appeared upon the snow-white deal tables of the men, as the officers and myself walked (by invitation) round the lower deck. Venison, beer, and a fresh stock of clay pipes, appeared to be the most prized luxuries; but the variety and abundance of the eatables, tastefully laid out, was such as might well support the delusion which all seemed desirous of imposing upon themselves—that they were in a land of plenty—in fact, *all but* at home! We contributed a large cheese and some preserves, and candles superseded the ordinary smoky lamps. With so many comforts, and the existence of so much genuine good feeling, their evening was a joyous one, enlivened also by songs and music.

Whilst all was order and merriment within the ship, the scene without was widely different. A fierce northwester howled loudly through the rigging, the snow-drift rustled swiftly past, no star appeared through the oppressive gloom, and the thermometer varied between 76° and 80° *below the freezing-point.* At one time it was impossible to visit the magnetic observatory, although only 210 yards distant, and with a rope stretched along, breast-high, upon poles the whole way. The officers discharged this duty for the quartermasters of the watches during the day and night.

1*st Jan.* 1859.—This being *Saturday night* as well as *New Year's Day*, "Sweethearts and Wives" were remembered with even more than the ordinary feeling. New year's eve was celebrated with all the joyfulness which

ardent hope can inspire : and we *have* reasonable ground
for *strong hope*.   At midnight the expiration of the old
year and commencement of the new one was announced to
me by *the band*—flutes, accordion, and gong—striking up
at my door.   Some songs were sung, and the performance
concluded with "God save the Queen ;" the few who could
find space in our mess-room sang the chorus; but this by no
means satisfied all the others who were without and unable
to show themselves to the officers, so they ·echoed the
chorus, and the effect was very pleasing.   Our new year's
day has been commemorated with all the substantials of
Christmas fare, but without so much display,—less tailoring
in pastry, not quite so much clipping of dough into roses, ·
and anchors, and nondescript animals, &c., &c.   The past
week has been cold and stormy; it now blows strong, and
the temperature is –44°.

On the 29th a few fresh tracks of animals and a ptarmigan were seen : yesterday I saw three ptarmigan.   December proved to be an unusually cold month, its mean temperature being –33° ; and it was rendered more than ordina-
rily dark and gloomy by continual mists from Bellot Strait.
This open water adds seriously to the drawbacks of a spot
already sufficiently cheerless, gameless, and "wind-loved."

9th.—Another week of uniform temperature of –40°, and
confinement to the ship by strong winds ; the atmosphere
is loaded with enveloping mists which impart a raw and
surprisingly keen edge to the chilling blasts, blasts that no
human nose can endure without blanching, be its propor-
tions what they may.   It is wonderful how the dogs stand
it, and without apparent inconvenience, unless their fur
happens to be thin.   They lie upon the snow under the lee
of the ship, with no other protection from the weather.

To-day, the winds being light and temperature *up to*
–30°, we enjoyed walks on shore, although the mist con-

tinued so dense as to limit our view to a couple of hundred yards.

I learn from Petersen that the natives of Smith's Sound are well acquainted with the continuation of its shores considerably beyond the farthest point reached by Kane's exploring parties, but unfortunately no one thought of getting them to delineate their local knowledge upon paper. They spoke much of a large island near the west coast called "Umingnak" (musk ox) Island, where there was much open water, abounding with walrus, and where some of their people formerly lived.*

Esquimaux exist upon the east coast of Greenland as far north as lat. 76°; how much farther north is not known. They are separated from the South Greenlanders by hundreds of miles of ice-bound coasts and impassable glaciers.

Many centuries ago a milder climate *may* and probably *did* exist, and a corresponding modification of glacier and a sea less ice-encumbered might have rendered the migration of these poor people from the south to their present isolated abodes practicable; but to me it appears much more easy to suppose that they migrated eastward from the northern outlet of Smith's Sound.

31st.—More pleasant weather since my last entry; and although last night the temperature fell to –47°, yet it has generally been mild; once it rose to –14°, but amply made amends by falling to –38° within twelve hours. We have enjoyed much of the moon's presence for the last ten days, but now she is waning and hastening away to the south. Daylight increases in strength and duration, consequently we walk more, and see more, and the winter's gloom gives place to activity and cheerfulness. Several ptarmigan, three or four hares, a snowy owl, and a bear-track, have at

* Petersen conversed with two men who had themselves been up to Umingmak Island.

various times been seen.   Young has shot four ptarmigan,
and I have shot a couple more and a hare, and the men
have trapped two foxes.

On board the ship the preparations for travelling take
precedence of all other occupations.

26th.—Part of the sun's disc loomed above the horizon
to-day, somewhat swollen and disfigured by the misty atmosphere, but looking benevolent withal.   I happened to be
diligently traversing the rocky hill-sides in the hope of
finding some solitary hare dozing in fancied security, when
the sun thus appeared in view, and halted to feast my eyes
upon the glorious sight, and scan the features of our returning friend.   Hope and promise mingled in his bright beams.
Again I moved upward, and with more elastic step ; for
now the sun of 1859 was shining upon all nature around
me.

2nd February.—A lovely, calm, bright day, and beautifully clear, except over the waterspace in Bellot Strait,
where rests a densely black mist, very strongly resembling
the West Indian rain-squall as it looms upon the distant
horizon.   The increasing sunlight is cheering, but void of
heat, and the mercury is often frozen.   A few more ptarmigan have been shot.

Our remaining serviceable dogs, twenty-two in number,
have been divided with great care into three teams of seven
each; the odd dog is added to my team, as my journey is
expected to be the longest.   The different sledge-parties
will now feed up their dogs without limit, so that the utmost
degree of work may be got out of them hereafter.

January has been slightly colder than December, mean
temperature being $-33\frac{1}{2}°$, but there has been rather less
wind.

8th.—All will be ready for the departure of Young and
myself upon our respective journeys upon the morning of
the 14th.

Mr. Petersen and Alexander Thompson accompany me, with two dog-sledges, and fifteen dogs, dragging twenty-four days' provisions. My object is to communicate with the Boothians in the vicinity of the magnetic pole. Young takes his party of four men and his dog-sledge; he will carry forward provisions for his spring exploration of the shores of Prince of Wales' Land, between the extreme points reached by Lieutenants Osborn and Brown in 1851.

On the 3d I walked for seven and a half hours, and saw two reindeer, but could not approach within shot. Young examined the water-space in the strait, and finds it washes both shores, but extends east and west only about one mile. The Doctor has seen a seal and a dovekie sporting in it.

For the last four days strong winds and intense cold have prevented us from rambling over the hills, besides which the minor preparations for travelling have given us more occupation on board.

James Pitcher has got a slight touch of scurvy; his gums are inflamed; and now it comes out that he dislikes preserved meats, and has not eaten any since he has been in the ship! He has lived upon salt meat and preserved vegetables, except for the very short periods in summer when birds could be obtained. He is rather a "used up" old fellow, too much so for our severe sledge-work, therefore is one of the few who will remain to take care of the ship. That he should have retained his health for seventeen months, under the circumstances, speaks well for the wholesomeness and quality of our provisions, and the ventilation and cleanliness of the ship.

10th.—Extremely cold, with dense mists from the open water. Yesterday eight ptarmigan and a sooty fox were seen. We have consumed the last of our venison; it supplied us for three days. We are drinking out a cask of sugar-beer, which is a very mild but agreeable beverage; we make it on board.

Sunday night, 13*th.*—To-morrow evening, if fine, Young and I set off upon our travels. He has advanced a portion of his sledge-load to the west side of the water in Bellot Strait, having been obliged to carry it overland for about a mile in order to get there. I have explored the route to the long lake, and find we can reach it without crossing elevated or uncovered land. I saw two reindeer, and Young saw about twenty ptarmigan.

The mean temperature of February up to this date is −33·2°, being an exact continuation of January. I confess to some anxiety upon this point, as hitherto the winter has been unusually severe, and the journeys to be performed will occupy more than twenty days. Besides, we shall be earlier in motion than any of the previous travellers, unless we are to make an exception in favor of Mr. Kennedy's trip of 30 miles from Batty Bay to Fury Beach, between the 5th and 10th of January, during which time the lowest temperature registered was only −25°. Should either Young or myself remain absent beyond the period for which we carry provisions, Hobson is to send a party in search of us. A sooty fox has been captured lately.

15*th.*—A strong N. W. wind, with a temperature of −40°, confines us on board. One cannot face these winds, therefore it is fortunate that we did not start, the ship being much more comfortable than a snow-hut.

*   *   *   *   *   *

20*th March.*—Already I have been a week on board, and so difficult is it to settle down to anything like sedentary occupation, after a period of continued vigorous action, that even now I can scarcely sit still to scribble a brief outline of my trip to Cape Victoria.

On the morning of the 17th February the weather moderated sufficiently for us to set out; the temperature throughout the day varied between −31° and −42½°. Leaving Young's party to pass on through the strait, I proceeded by way of the Long Lake, which I found to be $10\frac{1}{2}$ geographical miles in length, with an average width of half a mile.

We built our snow-hut upon the west coast, near Pemmican Rock, after a march of 19 or 20 geographical miles. We always speak of *geographical* miles with reference to our marches; six geographical are equal to seven English miles.

On the following day the old N. W. wind sprang up with renewed vigor, and the thermometer fell to –48°; the cold was therefore intense.

On the third day our dogs went lame in consequence of sore feet; the intense cold seems to be the principal, if not the only cause, having hardened the surface-snow beyond what their feet can endure. I was obliged to throw off a part of the provisions; still we could not make more than 12 or 18 miles daily. We of course walked, so that the dogs had only the remaining provisions and clothing to drag, yet several of them repeatedly fell down in fits.

For several days this severe weather continued, the mercury of my artificial horizon remaining frozen (its freezing point is –39°); and our rum, at first thick like treacle, required thawing latterly, when the more fluid and stronger part had been used. We travelled each day until dusk, and then were occupied for a couple of hours in building our snow-hut. The four walls were run up until $5\frac{1}{2}$ feet high, inclining inwards as much as possible; over these our tent was laid to form a roof; we could not afford the time necessary to construct a dome of snow.

Our equipment consisted of a very small brown-holland tent, mackintosh floor-cloth, and felt robes; besides this, each man had a bag of double blanketing, and a pair of fur boots, to sleep in. We wore mocassins over the pieces of blanket in which our feet were wrapped up, and, with the exception of a change of this foot-gear, carried no spare

clothes. The daily routine was as follows :—I led the way ;
Petersen and Thompson followed, conducting their sledges ;
and in this manner we trudged on for eight or ten hours
without halting, except when necessary to disentangle the
dog-harness When we halted for the night, Thompson
and I usually sawed out the blocks of compact snow and
carried them to Petersen, who acted as the master-mason
in building the snow-hut: the hour and a half or two
hours usually employed in erecting the edifice was the most
disagreeable of the day's labor, for, in addition to being
already well tired and desiring repose, we became thoroughly chilled whilst standing about. When the hut was
finished, the dogs were fed, and here the great difficulty
was to insure the weaker ones their full share in the
scramble for supper ; then commenced the operation of un-
packing the sledge, and carrying into our hut everything
necessary for ourselves, such as provision and sleeping-
gear, as well as all boots, fur mittens, and even the sledge
dog-harness to prevent the dogs from eating them during
our sleeping hours. The door was now blocked up with
snow, the cooking lamp lighted, foot-gear changed, diary
written up, watches wound, sleeping bags wriggled into,
pipes lighted, and the merits of the various dogs discussed,
until supper was ready ; the supper swallowed, the upper
robe or coverlet was pulled over, and then to sleep.

Next morning came breakfast, a struggle to get into
frozen mocassins, after which the sledges were packed, and
another day's march commenced.

In these little huts we usually slept warm enough, although
latterly, when our blankets and clothes became loaded with
ice, we felt the cold severely. When our low doorway was
carefully blocked up with snow, and the cooking-lamp
alight, the temperature quickly rose so that the walls became glazed, and our bedding thawed ; but the cooking
over, or the doorway partially opened, it as quickly fell

again, so that it was impossible to sleep, or even to hold
one's pannikin of tea, without putting our mitts on, so intense was the cold!

On the 21st I visited our main depot laid out last October; it was safe, but unfortunately had been carried far
into Wrottesley Inlet, and only 40 miles south of Bellot
Strait.

On the 22d an easterly gale prevented our marching, but
we had the good fortune to shoot a bear, so consoled ourselves with fresh steaks, and the dogs with an ample feed
of *unfrozen* flesh—a treat they had not enjoyed for many
months.

We coasted along a granitic land, deeply indented and
fringed with islands, and found it to be the general characteristic of the Boothian shore from Bellot Strait, until we
had accomplished half the distance to the magnetic pole;
limestone then appeared, and the remainder of our journey
was performed along a low, straight shore, which afforded
us much greater facility for sledging.

Throughout the whole distance we found a mixture of
heavy old ice and light ice of last autumn, in many places
squeezed up into pack; but as we advanced southward aged
floes were less frequently seen.

On the first of March we halted to encamp at about the position of the magnetic pole—for no cairn remains to mark the
spot. I had almost concluded that my journey would prove to
be a work of labor in vain, because hitherto no traces of Esquimaux had been met with, and in consequence of the
reduced state of our provisions and the wretched condition
of the poor dogs—six out of the fifteen being quite useless
—I could only advance one more march.

But we had done nothing more than look *ahead;* when
we halted, and turned round, great indeed was my surprise
and joy to see four men walking after us. Petersen and I
immediately buckled on our revolvers and advanced to meet

them. The natives halted, made fast their dogs, laid down
their spears, and received us without any evidence of surprise. They told us they had been out upon a seal hunt
on the ice, and were returning home : we proposed to join
them, and all were soon in motion again ; but another hour
brought sunset, and we learned that their snow village of
eight huts was still a long way off, so we hired them, at the
rate of a needle for each Esquimax, to build us a hut, which
they completed in an hour ; it was 8 feet in diameter, $5\frac{1}{2}$
feet high, and in it we all passed the night. Perhaps the
records of architecture do not furnish another instance of
a dwelling-house so cheaply constructed !

We gave them to understand that we were anxious to
barter with them, and very cautiously approached the real
object of our visit. A naval button upon one of their
dresses afforded the opportunity ; it came, they said, from
some white people who were starved upon an island where
there are salmon (that is, in a river) ; and that the iron of
which their knives were made came from the same place.
One of these men said he had been to the island to obtain
wood and iron, but none of them had seen the white men.
Another man had been to "Ei-wil-lik" (Repulse Bay), and
counted on his fingers seven individuals of Rae's party whom
he remembered having seen.

These Esquimaux had nothing to eat, and no other clothing
than their ordinary double dresses of fur ; they would not
eat our biscuit or salt pork, but took a small quantity of
bear's blubber and some water. They slept in a sitting
posture, with their heads leaning forward on their breasts.
Next morning we traveled about 10 miles further, by which
time we were close to Cape Victoria ; beyond this I would
not go, much as they wished to lead us on ; we therefore
landed, and they built us a commodious snow hut in half an
hour ; this done, we displayed to them our articles for barter
—knives, files, needles, scissors, beads, etc.—expressed our

desire to trade with them, and promised to purchase every thing which belonged to the starved white men, if they would come to us on the morrow. Notwithstanding that the weather was now stormy and bitterly cold, two of the natives stripped off their outer coats of reindeer skin and bartered them for a knife each.

Despite the gale which howled outside, we spent a comfortable night in our roomy hut.

Next morning the entire village population arrived, amounting to about forty-five souls, from aged people to infants in arms, and bartering commenced very briskly. First of all we purchased all the relics of the lost expedition, consisting of six silver spoons and forks, a silver medal, the property of Mr. A. M'Donald, assistant surgeon, part of a gold chain, several buttons, and knives made of the iron and wood of the wreck, also bows and arrows constructed of materials obtained from the same source. Having secured these, we purchased a few frozen salmon, some seals' blubber and venison, but could not prevail upon them to part with more than one of their fine dogs. One of their sledges was made of two stout pieces of wood, which might have been a boat's keel.

All the old people recollected the visit of the 'Victory.' An old man told me his name was "Ooblooria:" I recollected that Sir James Ross had employed a man of that name as a guide, and reminded him of it; he was, in fact, the same individual, and he inquired after Sir James by his Esquimaux name of "Agglugga."

I inquired after the man who was furnished with a wooden leg by the carpenter of the 'Victory:' no direct answer was given, but his daughter was pointed out to me. Petersen explained to me that they do not like alluding in any way to the dead, and that, as my question was not answered, it was certain the man was no longer amongst the living.

None of these people had seen the whites; one man said

he had seen their bones upon the island where they died, but some were buried. Petersen also understood him to say that the boat was crushed by the ice. Almost all of them had part of the plunder ; they say they will be here when we return, and will trade more with us ; also that we shall find natives upon Montreal Island at the time of our arriving there.

Next morning, 4th March, several natives came to us again. I bought a spear 6½ feet long from a man who told Petersen distinctly that a ship having three masts had been crushed by the ice out in the sea to the west of King William's Island, but that all the people landed safely ; he was not one of those who were eye witnesses of it ; the ship sunk, so nothing was obtained by the natives from her ; all that they have got, he said, came from the island in the river. The spear staff appears to have been part of the gunwale of a light boat. One old man, " Oo-na-lee," made a rough sketch of the coast-line with his spear upon the snow, and said it was eight journeys to where the ship sank, pointing in the direction of Cape Felix. I can make nothing out of his rude chart.

The information we obtained bears out the principal statements of Dr. Rae, and also accounts for the disappearance of one of the ships ; but it gives no clue to the whereabouts of the other, nor the direction whence the ships came. One thing is tolerably certain—the crews did not at any time land upon the Boothian shore.

These Esquimaux were all well clothed in reindeer dresses, and looked clean ; they appeared to have abundance of provisions, but scarcely a scrap of wood was seen amongst them which had not come from the lost expedition. Their sledges, with the exception of the one already spoken of, were wretched little affairs, consisting of two frozen rolls of seal-skins coated with ice, and attached to each other by bones, which served as the crossbars. The men were stout,

hearty fellows, and the women arrant thieves, but all were
good-humored and friendly. The women were decidedly
plain ; in fact, this term would have been flattering to most
of them ; yet there was a degree of vivacity and gentleness
in the manners of some that soon reconciled us to these
Arctic specimens of the fair sex. They had fine eyes and
teeth, as well as very small hands, and the young girls had
a fresh rosy hue not often seen in combination with olive
complexions.

Esquimaux mothers carry their infants on their backs
within their large fur dresses, and where the babes can only
be got at by pulling them out over the shoulder. Whilst
intent upon my bargaining for silver spoons and forks be-
longing to Franklin's expedition, at the rate of a few needles or a knife for each relic, one pertinacious old dame,
after having obtained all she was likely to get from me for
herself, pulled out her infant by the arm, and quietly held
the poor little creature (for it was perfectly naked) before
me in the breeze, the temperature at the time being 60°
below freezing point ! Petersen informed me that she was
begging for a needle for her child. I need not say I gave
it one as expeditiously as possible ; yet sufficient time
elapsed before the infant was again put out of sight to -
alarm me considerably for its safety in such a temperature.
The natives, however, seemed to think nothing of what
looked to me like cruel exposure of a naked baby.

We now returned to the ship with all the speed we could
command ; but stormy weather occasioned two days' delay,
so that we did not arrive on board until the 14th March.
Though considerably reduced in flesh, I and my companions
were in excellent health, and blessed with insatiable appetites. On washing our faces, which had become perfectly
black from the soot of our blubber lamp, sundry scars,
relics of frost-bites, appeared ; and the tips of our fingers,

from constant frost-bites, had become as callous as if seared
with hot iron.

In this journey of twenty-five days we traveled 360 geographical miles (420 English), and completed the discovery
of the coast-line of continental America, thereby adding
about 120 miles to our charts.   The mean temperature
throughout the journey was 30° below zero of Fahrenheit,
or 62° below the freezing point of water.

On reaching the ship, I at once assembled my small crew,
and told them of the information we had obtained, pointing
out that there still remained one of the ships unaccounted
for, and therefore it was necessary to carry out all our pro-
jected lines of search.

During this journey I acquired the Arctic accomplishment of eating frozen blubber, in delicate little slices, and
vastly preferred it to frozen pork.   At the present moment
I do not think I could even taste it, but the same privation
and hunger which induced me to eat of such food would
doubtless enable me again to partake of it *very kindly*.

I shot a couple of foxes which came playing about the
dogs; conscious of their superior speed, they were very im-
pudent, snapping at the dogs' tails, and passing almost
under their noses.   I shot these foxes, intending to eat
them; but the dogs anticipated me with respect to one;
the other we feasted off at our mess-table, and thought it
by no means bad; it was insipid, but decidedly better to
our taste than preserved meat.

Captain Allen Young and his party had returned on
board on the 3rd of March, having placed their depot upon
the shore of Prince of Wales' Land, about 70 miles S. W.
of the ship.   Young found the ice in Bellot Strait so rough
as to be impassable, and was obliged to adopt the lake
route.   Prince of Wales' Land was found to be composed
of limestone; the shore was low, and fringed for a distance
of ten miles to seaward with an ancient land-floe.   The

remaining width of the strait between this land (North Somerset) and Prince of Wales' Land was about 15 miles, and this space was composed of ice. formed since September last; this was the water we looked at so anxiously last autumn from Cape Bird and Pemmican Rock. His party lived in their tent, protected from the wind by snow walls, and, like ourselves, escaped with a few trivial frost-bites. So far all was very satisfactory, the general health good, and the eagerness of my crew to commence traveling quite charming.

Young proposed carrying out another depot to the northwest, in order to explore well up Peel Strait, and would have started on the 17th, but the weather was too severe. The day was spent in a fruitless search for three casks of sugar — a serious and unaccountable deficiency — but, as it was important to replace them with as little delay as possible, Young set off on the 18th, although it blew a N. W. gale at the time, with two men and eighteen dogs, for Fury Beach; failing to find the requisite quantity there, he will go on to Port Leopold.

CHAPTER XIII.

Dr. Walker's sledge journcy—Snow-blindness attacks Young's party—
Departure of all sledge-parties—Equipment of sledge-parties—Meet
the same party of natives—Intelligence of the second ship—My depot
robbed—Part company from Hobson—Matty Island—Deserted snow-
huts—Native sledges—Land on King William's Land.

DOCTOR WALKER'S zeal for traveling was not to be re-
strained; I therefore gladly availed myself of his willingness
to go with a party to Cape Airey and bring back the depot
of provisions left there in August last. These trips will
delay our spring journeys for a few days.

During my absence from the 'Fox' the weather was often
stormy, and temperature unusually low; the mean for the
month of February was −36°, showing it to be one of the
coldest on record. When possible the men were allowed to
go out shooting, and obtain fifty or sixty ptarmigan and a
hare; a few foxes were taken in traps, and two reindeer
were seen.

Yesterday two bears came near the ship, but were fright
ened away by the dogs. Hobson shot three ptarmigan.
To-day I rambled over the hills, the weather being fine, and
saw a hare.

29th.—Continued fine weather. A couple more foxes
and a lemming in its *brown* coat have been captured, and a
hare and four ptarmigan shot. This fine bright weather
seems to have awakened the lemmings and ermines; their
tracks, which were very rarely seen during the winter, are
now tolerably numerous; foxes appear in greater numbers,

probably following up the ptarmigan from the south; the
thermometer ranges between zero and -20°; it has once
been up to +13°. When exposed to a noonday sun against
the ship's side it rises 50° higher. The earth-thermometer
—placed 2 feet 2 inches beneath the surface—which gradually fell until the 10th of this month, has now begun to
ascend; its minimum was +½°; much snow also lay over
it, 6 feet deep at this season.

On the 25th Dr. Walker and his party returned, not
being able to find the depot. They found a barrel of flour
upon the beach a few miles south of Brentford Bay; it appeared to have lain there for years, just inside a shingle
projection, which kept off the ice pressure, so that it had
not been forced up high upon the beach; the ice which bore
it there—probably from Port Leopold—had disappeared,
and the cask was frozen in the shingle. The heading has
been brought on board, but the "scribing" upon it is very
indistinct, and unintelligible to us. The flour is of the
ordinary description used in the navy, and known as "seconds; most of it was good, and plain pudding made of it
for our mess could not be distinguished from fresh flour. A
specimen has been preserved with a view of identifying it
with the Fury Beach or Port Leopold stores of flour. With
the exception of a solitary bear, the party saw no living
creatures. The shore along which they traveled was a very
low, shingly limestone.

Last evening I was delighted to see Young and his two
dog-sledges heave in sight; he brought about 8 cwt. of
sugar from Fury Beach, but not without much difficulty,
owing to the roughness of the pack in Creswell Bay, and
also to the breaking down of one of his sledges; to avoid
this pack he found it necessary to travel nearly all round
Creswell Bay. Cape Garry he describes as a gradually
curved extent of flat land, and not the decided cape it appears to be upon the chart; two reindeer were seen near

it, and during the journey four bears; no other animals
were met with. His labors had been very severe; one
sledge broke down and all the sugar had to be piled upon
the other: the consequence was that the sledge was so
heavily loaded that it would only run freely after the dogs
on smooth ice; and directly any hummocks were encountered, the dogs, with their usual instinct, not to drag a
sledge unless it does run freely, would lie down, and oblige
Captain Young and his two men to unload and carry
the packages over the obstacle, upon their own backs.
After this, snow-blindness came on; Young and one of his
men became blind as kittens; and the third man had to
load, lead, and unload them, when these portages occurred.
Young's Esquimaux dog-driver, Samuel, was quite blind
when the party reached the ship.   Two dogs, not choosing
to allow themselves to be caught and put.in harness, had
been still left behind at the last encampment.

There still remains at Fury Beach an immense stack of
preserved vegetables and soups; the party supped off them
and found them good.   Young brought me back two specimen tins of "carrots plain" and "carrots and gravy." All
small casks and packages were covered with snow; of the
large ones which appeared through it, he saw thirty-four
casks of flour, five of split peas, five of tobacco, and four
of sugar. Only a very few tons of coals remained. There
were two boats, a short four-oared gig and a large cutter;
The former required nothing but caulking to make her
serviceable, but the latter had a large portion of one bow
and side cut out, as if for making or repairing flat sledges.
No record was found.

We have now enough sugar to last us for seven or eight
months, but by the survey of provisions which has just been
completed, we find a deficiency of many other articles,
including three casks of salt beef. Fortunately this is of
no consequence as we have abundance of both salt and

13

preserved meat, but it shows the alarming extent to which
a negligent Steward may lead one. This unfortunate man
has now got scurvy; want of exercise and fresh air is the
apparent cause, combined with irregular living; the spirits
have hitherto been in his charge.

The bustle of preparation for the extended searching
journeys has been exciting. Hobson's party and my own
are now all prepared, and Young having returned, we propose setting out on the 2d April—God willing. Young's
new sledge will be ready, and he will also start a few days
after us. All our winter defences of snow, our porches,
our deck-layer, and our external embankment, have been
removed. Dr. Walker, of necessity, remains in charge of
the ship, with two stewards, a cook, a carpenter, and a
stoker. My party, as well as Hobson's, will be provisioned,
including the depôts, for an absence of about eighty-four
days; but not being able to afford auxiliary or supporting
sledge-parties, much time will be occupied in transporting
our depôts further out, in order that we may start with as
much as we can possibly carry, from the Magnetic Pole,
besides leaving there a depôt for our return.

The declinometer was taken on board two days ago;
hourly observations have been made with it for more than
five months: we can no longer spare any one for this interesting duty.

*   *   *   *   *

24th June.—One thing is certain, the wild sort of tent-
life we lead in Arctic exploration quite unfits one for such
tame work as writing up a journal; my present attempt
will illustrate the fact,—yet with such ample materials what
a deeply interesting volume might be written! Since I last
opened this familiar old diary—the repository alike of dry
facts and the most trivial notes—winter has passed away,
summer is far advanced, and the glorious sun is again re-

turning southward. We too have endeavored to move on with the times and seasons.

As for myself—I have visited Montreal Island, completed the exploration and circuit of King William's Island, passing on foot through the only feasible North-West Passage; but all this is as nothing to the interest attached to the *Franklin records* picked up by Hobson, and now safe in my possession! We now know the fate of the 'Erebus' and 'Terror.' The sole object of our voyage has at length been completed, and we anxiously await the time when escape from these bleak regions will become practicable.

*　　*　　*　　*　　*

The morning of April 2nd was inauspicious, but as the day advanced the weather improved, so that Hobson and I were able to set out upon our journeys; we each had a sledge drawn by four men, besides a dog-sledge and dog-driver. Mr. Petersen having volunteered his services to drive my dogs,—an offer too valuable to be declined,—managed my dog-sledge throughout. Our five starveling puppies were harnessed, for the first time in their lives, to a small sledge which I drove myself, intending to sell them to the Esquimaux, if I could get them to drag their own supply of provisions so far. The procession looked imposing —it certainly was deeply interesting; there were five sledges, twelve men, and seventeen dogs, the latter of all sizes and shapes. The ship hoisted the Royal Harwich Yacht flag, and our sledges displayed their gay silk banners; mine was a very beautiful one, given me by Lady Franklin; it bears her name in white letters upon a red ground, and is margined with white embroidery; it was worked by the sisters of Captain Collinson.

The equipment of my sledge-party and the weights were as follows: those of Hobson and Young were almost precisely similar.

	lbs. weight.
Two sledges and fitting complete..	110
Tent, waterproof blanket, floorcloth, two sleeping-robes, and six blanket sleeping-bags..	90
Cooking-utensils, shovel, saw, snow-knife, and sundry small articles...	40
Sledge-gun and ammunition..	20
Magnetic and astronomical instruments.........................	60
Six knapsacks, containing spare clothing.....................	60
Various tins and bags, in which provision and fuel were stored...	50
Articles for barter..	40
Provisions	930
Total............................	1400

The load for each man to drag was fixed at 200 lbs., and for each dog 100 lbs. Our provisions consisted mainly of pemmican, biscuit, and tea, with a small addition of boiled pork, rum, and some tobacco.

The men being untrained to the work, and sledges heavily laden, our march was fatiguing and slow. We encamped that night upon the long lake. On the second day we reached the western sea, and upon the third, aided by our sledge-sails, we advanced some miles beyond Arcedeckne Island.

The various depôts carried out with so much difficulty and danger in the autumn, were now gathered up as we advanced, until at length we were so loaded as to be compelled to proceed with one-half at a time, going three times over the same ground. For six days this tedious mode of progression was persevered in, by which time (15th April) we reached the low limestone shore in latitude 71° 7' N., and which continues thence in almost a straight line southward for 60 or 70 miles. We now commenced laying down provisions for our consumption upon the return journey; and the snow being unusually level, we were able to advance with the whole of our remaining provisions, amounting to nearly sixty days' allowance.

Hitherto the temperature continued low, often nearly 30°
below zero, and at times with cutting north winds, bright
sun, and intensely strong snow glare. Although we wore
colored spectacles, yet almost all suffered great inconvenience and considerable pain from inflamed eyes. Our
faces were blistered, lips and hands cracked,—never were
men more disfigured by the combined effects of bright sun
and bitterly cold winds; fortunately no serious frost-bites
occurred, but frost-bitten faces and fingers were universal.

On the 20th April, in latitude $70\frac{1}{2}°$ N., we met two families of natives, comprising twelve individuals; their snow-
huts were upon the ice three-quarters of a mile off shore,
and their occupation was seal-hunting. They were the
same people with whom I had communicated at Cape Victoria in February.

Old Oo-na-lee laid his hands on Petersen's shoulders to
measure their width, and said, "He is fatter now:" true
enough, the February temperature and sharp marching had
caused us both at that time to shrink considerably.

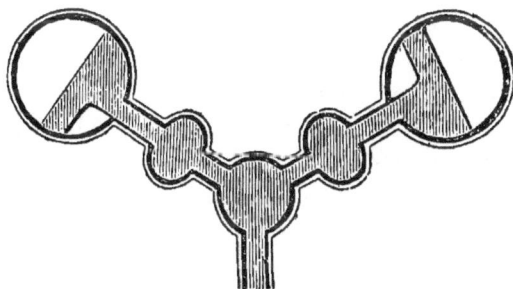

Their snow-huts were built in the above form, the common entrance and both passages being just sufficiently high
to get in without having to crawl upon our hands and
knees. A slab of ice in the roof admitted sufficient light.
A snow bank or bench two feet high, and occupying half

the area of each hut, was covered with reindeer skins, and formed the family place of repose. An angular snow bench served as the kitchen table, and immediately beside it sat the lady of the establishment attending the stone lamp which stood thereon, and the stone-cooking vessel suspended over it. The lamp was a shallow open vessel, the fuel seal oil, and the wick dried moss. Her " tinder-box " was a little seal-skin bag of soft dry moss, and with a lump of iron pyrites and a broken file she struck fire upon it. I purchased the file because it was marked with the Government broad arrow.

We saw two large snow shovels made of mahogany board, some long spear handles, a bow of English wood, two preserved-meat tins, and a deal case which might have once contained a large telescope or a barometer; it measured 3 feet 1 inch in length by 9 inches wide and $3\frac{1}{2}$ inches deep; there was no lid, but part of the brass hinges remained.

I also purchased a knife which had some indistinct markings upon it, such as ship's cutlasses or swords usually have; the man told us it had been picked up on the shore near where a ship lay stranded; that it was then about the length of his arm, but his countryman who picked it up broke it into lengths to make knives.

After much anxious inquiry we learned that two ships had been seen by the natives of King William's Island; one of them was seen to sink in deep water, and nothing was obtained from her, a circumstance at which they expressed much regret; but the other was forced on shore by the ice, where they suppose she still remains, but is much broken. From this ship they have obtained most of their wood, &c.; and Oot-loo-lik is the name of the place where she grounded.

Formerly many natives lived there, now very few remain. All the natives have obtained plenty of the wood.

The most of this information was given us by the young man who sold the knife. Old Oo-na-lee, who drew the rough chart for me in March, to show where the ship sank, now answered our questions respecting the one forced on shore ; not a syllable about her did he mention on the former occasion, although we asked whether they knew of only one ship ?   I think he would willingly have kept us in ignorance of the wreck being upon their coasts, and that the young man unwittingly made it known to us.

The latter also told us that the body of a man was found on board the ship; that he must have been a very large man, and had long teeth ; this is all he recollected having been told, for he was quite a child at the time.

They both told us it was in the fall of the year — that is, August or September — when the ships were destroyed; that all the white people went away to the " large river," taking a boat or boats with them, and that in the following winter their bones were found there.

These two Esquimaux families had been up as far north as the Tasmania Group* in latitude $71\frac{1}{4}°$ N., and were returning to Nëitchïllëe, hunting seals by the way; those we met at Cape Victoria had already gone there.   The nearest natives to us at present, they said, were residing at the island of Amitoke, ten days' journey distant from here. Can this Amitoke be Matty Island ?

We purchased some seal's blubber and flesh, as well as their two only dogs ; but next morning Oo-na-lee repented his bargain, or feigned to do so, but as he came without the knife to exchange back we retained his dog ; he tried to steal a tin vessel off one of the sledges, and perhaps it was for the purpose of regaining our favor that he made known to us, just as we were starting, that his countrymen had fol-

---

* These islands were so named by me at the request of Lady Franklin, in grateful acknowledgment of many proofs of affectionate sympathy received from the colony over which her husband presided for several years, and, in particular, of the large contributions raised there in aid of her expeditions of search.

lowed my homeward track in March, discovering my depôt of blubber, articles for barter, and two revolvers, and carried them all off to Nĕitchillĕe — by no means pleasant intelligence ; their dogs must have enabled them to find the blubber by scenting it, for it was buried under 4 feet of snow, and strong winds obliterated all traces upon the surface.

I was now glad we had purchased both the dogs of the men, as it would probably prevent their seeking for our depots to the northward ; the knowledge of the insecurity of *all* depots amongst these people will keep us on our guard for the future.   I regretted the loss of the pistols, as it left my party with no other arms than two guns.

Oo-na-lee told us when we first met him that one of his countrymen was very sick ; not seeing a sick man in their huts, we forgot all about it until after starting, when Petersen interpreted to me Oo-na-lee's parting information, and told me how he described that the breach of the revolver turned round ; it then occurred to me that one of the men might have been wounded,—they had discovered how to cock the locks, and the pistols were loaded and capped.

Oo-na-lee was well acquainted with the coast-line up to Bellot Strait, and had names for the different headlands, although he had never been so far north ; he made many inquiries about the position of our ship, her size, and the number of men.   Had he been able to travel so far with his wife and several young children, and without sledge or dogs, I think he certainly would have gone up to Port Kennedy : we did not give him any encouragement to do so. His wife was one of the most importunate of the many women we saw at Cape Victoria in March.   She was the woman who plucked out an infant by its arm from inside her dress, and exposed it regardless of –30° and a fresh wind, as I have previously told.

The information respecting *both* the missing ships was

DOG SLEDGE OR SCOUT PARTY

INTERIOR OF THE OBSERVATORY.

Drawn by Captain May.

most important, and it remained for us to discover, if possible, the stranded ship.

Continuing our journey, we crossed a wide bay upon level ice, and the most perfectly smooth hard snow I ever saw; there must have been much open water here late last autumn. Seven or eight snow huts, recently abandoned, were found near the magnetic pole. During the 25th, 26th, and 27th, we were confined to our tents by a very heavy south-east gale, with severe cold. Early on the 28th we reached Cape Victoria; here Hobson and I separated. He marched direct for Cape Felix, King William's Land, whilst I kept a more southerly course. Not daring to leave depots upon this coast, we carried on our whole supply, intending to deposit a small portion upon the Clarence Islands.

Hobson was unwell when we parted, complaining of stiffness and pain in the legs; neither of us then suspected the cause. I gave him directions to search the west coast of King William's Island for the stranded ship and for records, and to act upon such information as he might obtain in this way, or from the natives; but should that shore prove destitute of traces, to carry out, if possible, our original plan for the completion of discovery and search upon Victoria Land, comprising the blank space between the extremes visited by Captain Collinson and Mr. Wynniatt.

I soon found that my party had to labor across a rough pack; nor was it until the third day that we completed the traverse of the strait, and encamped near to the entrance of Port Parry, in King William's Island. Although the weather was clear, and that by our reckoning we passed directly over the assigned position of the two southern of the Clarence Islands, yet we saw nothing of them.

A day was devoted to securing a depot in a huge mass of grounded ice, and in repairing and drying equipments, or, to speak more correctly, in getting rid of the ice which encumbered our sleeping bags and gear; this we effected by beat-

ing them well and exposing them to the direct rays of the
sun.   Magnetic and other observations gave me ample employment, the only *immediate* result of which was my being
almost snow-blind for the two following days.

On May 2nd we set off again briskly ; our load being diminished to thirty days' provisions, and the sledge sail set,
we soon reached the land, and travelled along it for Cape
Sabine ; it was very thick weather, and we were unable to
see any distance in consequence of the mist and snow-drift.
The following day was no better, and the shore, which we
dared not leave to cross the bays, was extremely low.

We soon discovered that we had strayed inland ; but,
guided by the wind, continued our course.   Upon May 4th
we descended into Wellington Strait, and the weather being
tolerably clear, crossed over to the south-west extreme of
Matty Island, in the hope of meeting with natives, no traces
of them having been met with since leaving Cape Victoria.
Off this south-west point we found a deserted village of
nearly twenty snow-huts, besides several others, within a
few miles upon either side of it ; in all of them I found
shavings or chips of different kinds of wood from the lost
expedition ; they appeared to have been abandoned only
within a fortnight or three weeks.   Abundance of blubber
was gathered up to increase our stock of fuel, and had we
encamped here, the dogs would have feasted sumptuously
off the scraps and bones of seals strewed about.

The runners (or sides) of some old sledges left here were
very ingeniously formed out of rolls of seal-skin, about $3\frac{1}{2}$
feet long, and flattened so as to be 2 or 3 inches wide and 5
inches high ; the seal-skins appeared to have been well soaked
and then rolled up, flattened into the required form and al-

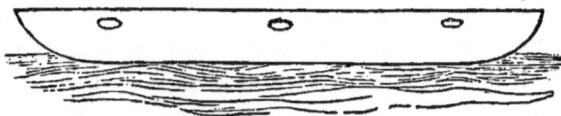

lowed to freeze. The underneath part was coated with a mixture of moss and ice laid smoothly on by hand before being allowed to freeze; the moss, I suppose, answering the purpose of hair in mortar, to make the compound adhere more firmly.

From this spot the shore-line of Matty Island turned sharply to the N. N. E.; there were some considerable islands to the east, but thinking the most southerly of this group, named "Owut-ta" by the Esquimaux, the most likely place to find the natives, I pushed on in that direction until we encamped. Thick fog enveloped us for the next two days; we could not find the island, but found a very small islet near it, off which was another snow-village very recently abandoned, the sledge tracks plainly showing that the inhabitants had gone to the E. N. E., which is straight for Nĕitchillĕe. It was now evident that these places of winter resort were deserted, and that here at least we should not find any natives; I was the more sorry at having missed them, as, from the quantity of wood chips about the huts, they probably had visited the stranded ship alluded to by the last Esquimaux we had met, and the route to which lies up an inlet visible from here, and then overland three or four days' journey to the westward, until the opposite coast of King William's Land is reached.

The largest huts measured 12 feet in diameter, by 6 or 7 feet high; the greater part were constructed in pairs, having a passage 20 or 25 feet long, serving as the common entrance; where the passage divides into two branches, there was a small hut, which served as a sort of ante-chamber for the reception of such articles as were intended to remain frozen.

CHAPTER XIV.

7th May.—To avoid snow-blindness, we commenced night-marching. Crossing over from Matty Island towards the King William Island shore, we continued our march south-ward until midnight, when we had the good fortune to arrive at an inhabited snow-village. We found here ten or twelve huts and thirty or forty natives of King William's Island ; I do not think any of them had ever seen white people alive before, but they evidently knew us to be friends. We halted at a little distance, and pitched our tent, the better to se-cure small articles from being stolen whilst we bartered with them.

I purchased from them six pieces of silver plate, bearing the crests or initials of Franklin, Crozier, Fairholme, and McDonald ; they also sold us bows and arrows of English woods, uniform and other buttons, and offered us a heavy sledge made of two short stout pieces of curved wood, which no mere boat could have furnished them with, but this of course we could not take away ; the silver spoons and forks were readily sold for four needles each.

They were most obliging and peaceably disposed, but could not resist the temptation to steal, and were importu-nate to barter every thing they possessed ; there was not a trace of fear, every countenance was lighted up with joy; even the children were not shy, nor backward either, in crowding about us, and poking in everywhere. One man got hold of our saw, and tried to retain it, holding it behind his back, and presenting his knife in exchange; we might have had some trouble in getting it from him, had not one of my men mistaken his object in presenting the knife towards me, and run out of the tent with a gun in his hand; the saw was instantly returned, and these poor people seemed to think they never could do enough to convince us of their friendliness; they repeatedly tapped me gently on the breast, repeating the words "Kammik toome" (We are friends).

Having obtained all the relics they possessed, I purchased some seal's flesh, blubber, frozen venison, dried and frozen salmon, and sold some of my puppies. They told us it was five days' journey to the wreck,—one day up the inlet still in sight, and four days overland; this would carry them to the western coast of King William's Land; they added that but little now remained of the wreck which was accessible, their countrymen having carried almost every thing away. In answer to an inquiry, they said she was without masts; the question gave rise to some laughter amongst them, and they spoke to each other about *fire*, from which Petersen thought they had burnt the masts through close to the deck in order to get them down.

There had been *many books* they said, but all have long ago been destroyed by the weather; the ship was forced on shore in the fall of the year by the ice. She had not been visited during the past winter, and an old woman and a boy were shown to us who were the last to visit the wreck; they said they had been at it during the winter of 1857–8.

Petersen questioned the woman closely, and she seemed anxious to give all the information in her power. She said many of the white men dropped by the way as they went to the Great River; that some were buried and some were not;

they did not themselves witness this, but discovered their bodies during the winter following.

We could not arrive at any approximation to the numbers of the white men nor of the years elapsed since they were lost.

This was all the information we could obtain, and it was with great difficulty so much could be gleaned, the dialect being strange to Petersen, and the natives far more inclined to ask questions than to answer them. They assured us we should find natives upon the south shore of King William's Island only three days' journey from here, and also at Montreal Island; moreover they said we might find some at the wreck. For these reasons I did not prolong my stay with them beyond a couple of hours. They seemed to have but little intercourse with other communities, not having heard of our visit to the Boothians two months before; one man even asked Petersen if he had seen his brother, who lived in Boothia, not having heard of him since last summer.

It was quite a relief to get away from these good-humored, noisy thieves, and rather difficult too, as some of them accompanied us for miles. They had abundance of food, were well clothed, and are a finer race than those who inhabit North Greenland, or Pond's Inlet: the men had their hair cropped short, with the exception of one long, straggling lock hanging down on each side of the face; like the Boothians, the women had lines tattooed upon their cheeks and chins.

We now proceeded round a bay which I named Latrobe in honor of the late Governor of Victoria, and of his brother, the head of the Moravian Church in London, both esteemed friends of Franklin.

Finding the "Mathison Island" of Rae to be a flat-topped hill, we crossed over low land to the west of it, and upon the morning of the 10th May reached a single snow hut off Point Booth. I was quite astonished at the number

of poles and various articles of wood lying about it, also at
the huge pile of walrus' and reindeer's flesh, seal's blubber,
and skins of various sorts. We had abundance of leisure
to examine these exterior articles before the inmates would
venture out; they were evidently much alarmed by our sudden appearance.

A remarkably fine old dog was tied at the entrance—the
line being made fast within the long passage—and although
he wagged his tail, and received us as old acquaintances, we
did not like to attempt an entrance. At length an old man
and an old woman appeared; they trembled with fear, and
could not, or would not, say any thing except "Kammik
toomee:" we tried every means of allaying their fears, but
their wits seemed paralyzed, and we could get no information. We asked where they got the wood? They purchased it from their countrymen. Did they know the Great
River? Yes, but it was a long way off. Were there natives
there now? Yes. They even denied all knowledge of white
people having died upon their shores. A fine young man
came out of the hut, but we could learn nothing of him;
they said they had nothing to barter, except what we saw,
although we tempted them by displaying our store of knives
and needles.

The wind was strong and fair, and the morning intensely
cold, and as I could not hope to overcome the fears of these
poor people without encamping, and staying perhaps a day
with them, I determined to push on, and presented the old
lady with a needle as a parting gift.

The principal articles which caught my attention here
were eight or ten fir poles, varying in length from 5 to 10
feet, and up to $2\frac{1}{2}$ inches in diameter (these were converted
into spear handles and tent poles), a kayak paddle constructed out of the blade of two ash oars, and two large
snow shovels 4 feet long, made of thin plank, painted white

or pale yellow; these might have been the bottom boards
of a boat. There were many smaller articles of wood.

Half a mile further on we found seven or eight deserted
snow huts. Bad weather had now fairly set in, accompanied
by a most unseasonable degree of cold. On the morning
of the 12th May we crossed Point Ogle, and encamped
upon the ice in the Great Fish River the same evening; the
cold and the darkness of our more southern latitude, having
obliged us to return to day-traveling. All the 13th we
were imprisoned in our tent by a most furious gale, nor was
it until late on the morning of the 14th that we could proceed; that evening we encamped 2 miles from some small
islands which lie off the north end of Montreal Island.

On the morning of the 15th we made only a short march
of 6 miles, as one of the men suffered severely from snow-
blindness, and I was anxious to recommence night-trav-
elling; encamped in a little bay upon the N. E. side of
Montreal Island. The same evening we again set out, although it was blowing very strongly, and "snowing for a
wager," as the men expressed it, but it was only necessary
for us to keep close along the shore of the island: we discovered, however, a narrow and crooked channel which led
us through to the west side of the island, and, one of the
men appearing seriously ill, we encamped about midnight.

Whilst encamped this day, explorations were made about
the N. E. quarter of the island; islets and rocks were seen
to abound in all directions; eventually it proved to be a
separate island upon which we had encamped. The only
traces or relics of Europeans found were the following articles, discovered by Petersen, beside a native mark (one large
stone set upright on the top of another), at the east side of
the Main—or Montreal Island :—A piece of preserved meat
tin, two pieces of iron hoop, some scraps of copper, and an
iron-hoop bolt. These probably are part of the plunder
obtained from the boat, and were left here until a more fa-

vorable opportunity should offer, or perhaps necessity should
compel the depositor to return for them.

All the 16th we were unable to move, not only because
Hampton was ill, but the weather was extremely bad, and
snow thickly falling with temperature at zero; certainly
strange weather for the middle of May! We have not had
a single clear day since the 1st of the month.

On the 17th the weather, though dull, was clear, so Mr.
Petersen, Thompson, and I, set off with the dog-sledge to
complete the examination of Montreal Island, leaving the
other three men with the tent: we hoped also to find natives,
but had not seen any recent traces of them since passing
Point Booth. Petersen drove the dog-sledge close along
shore round the island to the south, and as far up the east
side as to meet our previously explored portion of it, whilst
Thompson and I walked along on the land, the one close
down to the beach, and the other higher up, examining the
more conspicuous parts: in this order we traversed the remaining portion of the island.

Although the snow served to conceal from us any traces
which might exist in hollows or sheltered situations, yet it
rendered all objects intended to serve as marks proportion-
ably conspicuous; and we may remember that it was in its
winter garb that the retreating crews saw Montreal Island,
precisely as we ourselves saw it. The island was almost
covered with native marks, usually of one stone standing
upright upon another, sometimes consisting of three stones,
but very rarely of a greater number.

No trace of a cairn could be found.

In examining, with pickaxe and shovel, a collection of
stones which appeared to be arranged artificially, we found
a quantity of seal's blubber buried beneath; this old Esquimaux cache was near the S. E. point of the island. The
interior of the island and the principal islets adjacent were
also examined without success, nor was there the slightest

14

evidence of natives having been here during the winter : it is not to be wondered at that we returned in the evening to our tent somewhat dispirited. The total absence of natives was a bitter disappointment; circles of stones, indicating the sites of their tenting places in summer, were common enough.

Montreal Island is of primary rock, chiefly grey gneiss, traversed with whitish vertical bands in a N. and S. direction (by them I often directed my route when crossing the island). It is of considerable elevation, and extremely rugged. The low beaches and grassy hollows were covered with a foot or two of hard snow, whilst all the level, the elevated, or exposed parts were swept perfectly bare; had a cairn, or even a grave existed (raised as it must be, the earth being frozen hard as rock), we must at once have seen it. If any were constructed they must have been levelled by the natives; every doubtful appearance was examined with the pickaxe.

A remark made by my men struck me as being shrewd; they judged from the washed appearance of the rock upon the east side of Montreal Island that it must be often exposed to a considerable sea, such as would effectually remove everything not placed far above its reach; when looking over the smooth and frozen expanse one is apt to forget this.

Since our first landing upon King William's Island we have not met with any heavy ice; all along its eastern and southern shore, together with the estuary of this great river, is one vast unbroken sheet formed in the early part of last winter where *no ice previously existed;* this I fancy (from the accounts of Back and Anderson) is unusual, and may have caused the Esquimaux to vary their seal-hunting localities. Mr. Petersen suggested that they might have retired into the various inlets after the seals; and therefore I determined to cross over into Barrow's Inlet as soon as we had examined the Point Ogle Peninsula.

Upon Montreal Island I shot a hare and a brace of willow-grouse. Up to this date we had shot during our journey only one bear and a couple of ptarmigan. The first recent traces of reindeer were met with here.

On the 18th May we crossed over to the mainland near Point Duncan, but Hampton again complaining, I was obliged to encamp. When away from my party, and exploring along the shore towards Elliot Bay, I saw a herd of eight reindeer and succeeded in shooting one of them. In the evening Petersen saw another. Some willow-grouse also were seen. Here we found much more vegetation than upon King William's Island, or any other Arctic land I have yet seen.

On the evening of the 19th we commenced our return journey, but for the three following weeks our route led us over new ground. Hampton being unable to drag, I made over my puppy-team to him, and was thus left free to explore and fully examine every doubtful object along our route. I shall not easily forget the trial my patience underwent during the six weeks that I drove that dog-sledge. The leader of my team, named "Omar Pascha," was very willing, but very lame; little "Rose" was coquettish, and fonder of being caressed than whipped; from some cause or other she ceased growing when only a few months old; she was therefore far too small for heavy work; "Darky" and "Missy" were mere pùps; and last of all came the two wretched starvelings, reared in the winter, "Foxey" and "Dolly." Each dog had its own harness, formed of strips of canvas, and was attached to the sledge by a single trace 12 feet long. None of them had ever been yoked before, and the amount of cunning and perversity they displayed to avoid both the whip and the work, was quite astonishing. They bit through their traces, and hid away under the sledge, or leaped over one another's backs, so as to get into the middle of the team out of the way of my whip, until the traces became plaited up, and the dogs were almost knotted together; the consequence was I had to halt every few minutes, pull off my mits, and, at the risk of frozen fingers, disentangle the lines. I persevered, however, and, without breaking any of their bones, succeeded in getting a surprising amount of work out of them. Hobson drove his own dog-sledge likewise, and as long as we were together we helped each other out of difficulties, and they were frequently occurring, for, apart from those I have above mentioned, directly a dog-sledge is stopped by hummocks, or sticks fast in deep snow, the dogs, instead of exerting themselves, lie down, looking perfectly delighted at the circumstance, and the driver has to extricate the sledge with a hearty one, two, three haul! and apply a little gentle persuasion to set his canine team in motion again.

Having searched the east shore of this land for 7 or 8 miles further north, we crossed over into Barrow's Inlet, and spent a day in its examination, but not a trace of natives were met with

Regaining the shore of Dease and Simpson's Strait, some miles to the west of Point Richardson, we crossed over to King William's Island upon the morning of the 24th, striking in upon it a short distance west of the Peffer River. The south coast was closely examined as we marched along towards Cape Herschel. Upon a conspicuous point, to the westward of Point Gladman, a cairn nearly five feet high was seen, which, although it did not appear to be a recent construction, was taken down, stone by stone, and carefully examined, the ground beneath being broken up with the pickaxe, but nothing was covered.

The ground about it was much exposed to the winds, and consequently devoid of snow, so that no trace could have escaped us. Simpson does not mention having landed here, or anywhere upon the island except at Cape Herschel, yet it seemed to me strange that natives should construct such a mark here, since a huge boulder, which would equally serve their purpose, stood upon the same elevation, and within a couple of hundred yards. We had previously examined a similar but smaller cairn, a few miles to the eastward.

We were now upon the shore along which the retreating crews must have marched. My sledges of course travelled upon the sea-ice close along the shore; and, although the depth of snow which covered the beach deprived us of almost every hope, yet we kept a very sharp look-out for traces, nor were we unsuccessful. Shortly after midnight of the 24th May, when slowly walking along a gravel ridge near the beach, which the winds kept partially bare of snow, I came upon a human skeleton, partly exposed, with here and there a few fragments of clothing appearing through the snow. The skeleton—now perfectly bleached —was lying upon its face, the limbs and smaller bones either dissevered or gnawed away by small animals.

A most careful examination of the spot was of course made, the snow removed, and every scrap of clothing gathered up. A pocket-book afforded strong grounds of hope that some information might be subsequently obtained respecting the unfortunate owner and the calamitous march of the lost crews, but at the time it was frozen hard. The substance of that which we gleaned upon the spot may thus be summed up :

This victim was a young man, slightly built, and perhaps above the common height; the dress appeared to be that of a steward or officer's servant, the loose bow-knot in which his neck-handkerchief was tied not being used by seamen or officers. In every particular the dress confirmed our conjectures as to his rank or office in the late expedition,—the blue jacket with slashed sleeves and braided edging, and the pilot-cloth great-coat with plain covered buttons. We found, also, a clothes-brush near, and a horn pocket-comb. This poor man seems to have selected the bare ridge top, as affording the least tiresome walking, and to have fallen upon his face in the position in which we found him.

It was a melancholy truth that the old woman spoke when she said, "they fell down and died as they walked along."

I do not think the Esquimaux had discovered this skeleton, or they would have carried off the brush and comb ; superstition prevents them from disturbing their own dead, but would not keep them from appropriating the property of the white man, if in any way useful to them. Dr. Rae obtained a piece of flannel, marked " F. D. V., 1845," from the Esquimaux of Boothia or Repulse Bay : it had doubtless been a part of poor Des Vœux's garments.

At the time of our interview with the natives of King William's Island, Petersen was inclined to think that the retreat of the crews took place in the fall of the year, some of the men in boats, and others walking along the shore ; and as only five bodies are said to have been found upon Montreal Island with the boat, this fact favored his opinion, because so small a number could not have dragged her there over the ice, although they could very easily have taken her there by water. Subsequently this opinion proved erroneous. I mention it because it shows how vague our information was—indeed all Esquimaux accounts are naturally so—and how entirely we were dependent upon our own exertions for bringing to light the mystery of their fate.

The information obtained by Dr. Rae was mainly derived second-hand from the Fish River Esquimaux, and should not be confounded with that received by us from the King William's Island Esquimaux. These people told us they did not find the bodies of the white men (that is, they did not know any had died upon the march) until the following

M'CLINTOCK'S TRAVELLING PARTY DISCOVERING THE REMAINS OF CAIRN AT CAPE HERSCHEL.

winter. This is probably true, as it is only in winter and early spring they can travel overland to the west shore, or that they make a practice of wandering along the shore in search of seals and bears.

The remains of those who died in the Fish River may very probably have been discovered in the summer shortly after their decease.

Along the south coast of King William's Land, as upon the mainland, I was sadly disappointed in my expectation of meeting natives. We found only six or eight deserted snow huts, showing that they had recently been here, and consequently there was less chance of meeting with them on our further progress, as the season had now arrived when they seek the rivers and the favorite haunts and passes of the reindeer in their northern migration.

Hobson was, however, upon the western coast, and I hoped to find a note left for me at Cape Herschel, containing some piece of good news. After minutely examining the intervening coast-line, it was with strong and reasonable hope I ascended the slope which is crowned by Simpson's conspicuous cairn. This summit of Cape Herschel is perhaps 150 feet high, and about a quarter of a mile within the low stony point which projects from it, and on which there was considerable ice pressure and a few hummocks heaped up, the first we had seen for three weeks. Close round this point, or by cutting across it as we did, the retreating party *must* have passed ; and the opportunity afforded by the cairn of depositing in a known position—and that, too, where their own discoveries terminated—some record of their own proceedings, or, it might be, a portion of their scientific journals, would scarcely have been disregarded.

Simpson makes no mention of having left a record in this cairn, nor would Franklin's people have taken any trouble to find it if he had left one ; but what now remained of this once " ponderous cairn" was only four feet high ; the south

side had been pulled down and the central stones removed,
as if by persons seeking for something deposited beneath.
After removing the snow with which it was filled, and a few
loose stones, the men laid bare a large slab of limestone;
with difficulty this was removed, then a second, and also a
third slab, when they came to the ground.   For some time
we persevered with a pickaxe, in breaking up the frozen
earth, but nothing whatever was found, nor any trace of
European visitors in its vicinity.   There were many old
caches and low stone walls, such as natives would use to
lurk behind for the purpose of shooting reindeer; and we
noticed some recent tracks of those animals which had
crossed direct hither from the mainland.

CHAPTER XV.

The cairn found empty—Discover Hobson's letter—Discovery of Crozier's record—The deserted boat—Articles discovered about the boat—
The skeleton and relics—The boat belonged to the 'Erebus'—Conjectures.

As the Esquimaux of this land, as well as those of
Boothia and Pond's Inlet, have long since given up the
practice of building stone dwellings—passing their winters
in snow huts, and summers in tents—no other traces of them
than those described remain ; so that when or in what numbers they may have been here one cannot form any opinion,
the same caches and hiding-places serving for generations.

I cannot divest myself of the belief that *some record was
left here* by the retreating crews, and perhaps some most
valuable documents which their slow progress and fast
failing strength would have assured them could not be carried much further.   If any such were left they have been
discovered by the natives, and carried off, or thrown away
as worthless.   Doubtless the natives, when they ascertained
that famine and fatigue had caused many of the white men
"to fall down and die" upon their fearful march, and heard,
as they might have done, of its fatal termination upon the
mainland, lost no time in following up their traces, examining every spot where they halted, every mark they put up,
or stone displaced.

It is easy to tell whether a cairn has been put up or
touched within a moderate period of years ; if very old,
the outer stones have a weathered appearance, lichens will
have grown upon the sheltered portions and moss in the

crevices ; but if recently disturbed, even if a single stone is
turned upside down, these appearances are altered.   If a
cairn has been recently built it will be evident, because the
stones picked up from the neighborhood would be bleached
on top by the exposure of centuries, whilst underneath they
would be colored by the soil in which they were imbedded.

To the eye of the native hunter these marks of a recent
cairn are at once apparent : and unless Simpson's cairn
(built in 1839) had been disturbed by Crozier, I do not
think the Esquimaux would have been at the trouble of
pulling it down to plunder the cache ; but having commenced to do so, would not have left any of it standing,
unless they found what they sought.

I noticed with great care the appearance of the stones,
and came to the conclusion that the cairn itself was of old
date, and had been erected many years ago, and that it was
reduced to the state in which we found it by people having
broken down one side of it ; the displaced stones, from
being turned over, looking far more fresh than those in that
portion of the cairn which had been left standing.   It was
with a feeling of deep regret and much disappointment that
I left this spot without finding some certain record of those
martyrs to their country's fame.   Perhaps in all the wide
world there will be few spots more hallowed in the recollection of English seamen than this cairn on Cape Herschel.

A few miles beyond Cape Herschel the land becomes
very low ; many islets and shingle-ridges lie far off the
coast ; and as we advanced we met with hummocks of unusually heavy ice, showing plainly that we were now travelling upon a far more exposed part of the coast-line.   We
were approaching a spot where a revelation of intense interest was awaiting me.

About 12 miles from Cape Herschel I found a small
cairn built by Hobson's party, and containing a note for
me.   He had reached this his extreme point, six days pre-

viously, without having seen anything of the wreck, or of natives, but he had found a record—the record so ardently sought for, of the Franklin Expedition—at Point Victory, on the N. W. coast of King William's Land

That record is indeed a sad and touching relic of our lost friends, and, to simplify its contents, I will point out separately the double story it so briefly tells. In the first place, the record paper was one of the printed forms usually supplied to discovery ships for the purpose of being enclosed in bottles and thrown overboard at sea, in order to ascertain the set of the currents, blanks being left for the date and position ; any person finding one of these records is requested to forward it to the Secretary of the Admiralty, with a note of time and place ; and this request is printed upon it in six different languages.   Upon it was written apparently by Lieutenant Gore, as follows :

"28 of May,   { H. M. ships 'Erebus' and 'Terror' wintered in the ice in
    1847.   {   lat. 70° 05' N.; long. 98° 23' W.

Having wintered in 1846–7 at Beechey Island, in lat. 74° 43' 28" N.; long. 91° 39' 15" W., after having ascended Wellington Channel to lat. 77°, and returned by the west side of Cornwallis Island.
 "Sir John Franklin commanding the expedition.
 "All well.
 "Party consisting of 2 officers and 6 men left the ships on Monday, 24th May, 1847.
                        "GM. GORE, Lieut.
                        "CHAS. F. DES VŒUS, Mate."

There is an error in the above document, namely, that the 'Erebus' and 'Terror' wintered at Beechey Island in 1846–7,—the correct dates should have been 1845–6 ; a glance at the date at the top and bottom of the record proves this, but in all other respects the tale is told in as few words as possible of their wonderful success up to that date, May, 1847.

We find that, after the last intelligence of Sir John

Franklin was received by us (bearing date of July, 1845), from the whalers in Melville Bay, that his Expedition passed on to Lancaster Sound, and entered Wellington Channel, of which the southern entrance had been discovered by Sir Edward Parry in 1819. The 'Erebus' and 'Terror' sailed up that strait for one hundred and fifty miles, and reached in the autumn of 1845 the same latitude as was attained eight years subsequently by H. M. S. 'Assistance' and 'Pioneer.' Whether Franklin intended to pursue this northern course, and was only stopped by ice in that latitude of 77° north, or purposely relinquished a route which seemed to lead away from the known seas off the coast of America, must be a matter of opinion ; but this the document assures of, that Sir John Franklin's Expedition, having accomplished this examination, returned southward from latitude 77° north, which is at the head of Wellington Channel, and re-entered Barrow's Strait by a new channel between Bathurst and Cornwallis Islands.

Seldom has such an amount of success been accorded to an Arctic navigator in a single season, and when the 'Erebus' and 'Terror' were secured at Beechey Island for the coming winter of 1845–6, the results of their first year's labor must have been most cheering. These results were the exploration of Wellington and Queen's Channel, and the addition to our charts of the extensive lands on either hand. In 1846 they proceeded to the southwest, and eventually reached within twelve miles of the north extreme of King William's Land, when their progress was arrested by the approaching winter of 1846–7. That winter appears to have passed without any serious loss of life ; and when in the spring Lieutenant Gore leaves with a party for some especial purpose, and very probably to connect the unknown coast-line of King William's Land between Point Victory and Cape Herschel, those on board the 'Erebus' and

'Terror' were "all well," and the gallant Franklin still commanded.

But, alas! round the margin of the paper upon which Lieutenant Gore in 1847 wrote those words of hope and promise, another hand had subsequently written the following words :—

"April 25, 1848.—H. M. ships 'Terror' and 'Erebus' were deserted on the 22d April, 5 leagues N. N. W. of this, having been beset since 12th September, 1846. The officers and crews, consisting of 105 souls, under the command of Captain F. R. M. Crozier, landed here in lat. 69° 37' 42" N., long. 98° 41' W. Sir John Franklin died on the 11th June, 1847 ; and the total loss by deaths in the expedition has been to this date 9 officers and 15 men.
(Signed)   (Signed)
  " F. R. M. CROZIER,   " JAMES FITZJAMES,
" Captain and Senior Officer.   " Captain H. M. S. Erebus.
  "and start (on) to-morrow, 26th, for
              Back's Fish River."

The marginal information was evidently written by Captain Fitzjames, excepting only the note stating when and where they were going, which was added by Captain Crozier.

There is some additional marginal information relative to the transfer of the document to its present position (viz., the site of Sir James Ross's pillar) from a spot four miles to the northward, near Point Victory, where it had been originally deposited by the *late* Commander Gore. This little word *late* shows us that he too, within the twelvemonth, had passed away.

In the short space of twelve months how mournful had become the history of Franklin's expedition ; how changed from the cheerful "All well" of Graham Gore ! The spring

of 1847 found them within 90 miles of the known sea off
the coast of America; and to men who had already in two
seasons sailed over 500 miles of previously unexplored waters, how confident must they have felt that that forthcoming
navigable season of 1847 would see their ships pass over
so short an intervening space! It was ruled otherwise.
Within a month after Lieutenant Gore placed the record on
Point Victory, the much-loved leader of the expedition, Sir
John Franklin, was dead; and the following spring found
Captain Crozier, upon whom the command had devolved at
King William's Land, endeavoring to save his starving men,
105 souls in all, from a terrible death, by retreating to the
Hudson Bay territories up the Back or Great Fish River.

A sad tale was never told in fewer words. There is something deeply touching in their extreme simplicity, and they
show in the strongest manner that both the leaders of this
retreating party were actuated by the loftiest sense of duty,
and met with calmness and decision the fearful alternative
of a last bold struggle for life, rather than perish without
effort on board their ships; for we well know that the 'Erebus' and 'Terror' were only provisioned up to July, 1848.

Another discrepancy exists in the second part of the record written by Fitzjames. The original number composing
the expedition was 138 souls,* and the record states the
total loss by deaths to have been 9 officers and 15 men,
consequently that 114 officers and men remained; but it
also states that 105 only landed under Captain Crozier's
command, so that 9 individuals are unaccounted for.

Lieutenant Hobson's note told me that he found quantities of clothing and articles of all kinds lying about the
cairn, as if these men, aware that they were retreating for
their lives, had there abandoned every thing which they considered superfluous.

---

* See Conclusion, p.

Hobson had experienced extremely bad weather—constant gales and fogs—and thought he might have passed the wreck without seeing her; he hoped to be more successful upon his return journey.

Encouraged by this important news, we exerted our ut most vigilance in order that no trace should escape us.

Our provisions were running very short, therefore the three remaining puppies were of necessity shot, and their sledges used for fuel. We were also enabled to lengthen our journeys, as we had very smooth ice to travel over, the off-lying islets keeping the rough pack from pressing in upon the shore.

Upon the 29th of May we reached the western extreme of King William's Island, in lat. 69° 08' N., and long. 100° 08' W. I named it after Captain Crozier of the 'Terror,' the gallant leader of that "Forlorn Hope" of which we now just obtained tidings. The coast we marched along was extremely low—a mere series of ridges of lime-stone shingle, almost destitute of fossils. The only tracks of amimals seen were those of a bear and a few foxes—the only living creatures a few willow grouse. Traces even of the wandering Esquimaux became much less frequent after leaving Cape Herschel. Here were found only a few circles of stones, the sites of tenting-places, but so moss-grown as to be of great age. The prospect to seaward was not less forbidding—a rugged surface of crushed-up pack, including much heavy ice. In these shallow ice-covered seas, seals are but seldom found: and it is highly probable that all animal life in them is as scarce as upon the land.

From Cape Crozier the coast-line was found to turn sharply away to the eastward; and early in the morning of the 30th May we encamped alongside a large boat—another melancholy relic which Hobson had found and examined a few days before, as his note left here informed me: but he

had failed to discover record, journal, pocket-book, or mem-
orandum of any description.

A vast quantity of tattered clothing was lying in her, and
this we first examined. Not a single article bore the name
of its former owner. The boat was cleared out and carefully swept that nothing might escape us. The snow was
then removed from about her, but nothing whatever was
found.

This boat measured 28 feet long, and 7 feet 3 inches wide;
she was built with a view to lightness and light draught of
water, and evidently equipped with the utmost care for the
ascent of the Great Fish River; she had neither oars nor
rudder, paddles supplying their place, and as a large remnant of light canvas, commonly known as No. 8, was found,
and also a small block for reeving a sheet through, I suppose she had been provided with a sail. A sloping canvas
roof or rain-awning had also formed part of her equipment.
She was fitted with a weather-cloth 9 inches high, battened
down all round the gunwale, and supported by 24 iron
stanchions, so placed as to serve likewise for rowing
thowells. There were 50 fathoms of deep-sea sounding-line
near her, as well as an ice grapnel. She appeared to have
been originally "carvel" built; but for the purpose of re-
ducing weight, very thin fir planks had been substituted for
her seven upper strakes, and put on "clincher" fashion.

The weight of the boat alone was about 700 or 800 lbs.
only, but she was mounted upon a sledge of unusual weight
and strength. It was constructed of two oak planks 23
feet 4 inches in length, 8 inches in width, and with an average thickness of 2½ inches. These planks formed the sides
or runners of the sledge; they were connected by five cross-
bars of oak, each 5 feet long, and 4 inches by 3½ inches
thick, and bolted down to the runners; the underneath
parts of the latter were shod with iron. Upon the cross-
bars five saddles or supporting chocks for the boat were

lashed, and the drag-ropes by which the crew moved this massive sledge, and the weights upon it, consisted of $2\frac{3}{4}$ inch whale line.

I have calculated the weight of this sledge to be 650 lbs. ; it could not have been less, and may have been considerably more.   The total weight of boat and sledge may be taken at 1400 lbs., which amounts to a heavy load for seven strong healthy men.

The only markings about the boat were those upon her stem, by which we learned that she was built by contract,

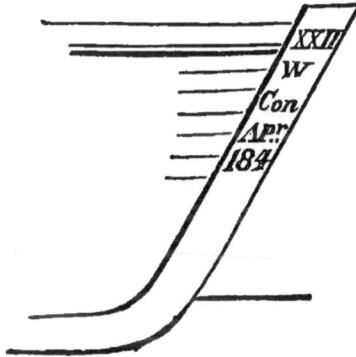

was received into Woolwich Dockyard in April, 184 ,* and was numbered 61.   There may have been a fourth figure to the right hand, as the stem had been reduced in order to lighten the boat.   The ground the sledge rested upon was the usual limestone shingle, perfectly flat, and probably overflowed at times every summer, as the stones were im-bedded in ice.

The boat was partially out of her cradle upon the sledge, and lying in such a position as to lead me to suppose it the

---

* Only the first three figures of the date upon her stem remained, thus ·—184 .

15

effect of a violent northwest gale. She was barely, if at all, above the reach of occasional tides.

One hundred yards from her, upon the land side, lay the stump of a fir-tree 12 feet long, and 16 inches in diameter at 3 feet above the roots. Although the ice had used it roughly during its drift to this shore, and rubbed off every vestige of bark, yet the wood was perfectly sound. It may have been and probably has been lying there for twenty or thirty years, and during such a period would suffer less decay in this region of frost than in one-sixth of the time at home. Within two yards of it I noticed a few scanty tufts of grass.

But all these were after observations; there was that in the boat which transfixed us with awe. It was portions of two human skeletons. One was that of a slight young person; the other of a large, strongly-made, middle-aged man. The former was found in the bow of the boat, but in too much disturbed a state to enable Hobson to judge whether the sufferer had died there; large and powerful animals, probably wolves, had destroyed much of this skeleton, which may have been that of an officer. Near it we found the fragment of a pair of worked slippers, of which I give the pattern, as they may possibly be identified. The lines were white, with a black margin; the spaces white, red, and yellow. They had originally been 11 inches long, lined with calf-skin with the hair left on, and the edges bound with red silk ribbon. Besides these slippers there were a pair of small strong shooting half-boots. The other skeleton was in a somewhat more perfect state,* and was enveloped with clothes and furs; it lay across the boat, under the after-thwart. Close beside it were found five watches; and there were two double-barrelled guns —

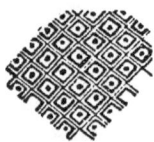

---

* No part of the skull of either skeleton was found, with the exception only of the lower jaw of each.

one barrel in each loaded and cocked — standing muzzle upward against the boat's side.   It may be imagined with what deep interest these sad relics were scrutinised, and how anxiously every fragment of clothing was turned over in search of pockets and pocket-books, journals, or even names. Five or six small books were found, all of them scriptural or devotional works, except the ' Vicar of Wakefield.'   One little book, ' Christian Melodies,' bore an inscription upon the titlepage from the donor to G. G. (Graham Gore ?) A small Bible contained numerous marginal notes, and whole passages underlined.   Besides these books, the covers of a New Testament and Prayerbook were found.

Amongst an amazing quantity of clothing there were seven or eight pairs of boots of various kinds — cloth winter boots, sea boots, heavy ankle boots, and strong shoes.   I noted that there were silk handkerchiefs — black, white, and figured — towels, soap, sponge, tooth-brush, and hair-combs ; mackintosh gun-cover, marked outside with paint A 12, and lined with black cloth.   Besides these articles we found twine, nails, saws, files, bristles, wax-ends, sailmakers' palms, powder, bullets, shot, cartridges, wads, leather cartridge-case, knives — clasp and dinner ones — needle and thread cases, slow-match, several bayonet-scabbards cut down into knife-sheaths, two rolls of sheet-lead, and, in short, a quantity of articles of one description and another truly astonishing in variety, and such as, for the most part, modern sledge-travelers in these regions would consider a mere accumulation of dead weight, but slightly useful, and very likely to break down the strength of the sledge-crews.

The only provisions we could find were tea and chocolate ; of the former very little remained, but there were nearly 40 pounds of the latter.   These articles alone could never support life in such a climate, and we found neither biscuit nor meat of any kind.   A portion of tobacco and an empty

pemmican-tin, capable of containing 22 pounds weight,
were discovered. The tin was marked with an E; it had
probably belonged to the 'Erebus.' None of the fuel originally brought from the ships remained in or about the boat,
but there was no lack of it, for a drift-tree was lying on the
beach close at hand, and had the party been in need of fuel
they would have used the paddles and bottom-boards of the
boat.

In the after part of the boat we discovered eleven large
spoons, eleven forks, and four teaspoons, all of silver; of
these twenty-six pieces of plate, eight bore Sir John Franklin's crest, the remainder had the crests or initials of nine
different officers, with the exception of a single fork which
was not marked ; of these nine officers, five belonged to the
'Erebus,'— Gore, Le Vesconte, Fairholme, Couch, and
Goodsir. Three others belonged to the 'Terror,'— Crozier,
(a teaspoon only,) Hornby, and Thomas. I do not know
to whom the three articles with an owl engraved on them
belonged, nor who was the owner of the unmarked fork,
but of the owners of those we can identify, the majority
belonged to the 'Erebus.' One of the watches bore the
crest of Mr. Couch, of the 'Erebus,' and as the pemmican
tin also came from that ship, I am inclined to think the boat
did also ; the authorities at Woolwich could tell (by her
number) to which ship she was supplied ; and as one of the
pocket chronometers found in the boat was marked, "Park-
inson and Frodsham 980," and the other "Arnold 2020,"
it could also be ascertained to which ship they had been
issued.*

Sir John Franklin's plate perhaps was issued to the men
for their use, as the only means of saving it; and it seems
probable that the officers generally did the same, as not a

---

* These chronometers, according to the receipts in office, were supplied
one to each ship in 1845 ; but it is impossible to tell to which ship the
boat belonged, as the number is imperfect.

single iron spoon, such as sailors always use, has been found. Of the many men, probably twenty or thirty, who were attached to this boat, it seemed most strange that the remains of only two individuals were found, nor were there any graves upon the neighboring flat land ; indeed, bearing in mind the season at which these poor fellows left their ships, it should be remembered that the soil was then frozen hard, and the labor of *cutting* a grave very great indeed.

I was astonished to find that the sledge was directed to the N. E., exactly for the next point of land for which we ourselves were travelling !

The position of this abandoned boat is about 50 miles— as a sledge would travel—from Point Victory, and therefore 65 miles from the position of the ships ; also it is 70 miles from the skeleton of the steward, and 150 miles from Montreal Island ; it is moreover in the depth of a wide bay, where, by crossing over 10 or 12 miles of very low land, a great saving of distance would be effected, the route by the coast-line being about 40 miles.

A little reflection led me to satisfy my own mind at least, that the boat was returning to the ships : and in no other way can I account for two men having been left in her, than by supposing the party were unable to drag the boat further, and that these two men, not being able to keep pace with their shipmates, were therefore left by them supplied with such provisions as could be spared, to last until the return of the others from the ship with a fresh stock.

Whether it was the intention of the retroceding party to await the result of another season in the ships, or to follow the track of the main body to the Great Fish River, is now a matter of conjecture. It seems highly probable that they had purposed revisiting the boat, not only on account of the two men left in charge of it, but also to obtain the chocolate, the five watches, and many other articles which would otherwise scarcely have been left in her.

The same reasons which may be assigned for the return
of this detachment from the main body, will also serve to
account for their not having come back to their boat. In
both instances they appear to have greatly overrated their
strength, and the distance they could travel in a given
time.

Taking this view of the case, we can understand why
their provisions would not last them for anything like the
distance they required to travel; and why they would be
obliged to send back to the ships for more, first taking from
the detached party all provisions they could possibly spare.
Whether all or any of the remainder of this detached party
ever reached their ships is uncertain; all we know is, that
they did not revisit the boat, and which accounts for the
absence of more skeletons in its neighborhood, and the
Esquimaux report that there was no one alive in the ship
when she drifted on shore, and that but one human body
was found by them on board of her.

After leaving the boat we followed an irregular coast-
line to the N. and N. W., up to a very prominent cape,
which is probably the extreme of land seen from Point Victory by Sir James Ross, and named by him Point Franklin, which name, as a cape, it still retains.

I need hardly say that throughout the whole of my journey along the shores of King William's Land I caused a
most vigilant look-out to be kept to seaward for any appearance of the stranded ship spoken of by the natives: our
search was however fruitless in that respect.

CHAPTER XVI.

Errors in Franklin's records—Relics found at the cairn—Reflections on the retreat—Returning homeward—Geological remarks—Difficulties of summer sledging—Arrive on board the 'Fox'—Navigable N. W. Passage—Death from scurvy—Anxiety for Captain Young—Young returns safely.

ON the morning of 2nd June we reached Point Victory. Here Hobson's note left for me in the cairn informed me that be had not found the slightest trace either of a wreck anywhere upon the coast, or of natives to the north of Cape Crozier.

Although somewhat short of provisions, I determined to remain a day here in order to examine an opening at the Bottom of Back Bay, called so after Sir George Back, by his friend Sir James Ross, and which had not been explored. This proved to be an inlet nearly 13 miles deep, with an average width of $1\frac{1}{2}$ or 2 miles; I drove round it upon the dog sledge, but found no trace of human beings; it was filled with heavy old ice, and was therefore unfavorable for the resort of seals, and consequently of natives also.

The direction of the inlet is to the E. S. E.; we found the land on either side rose as we advanced up it, and attained a considerable elevation, except immediately across its head, where alone it was very low; I have conferred upon it the name of Collinson, after one who will ever be distinguished in connection with the Franklin search, and who kindly relieved Lady Franklin of much trouble by taking upon himself the financial business of this expedition.

An extensive bay, westward of Cape Herschel, I have named after Captain Washington, the hydrographer, a steadfast supporter of this final seerch.

All the intermediate coast-line, along which the retreating crews performed their fearful march, is sacred to their names alone.

Hobson's note informed me of his having found a second record, deposited also by Lieutenant Gore in May, 1847, upon the south side of Back Bay, but it afforded no additional information.

It is strange that both these papers state the ships to have wintered in 1846–7 at Beechey Island! So obvious a mistake would hardly have been made had any importance been attached to these documents. They were soldered up in thin tin cylinders, having been filled up on board prior to the departure of the travellers; consequently the day upon which they were *deposited* was not filled in; but already the papers were much damaged by rust,—a very few more years would have rendered them wholly illegible. When the record left at Point Victory was opened to add thereto the supplemental information which gives it its chief value, Captain Fitzjames, as may be concluded by the color of the ink, filled in the date—28th—in May, when the record was originally deposited. The cylinder containing the record had not been soldered up again; I suppose they had not the means of doing so; it was found on the ground amongst a few loose stones which had evidently fallen along with it from the top of the cairn. Hobson removed every stone of this cairn down to the ground and rebuilt it.

Brief as these records are, we must needs be contented with them; they are perfect models of official brevity. No log-book could be more provokingly laconic. Yet, that *any record at all* should be deposited after the abandonment of the ships, does not seem to have been intended; and we should feel the more thankful to Captains Crozier and Fitzjames, to whom we are indebted for the invaluable supplement; and our gratitude ought to be all the greater when we remember that the ink had to be thawed, and that writing in a tent during an April day in the Arctic regions is by no means an easy task.

Besides placing a copy of the record taken away by Hobson from the cairn, we both put records of our own in it; and I also buried one under a large stone ten feet true north from it, stating the explorations and discoveries we had made.

A great quantity and variety of things lay strewed about the cairn, such as even in their three days' march from the ships the retreating crews found it impossible to carry further.   Amongst these were four heavy sets of boat's cooking stoves, pickaxes, shovels, iron-hoops, old canvas, a large single block, about four feet of a copper lightning conductor, long pieces of hollow brass curtain rods, a small case of selected medicines containing about twenty-four phials, the contents in a wonderful state of preservation ; a dip circle. by Robinson, with two needles, bar magnets, and light horizontal needle all complete, the whole weighing only nine pounds ; and even a small sextant engraved with the name of " Frederick Hornby" lying beside the cairn without its case.   The colored eye-shades of the sextant had been taken out, otherwise it was perfect ; the movable screws and such parts as come in contact with the observer's hand were neatly covered with thin leather to prevent frostbite in severe weather.

The clothing left by the retreating crews of the 'Erebus' and 'Terror' formed a huge heap four feet high ; every article was searched, but the pockets were empty, and not one of all these articles were marked,—indeed sailors' warm clothing seldom is.   Two canteens, the property of marines, were found, one marked " 88 C°. Wm. Hedges," and the other " 89 C°. Wm. Hether."   A small panniken made out of a two-pound preserved-meat tin had scratched on it "W. Mark."

When continuing my homeward march, and, as nearly as I could judge, 2½ or 2¾ miles to the north of Point Victory, I saw a few stones placed in line, as if across the head of a tenting place to afford some shelter; here it was I think that Lieutenant Gore deposited the record in May, 1847, which was found in 1848 by Lieutenant Irving, and finally deposited at Point Victory. Some scraps of tin vessels were lying about, but whether they had been left by Sir James Ross' party in May, 1830, or by the Franklin Expedition in 1847 or 1848, is uncertain."*

Here ended my own search for traces of the lost ones. Hobson found two other cairns, and many relics, between this position and Cape Felix. From each place where any trace was discovered the most interesting of the relics were taken away, so that the collection we have made is very considerable.

Of these northern cairns I will write a description when I have received Hobson's account of his journey; but here it is as well to state his opinion, as well as my own, that no part of the coast between Cape Felix and Cape Crozier has been visited by Esquimaux since the fatal march of the lost crews in April, 1848; none of the cairns or numerous articles strewed about—which would be invaluable to the natives—or even the drift-wood we noticed, had been touched by them. From this very significant fact it seems quite certain that they had not been discovered by the Esquimaux, whose knowledge of the "white men falling down and dying as they walked along" must be limited to the shore-line southward and eastward of Cape Crozier, and where,

---

* It is a remarkable circumstance that when, in 1830, Sir James Ross discovered Point Victory, he named two points of land, then in sight, Cape Franklin and Cape Jane Franklin respectively. Eighteen years afterwards Franklin's ships perished within sight of those headlands.

of course, no traces were permitted to remain for us to find. It is not probable that such fearful mortality would have overtaken them so early in their march as within 80 miles by sledge-route from the abandoned ships—such being their distance from Cape Crozier; nor is it probable that we could have passed the wreck had she existed there, as there are no off-lying islands to prevent a ship drifting in upon the beach; whilst to the southward they are very numerous; so much so that a drifting ship could hardly run the gauntlet between them so as to reach the shore.

The coast from Point Victory northward is considerably higher than that upon which we have been so many days; the sea also is not so shallow, and the ice comes close in; to seaward all was heavy close pack, consisting of all descriptions of ice, but for the most part old and heavy.

From Walls' Bay I crossed overland to the eastern shore, and reached my depot near the entrance of Port Parry on the 5th June, after an absence of thirty-four days. Hence I purposed travelling alongshore to Cape Sabine, in order to avoid the rough ice which we encountered when crossing direct from Cape Victoria in April, and also hoping to obtain a few more observations for the magnetic inclination.

The weather became foggy as we approached Prince George's Bay, therefore we were obliged to go well into it before attempting to cross. We gained the land—upon the opposite side, as I supposed—and which would lead us direct to Cape Sabine; but when the weather cleared up we saw a long low island to seaward of us, which puzzled me much. Eventually I found we had discovered a strait leading from Prince George's Bay into Wellington Strait, about 8 miles south of Cape Sabine.

This discovery cost us a day's delay, and was therefore unwelcome, as we were then in daily expectation and dread of the thaw, which renders all travelling so very difficult; and we were still 230 long miles from our ship. In this strait

we found a deserted snow village of seventeen huts; one of
tnem was unusually large, its internal diameter being 14
feet.   The men soon scraped together enough blubber to
supply us with fuel for our homeward march.   Strewed
about on the ice or in every snow hut were shavings and
chips of fresh wood; in one of them I found a child's toy
—a miniature sledge—made of wood.   No traces of natives
were found upon either shore of this place, nor had I met
with any since leaving the western coast of the island to the
southward of Cape Crozier.

Having passed through nearly to the eastern end of the
strait, we cut off some distance by crossing overland, so as to
reach the sea-coast 3 or 4 miles southward of Cape Sabine.
A few willow grouse, two foxes, and a young reindeer were
seen.   There was some vegetation upon the land, and animals appeared to resort to this locality in tolerable abundance; the contrast between it and the low, barren shore we
had so recently come from was striking indeed !

Nothing can exceed the gloom and desolation of the western coast of King William's Island: Hobson and myself
had some considerable experience of it; his sojourn there
exceeded a month; its climate seems different from that of
the eastern coast; it is more exposed to north-west winds,
and the air was almost constantly loaded with chilling fogs.
Everywhere upon the shores of the island I noticed boulders of dark gneiss ; upon the west coast they were generally small, and of a dark gray color.   About the north
part of the island Hobson found a good deal of sandstone,
the probable result of ice-drift from Melville Island or
Banks Land.

This land gives one the idea of its having risen within a
recent geological period of the sea—not suddenly, but at regular intervals ; the numerous terraces or beach-marks form
long horizontal lines, rising very gradually, and in due proportion as their distance increases from the sea; near the

ISOLATED ICEBERG.

shore they are, of course, most distinct. Upon the west coast some fossils were picked up, chiefly impressions of shells.

King William's Island is for the most part extremely barren, and its surface dotted over with innumerable ponds and lakes. It is not by any means "the land abounding with reindeer and musk oxen" which we expected to find : the natives told us there were none of the latter and very few of the former upon it.

On the 8th of June the first ducks and brent geese were seen flying northward. Passing over the extreme point of Cape Victoria, Boothia Land, near which we saw the deserted snow huts of our March acquaintances, and shortly afterwards crossing the mouth of the deep bay to the north of it, in which, sheltered by the island, a ship would find security from the ice pressure, and very tolerable winter quarters, we again reached the straight low limestone coast of Boothia Felix.

I was unable to make any delay at the Magnetic Pole, nor could I find a trace of Ross' cairn ;* but at each of our encampments along the coast the magnetic inclination was carefully observed. Throughout my whole journey I availed myself of every opportunity of obtaining these most interesting observations, often remaining up, after we had encamped for rest, six or seven hours in order to do so ; but the instruments supplied for this purpose were not well adapted, and occasioned me a vast deal of labor and loss of time, so as to diminish to almost one-third the results I should otherwise have obtained. Much snow has disappeared off the land ; and the ridges or ancient beaches, being the parts most free from snow, showed out strongly in

---

* This cairn, as well as the one built on Point Victory in 1830, was removed by the natives ; fortunately they had not visited Point Victory whilst the Franklin cairn and record remained there, otherwise neither cairn nor record would have remained for us to discover.

long, dark, horizontal lines, rising above each other until lost to view in the interior. Here and there a few fossil shells and corals were picked up, and four or five willow grouse shot.

13th June.—We passed from limestone to granite in lat. 71° 10' N. Here the land attains to considerable elevation. In the hollows of the dark granite rocks we found abundance of water, and also in a few places upon the sea-ice; it was quite evident that in another day or two the snow would altogether yield to the warmth of summer; birds were now frequently seen.

We discovered a narrow channel to the eastward of the one between the Tasmania Group, through which we had passed with so much difficulty in April; our new channel was covered with smooth ice, and was also much shorter.

At one of our depots lately visited, a note left by Hobson informed me of his being six days in advance of me, and also of his own serious illness; for many days past he had been unable to walk, and was consequently conveyed upon the sledge; his men were hastening home with all their strength and speed, in order to get him under the Doctor's care. We also were doing our best to push on, lest the bursting out of melting snow from the various ravines should render the ice impassable.

On the 15th the snow upon the ice everywhere yielded to the effects of increased temperature; I was, indeed, most thankful at its having remained firm so long. To make any progress at all after this date was of course a very great labor, requiring the utmost efforts of both the men and the dogs; nor was the freezing mixture through which we trudged by any means agreeable; we were often more than knee-deep in it.

We succeeded in reaching False Strait on the morning of the 18th June, and pitched our tent just as heavy rain began to descend; it lasted throughout the greater part of the day. After traveling a few miles upon the Long Lake, further progress was found to be quite impossible, and we were obliged to haul our sledges up off the flooded ice, and commence a march of 16 or 17 miles overland for the ship. The poor dogs were so tired and sore-footed, that we could not induce them to follow us ; they remained about the sledges. After a very fatiguing scramble across the hills and through the snow valleys, we were refreshed with a sight of our poor dear lonely little ' Fox,' and arrived on board in time for a late breakfast on the 19th June.

With respect to a *navigable* North-West Passage, and to the probability of our having been able last season to make any considerable advance to the southward, had the barrier of ice across the western outlet of Bellot Strait permitted us to reach the open water beyond, I think, judging from what I have since seen of the ice in the Franklin Strait, that the chances were greatly in favor of our reaching Cape Herschel on the S. side of King William's Land, by passing (as I intended to do) *eastward* of that island.

From Bellot Strait to Cape Victoria we found a mixture of old and new ice, showing the exact proportion of pack and of clear water at the setting in of winter. Once to the southward of the Tasmania Group, I think our chief difficulty would have been overcome ; and south of Cape Victoria I doubt whether any further obstruction would have been experienced, as but little, if any, ice remained. The natives told us the ice went away, and left a clear sea every year. As our discoveries show the Victoria Strait to be but little more than 20 miles wide, the ice pressed southward through so narrow a space could hardly have prevented our crossing to Victoria Land, and Cambridge Bay, the wintering place reached by Collinson, from the *west*.

No one who sees that portion of Victoria Strait which lies between King William's Island and Victoria Land, as we saw it, could doubt of there being but one way of getting a ship through it, that way being the *extremely* hazardous one of drift through in the pack.

The wide channel between Prince of Wales' Land and Victoria Land admits a vast and continuous stream of very heavy ocean-formed ice, from the N. W., which presses upon the western face of King William's Island, and chokes up Victoria Strait in the manner I have just described. I do not think the North-West Passage could ever be sailed through by passing westward—that is, to windward—of King William's Island.

If the season was so favorable for navigation as to open the northern part of this western sea* (as, for instance, in 1846, when Sir John Franklin sailed down it), I think but comparatively little difficulty would be experienced in the more southern portion of it until Victoria Strait was reached. Had Sir John Franklin known that a channel existed eastward of King William's *Land* (so named by Sir John Ross), I do not think he would have risked the besetment of his ships in such very heavy ice to the westward of it; but had he attempted the north-west passage by the *eastern* route, he would probably have carried his ships safely through to Behring's Straits. But Franklin was furnished with charts which indicated no passage to the eastward of King William's Land, and made that land (since discovered by Rae to be an island) a peninsula attached to the continent of North America; and he consequently had but one course open to him, and that the one he adopted.

My own preference for the route by the east side of the island is founded upon the observations and experience of Rae and Collinson in 1851-2-4. I am of opinion that the barrier of ice off Bellot Strait, some 3 or 4 miles wide, was

---

* This channel is now named after the illustrious navigator, Admiral Sir John Franklin.

the only obstacle to our carrying the 'Fox,' according to my original intention, southward to the Great Fish River, passing *east* of King William's Island, and from thence to a wintering position on Victoria Land. Perhaps some future voyager, profiting by the experience so fearfully and fatally acquired by the Franklin expedition, and the observations of Rae, Collinson, and myself, may succeed in carrying his ship through from sea to sea: at least he will be enabled to direct all his efforts in the true and only direction. In the meantime to Franklin must be assigned the earliest discovery of the North-West Passage, though not the actual accomplishment of it in his ships.*

Saturday, 2nd July.—Upon my arrival on board on the morning of the 19th June, my first inquiries were about Hobson; I found him in a worse state than I expected. He reached the ship on the 14th, unable to walk, or even stand without assistance; but already he was beginning to amend, and was in excellent spirits. Christian had shot several ducks, which, with preserved potato, milk, strong ale, and lemon-juice, completed a very respectable dietary for a scurvy-stricken patient. All the rest were tolerably well; slight traces only of scurvy in two or three of the men. The ship was as clean and trim as I could expect, and all had well and cheerfully performed their duties during my absence; hardly any game had been shot, except one bear.

The Doctor now acquainted me with the death of Thomas

---

* This will be understood when it is recollected that W. of Simpson's Straits or Victoria Land, a navigable passage to Behring's Straits is known to exist along the coast of North America. Franklin himself, with his companion Richardson, surveyed by far the greater portion of that distance. Franklin's and Parry's discoveries overlap each other in longitude, and for the last thirty years or more the discovery of the North-West Passage has been reduced to the discovery of a link uniting the two.

Blackwell, ship's steward, which occurred only five days previously, and was occasioned by scurvy. This man had scurvy when I left the ship in April, and no means were left untried by the Doctor to promote the recovery and rally his deponding energies ; but his mind, unsustained by hope, lost all energy, and at last he had to be forcibly taken upon deck for fresh air. For months past the ship's spirits had been of necessity removed from under his control.

When too late his shipmates made it known that he had a dislike to preserved meats, and had lived the whole winter upon salt pork ! He also disliked preserved potato, and would not eat it unless watched, nor would he put on clean clothes which others in charity prepared for him. Yet his death was somewhat unexpected ; he went on deck as usual to walk in the middle of the day, and, when found there, was quite dead. His remains were buried beside those of our late shipmate Mr. Brand.

The news of our success to the southward in tracing the footsteps of the lost expedition greatly revived the spirits of my small crew ; we wished only for the safe and speedy return of Young and his party.

Captain Young commenced his spring explorations on the 7th April, with a sledge party of four men, and a second sledge drawn by six dogs under the management of our Greenlander, Samuel ; finding in his progress that a channel existed between Prince of Wales' Land and Victoria Land whereby his discovery and search would be lengthened, he sent back one sledge, the tent, and four men to the ship, in order to economise provisions, and for forty days journeyed with one man (George Hobday) and the dogs, encamping in such snow lodges as they were able to build.

This great exposure and fatigue, together with extremely bad weather, and a most difficult coastline to trace, greatly injured his health ; he was compelled to return to the ship on 7th June for medical aid, but proposing at all hazards to renew his explorations almost immediately.   Dr. Walker met this determination by a strong protest in writing against his leaving the ship again, his health being quite unequal to it; but after three days Young felt himself somewhat better, and, with a zeal which knew no bounds, set off to complete his branch of the search, taking with him both his sledge parties.

From the Doctor's account I felt most anxious for his return, lest his health, or that of his companions, should receive permanent injury; in fact this was now. my only cause of anxiety.   The season was rather forward here, and advancing with unusual rapidity, rain and wind dissolving the snow and ice; there was much water in Bellot Strait, extending from Half-way Island eastward to the table-land, and thence in a narrow lane to Long Island.   After a day or two I could perceive a vast improvement in Hobson; and my own four men, with the exception of Hampton, who required rest, were in sound health; so also was my companion Petersen.   On 24th June Christian shot two small reindeer, which gave us 170 lbs. of meat; a few days before that he shot a seal, which afforded two sumptuous meals for all on board.

The time having elapsed during which Young expected to remain absent, and the difficulties of the transit from the western sea having become greatly increased, I set off early on the 25th June with my four men, intending to visit Pemmican Rock; but failing to come across him there, I resolved to carry on provisions as far as Four River Point, in the hope of meeting with him, and facilitating his return. To our surprise the water had all drained off the frozen surface of the Long Lake, and it therefore afforded excellent travelling.   We found the poor dogs lying quietly beside our sledges; they had attacked the pemmican, and devoured a small quantity which was not secured in tin, also some blubber, some leather straps, and a gull that I had shot for a specimen; but they had not apparently relished the biscuit. Poor dogs! they have a hard life of it in these regions. Even Petersen, who is generally kind and humane, seems to fancy they must have little or no feeling: one of his theories is, that you may knock an Esquimaux dog about the head with any article, however heavy, with perfect impunity to the brutes. One of us upbraided him the other day because he broke his whip-handle over the head of a dog. *"That was nothing at all,"* he assured us: some friend of his in Greenland found he could beat his dogs over the head with a heavy hammer,—it stunned them certainly,—but by laying them with their mouths open to the wind, they soon revived, got up and ran about *"all right."*

We lost no time in giving them a good feed, the first for seven days, yet they did not seem unusually hungry, and soon coiled themselves up to sleep again. Whilst the men and dogs were employed next day in conveying a sledge to the east end of the lake, I walked to Cape Bird to look out for the absent party, but they had not yet returned to Pemmican Rock.

When vainly endeavoring, with felonious intentions, to climb up a steep cliff to the breeding-places of some silvery gulls, I saw and shot a brent goose, seated upon an accessible ledge, and made a prize of four eggs; it seems strange that this bird should have selected so unusual a breeding-place. Many seals were basking on the ice, and the watercourse by which our sledges ascended a week before to the Long Lake was now a strong and rapid stream. A few reindeer were seen.

On the 27th I sent three of the men back to the ship, and with Thompson and the dogs went on to Pemmican Rock, where, to our great joy, we happily met Young and his party, who had but just returned there, after a long and successful journey the particulars of which I will give hereafter.

Young was greatly reduced in flesh and strength, so much weakened indeed that for the last few days he had travelled on the dog-sledge; Harvey—also far from well—could just manage to keep pace with the sledge; his malady was scurvy. Their journeys had been very depressing; most dismal weather, low, dreary limestone shores devoid of game, and no traces of the lost expedition. The news of our success in the southern journeys greatly cheered them. On the following day we were all once more on board, and indulging in such rapid consumption of eatables as only those can do who have been much reduced by long-contin ued fatigue and exposure to cold. Venison, ducks, beer and lemon-juice, daily; preserved apples and cranberries three times a week; and pickled whaleskin—a famous anti-scorbutic—*ad libitum* for all who liked it. The weather, which for the last week had been wet, windy, and miserable, now set in fair. The carpenter's hammer, and the men's voices at their work, were new and animating sounds.

CHAPTER XVII.

To-day (*2nd July*) I took a long and delightful walk, but shot only two ducks; Petersen went in another direction, and got nothing; Christian, after toiling all day in his kayak, returned with only two divers and a duck. Lately he has obtained for us several king and long-tailed ducks (no eider-ducks have been seen); two red-throated divers, and two brent geese, and caught an ermine in its summer coat. Yesterday one of the men brought on board a trout weighing 2 lbs; he saw a glaucous gull and a fox disputing for it; the former seems to have killed and brought it to land.

The water now washes the south side of the Fox Islands, and extends to the south point of Long Island. The month of June has been somewhat warmer than usual, its mean temperature being $+35\frac{1}{2}°$.

9th.—The ship has been thoroughly cleaned and restowed, remaining · provisions examined, tanks filled with fresh water, 12 tons of stone ballast taken in, and everything brought on board that was landed last autumn. Hobson is the only one upon the sick list; but he is able to walk about and does duty. Very few birds, and only one small seal, have been obtained during the week; an occasional great northern diver is seen, and a rare land bird has been shot. We cannot discover the nests of either ducks or geese, and the breeding cliffs of the gulls being inaccessible, we have not got any eggs. I am a close prisoner at the corner of my table, poring over my observation and angle book, and have at length laid down upon paper the west coast of King William's Land to my satisfaction. Tidal observations are commenced; and the aneroid and mercurial barometers are again being compared in order to verify the former.

16th. *Saturday night.*—We are now almost ready for sea. There is now a much larger space of water in Bellot Strait, reaching within 300 or 400 yards of us. Long cracks or lanes of water have been seen in Prince Regent's Inlet. The decay of the ice continues, though not with equal rapidity, yet with very satisfactory despatch. Westerly winds and clear weather prevail. Christian has seen two reindeer this week, and has shot a very few birds, and seven seals. As these creatures lie basking upon the ice, he crawls up to them behind a small calico screen, fitted upon a miniature sledge about a foot long, on which there is a rest for the muzzle of his rifle, and a slit in the calico, through which he fires it. The seals afford an average weight of thirty pounds of excellent fresh meat, which we relish greatly, and consider much better suited to our present condition than such poor venison as reindeer would furnish at this season. A single hare has been shot; the white fur has nearly all disappeared, and left exposed the summer coat of dull lead color. Several small birds not common to the northward are found here. Insects abound; the Doctor is perpetually in chase, unless busily occupied in grubbing up plants. Young is surveying the harbor. Hobson fully occupied in preparing the ship for sea. I have been giving some attention to the engines and boiler, and hope, with the help of the two stokers, to be able to make use of our steam power

The men have received my hearty thanks for their great exertions during the traveling period. I told them I considered every part of our search to have been fully and efficiently performed. Our labors have determined the exact position of the extreme northern promontory of the continent of America; I have affixed to it the name of Murchison, after the distinguished President of the Royal Geographical Society—the strenuous advocate for this " further search"—and the able champion of Lady Franklin when she needed all the support which private friendship and public spirit could bestow.

22rd.—The ice in Prince Regent's Inlet is broken up into pack, but the prevalence of easterly winds keeps it close upon the shore. The ice about us is very much decayed, holes through it in many places. No reindeer seen this week, and only two seals procured; one of them shot by Christian, the other was killed by a bear, which ran off before Samuel could come within shot of him. A fox, a gull, a couple of ducks, and one or two lemmings, complete our game list for the week, yet our two Esquimaux are indefatigable in the pursuit. We eat all the birds and seals we can shoot, as well as mustard and cress as fast as we can grow it, but the quantity is very small. We sometimes refresh ourselves with a salad of sorrel leaves, or roots of the little plant with lilac flower of snapdragon shape, named *Pedicularis hirsuta.*

The seine has been hauled in the narrow lake at the head of the harbor, but as it was not well managed, only a dozen small trout were taken, though several were seen. We have tried for rock-cod, but without success. The relics of the lost expedition have been aired, exhibited to the crew, labelled, and packed away. The Doctor has been dredging lately. A record detailing our proceedings has been placed in a cairn upon the west point of Depot Bay.

1st August—A long continuance of unusually calm,

bright, and warm weather has been favorable to our painting and cleaning the ship, scraping masts, and so forth.
the result is that she looks unusually smart and gay, and
our impatience to exhibit her, and *ourselves* at home is
much increased.   With the exception of a few gulls, and a
duck, our hunters have shot nothing lately, although constantly out, either darting about in their kayaks or ranging
over the hills ; in fact there is nothing which they *can*
shoot ; the ducks are tolerably numerous, but extremely
wild ; the valleys are respectably clothed with vegetation,
yet only one animal—a hare—has been seen.   I was so fortunate as to shoot a snowy owl, the flesh of which was white
and tender, but to my palate, tasteless, although Petersen
considers that " owl is the best beef in the country."

On Thursday night we found the harbor-ice to be quietly
drifting out, of course taking us with it.   The night was
calm, the current in Bellot Strait was very strong : we were
almost helpless under the circumstances, and therefore felt
the danger of our position.   To warp the ship along the ice-
edge, out of the way of the shore and rocks as it turned
round and drifted along the cliffs to the westward, gave us
some hours' occupation.   At length it stuck fast between
Fox Island and the main.

At turn of tide on Friday morning it began to drift eastward, and by this time being much broken up, and a breeze
coming to our aid, we managed to extricate ourselves and
reach a secure anchorage in Point Kennedy.

On Saturday night some ice that was left came drifting
out of the inner harbor, and obliged us to slip our cable ;
but after a few hours we regained our berth in safety, and
have since been undisturbed.   There is no immediate prospect of escape, but we expect a prodigious smashing up of
the ice whenever a strong wind springs up to set it in motion.   To-day the steam was got up, and with the help of
our two stokers I worked the engines for a short time.   It

is very cheering to know that we still have steam power at our command, although, by the deaths of poor Mr. Brand and Robert Scott, we were deprived of our engineer and engine-driver.

The mean temperature for July has been 40°·14, which is above the average for this region; the July temperatures have usually varied from 36° to 42°.

All are now in good health, but Hobson still a little lame. The issue of lemon-juice has been reduced to the ordinary allowance of half an ounce daily (as we have but little that is really good), lest another winter should become inevitable, which, I can devoutly say, may God forbid!

Monday night, 8th.—Very anxiously awaiting an opportunity to escape. We have constantly watched the ice from the neighboring hills, including the lofty summit of Mount Walker—named after the Doctor, who was the first to ascend it (1123 feet)—from which Fury Point can be distinguished, but nothing very cheering has been seen. We had a N. E. gale, accompanied by rain and a considerable fall of the barometer, a few days ago; and as it blew freshly from the westward this morning, I went to a hill-top and saw that much ice had been broken up in Brentford Bay, and that there were streaks of water along the land between Possession Point and Hazard Inlet; this water, however, was not accessible to us.

The ice about Pemmican Rock was much in the same position as we found it last year, but Bellot Strait was perfectly clear. All the ice in this harbor, in Depôt Bay, and Hazard Inlet, is gone, by far the greater part having decayed, not drifted away.

Later in the day and from loftier hill-tops, a good deal of water was seen off Cape Garry, and a water-sky beyond. It now blows very strongly from the S. W., the most desirable quarter; and as the anxious desire to escape has become oppressive, it is not to be wondered at that now our hopes have become extravagant. We may even make a start to-morrow ! On the other hand, a careful examination of our provision store shows that, should we be obliged to spend another winter here, we must curtail our allowance of meat—fresh and salt—to three-quarters of a pound, and have to use but very indifferent lemon-juice. The spirits, I rejoice to say, will very shortly be entirely expended.

On the morning of the 3d instant, when the rain ceased and N. E. gale sprang up, two claps of thunder were distinctly heard ; this occurs but very rarely in these latitudes. There is ample occupation for the men but not much for the officers ; as for myself, I write a great deal, and work occasionally at our chart of discoveries ; the only refreshment I indulge in is an occasional dive into packets of old letters. All yesterday the harbor was full of ice set in by southerly and westerly winds, and so closely packed that one might have walked over it to the shore ; to-day it has nearly all drifted out again. The subjoined list will show what game we have been able to obtain by constant and arduous labor from the resources of these regions during nearly two years' sojourn.

GAME LIST.

8 Months in the Pack, 1857–8.				11 Months in Port Kennedy, 1858–9.						
Bears.	Seals.	Dovekies.	Foxes.	Bears.	Deer.	Hares.	Foxes.	Ptarmigan.	Wild Fowl.	Seals.
2	73	38	1	2	8	9	19	82	98	18

At Port Kennedy several ermines and lemmings were also caught.
The ptarmigan all disappeared after 1st April.
Only 2 dovekies were seen, 1 in winter and 1 in summer plumage
A few seals were seen as early as the month of February.
Ducks, geese, and gulls, were the usual kind of wild fowl killed.
During the four months occupied in sailing from Davis Strait to Bellot Strait, many looms and rotchies, and 5 or 6 bears were shot.

Wednesday, 10th.—The S. W. wind proved a good friend to us ; by the morning of the 9th it had moved the ice off shore, and cleared away a passage for us out of Brentford

Bay. We started under steam at eleven o'clock yesterday
morning, and, passing round Long Island, made sail along
the land towards Cape Garry, there being a channel about
2 or 3 miles wide between the pack and the shore.

The wind now failed us, and I experienced some little
difficulty in the management of the engines and boiler; the
latter primed so violently as to send the water over our top
gallant yard, and the tail valve of the condenser by some
means had got out of its seat, and admitted air to the condenser; but eventually we got the engines to work well, and
steamed across Cresswell Bay during the night. The pack
rested against Fury Point, and an east wind springing up,
we made fast to a large grounded mass of ice in Adelaide
Bay, about ¼ mile off shore, and in 3 fathoms water, at
eleven o'clock this morning. Having managed the engines
for twenty-four consecutive hours, I was not sorry to get
into bed. We were hardly out of Brentford Bay when fulmar petrels and white whales were seen; the first we have
noticed for eleven and a half months. Dovekies are likewise abundant, and a seal has already been shot. Cresswell Bay is perfectly clear of ice, but this pale limestone
land is the perfection of sterility, even with the rugged hills
of Brentford Bay in lively recollection.

Upon the east side of Port Kennedy the bones of whales
were found in two places a mile apart from each other; the
lowest of them was 180 feet above the sea, the second was
more than 300 feet high. The latter I examined, and found
a jawbone, two ribs, a joint of the vertebræ, and fragments
of other bones, all more or less buried in the soil, and much
heavier than the bones of a recent animal; they lay within
40 or 60 yards of each other, and upon a little flat patch of
rather rich earth, a rocky hill above, and steep slope below;
—they are also nearly a mile inland.

Of the traces which we have left behind us, the most considerable are the graves of our two shipmates within the

western point of our little harbor; they were tastefully
sodded round, and planted over with the usual Arctic flowers. There is our record in a conspicuous cairn at the west
point of Depôt or Transition Bay : we left also three cases
of pemmican near the east end of the Long Lake, and our
traveling boat near its west end, at .the head of False
Strait.

Monday, 15th.—Strong east winds, with much rain, have
imprisoned us here for the last four days, and driven the
whole pack close in, completely filling up Cresswell Bay.
We remain fast to the grounded ice, which shields us from
pressure, otherwise we should have been driven irretrievably
on shore. A couple more seals and a white whale have
been shot; the latter measured $13\frac{1}{2}$ feet long, and proved to
be a female of ordinary dimensions, and of an uniform cream
color ; the eyes are extremely small, and orifices of the ears
scarcely large enough to admit a crow-quill. We dined off
steaks of the flesh, and prefer it to seal, which it very much
resembles, but it is not quite so tender; the skin is greatly
prized by the Greenlanders as an antiscorbutic ; it is a sort
of gristly gelatinous substance, nearly half an inch thick,
and possessing very little taste; fried and eaten with
fish-sauce, it reminded me of cod sound, though not so
good.

The blubber fills two twenty-gallon casks; it produces
oil of a quality superior to seal oil; not an ounce of the
flesh or skin of this huge animal has been thrown away, the
men having a wholesome dread of scurvy, and unbounded
confidence in "blood-meat," such as this ! The Doctor has
picked up a few fossils very similar to those formerly
brought home from Port Leopold.

To our great joy the east wind died away this morning,
and immediately a west wind sprang up, which very quickly
freshened to a smart gale. At four o'clock this afternoon
we were able to make sail, the ice having moved about 3

miles off shore.   Passed within a mile of Fury Beach two
hours afterward, and saw the framing of the house, the boats
and casks very distinctly.

17*th.*—After passing Fury Beach it fell . calm, so we
steamed up as far as Batty Bay.   On Tuesday afternoon we
were off Port Leopold, running fast, when thick fog came
on, and we got involved in loose ice, and seriously damaged
our rudder.   The boats and stores at Port Leopold appeared to remain as we left them last year.   The flag-staff
on the summit of the North-east Cape (over Whale Point)
is still standing, but not erect.

Fog and ice obstructed our progress during the night;
but this morning when I came on deck at eight o'clock, the
day was bright, clear, and charming; no ice visible, except
about Leopold Island, which was now some miles behind us.
Towards evening the wind became contrary.

Sunday evening, 21*st.*—At sea—out of sight of land!

On the 19th we were somewhat delayed by loose ice off
Cape Hay, but by noon yesterday were close off Cape
Burney, and whilst almost becalmed there, a mother bear
swam off to us with two interesting cubs about the size of
very large dogs.   Foolish creatures! a volley of rifles decided their fate in a very few seconds.   Not finding any
whaling vessels off Pond's Inlet, the land-ice which shelters
the whales having all disappeared, we therefore concluded
that the whalers had left in consequence, so, without seeking
for them further south, at once changed our course for
Disco.

To-day only a few icebergs have been seen.   There is a
good deal of swell, so we tumble about.   Roast *veal* has
appeared amongst the delicacies of our table since the bat-
tue of yesterday, and Christian has asked for a portion of
the old bear to carry home to his mother.   Bear's flesh is
really considered a delicacy in Greenland.

25*th.*—Becalmed off Hare Island, and getting the steam

ready. We are only 108 miles from Godhavn, and the
anxiety to clutch our letters has become intolerable. No
pack-ice has been met with in our passage across Baffin's
Bay, but many icebergs. This morning the lofty snow-clad
land of Noursoak and Disco was beautifully distinct; and
at the same time the wind died away, leaving us, at least,
the opportunity to contemplate at our *leisure* their gloomy
grandeur.

26*th.*—Steamed for ten hours last night. Fair winds and
calms have alternated since then, but this evening we are
within 20 miles, and hope soon to get into port. I have
been reading over Young's report of his spring journey. It
comprises seventy-eight days of sledge-traveling, and certainly under most discouraging circumstances. Leaving the
ship on the 7th April, he crossed the western strait to
Prince of Wales' Land, and thence traced its shore to the
south and west. On reaching its southern termination—
Cape Swinburne, so named in honor of Rear-Admiral
Swinburne, a much-esteemed friend of Sir J. Franklin, and
one of the earliest supporters of this final expedition--he
describes the land as extremely low and deeply covered with
snow, the heavy grounded hummocks which fringed its monotonous coast alone indicating the line of demarcation
betwixt land and sea. To the north-east of this terminal
cape the sea was covered with level floe formed in the fall
of last year, whilst all to the north-westward of the same
cape was pack consisting of heavy ice-masses, formed perhaps years ago in far distant and wider seas.

Young attempted to cross the channel which he discovered
between Prince of Wales' Island and Victoria Land; but
from the rugged nature of the ice, found it quite impracticable with the means and time remaining at his disposal.
Young expresses his firm conviction that this channel is so
constantly choked up with unusually heavy ice as to be quite
unnavigable; it is, in fact a *continuous ice-stream* from the

N. W. His opinion coincides with my own, and with those of Captains Omanney and Osborn, when those officers explored the north-western shores of Prince of Wales' Land in 1851.

Fearing that his provisions might run short, he sent back one sledge with four men, and continued his march with only one man and the dogs for forty days! They were obliged to build a snow-hut each night to sleep in, as the tent was sent back with the men ; but latterly, when the weather became more mild, they preferred sleeping on the sledge, as the constructing of a snow-hut usually occupied them for two hours. Young completed the exploration of this coast beyond the point marked upon the charts as Osborn's farthest, up nearly to lat. 73° N., but no cairn was found. Young, however, recognized the remarkably shaped conical hills spoken of by Osborn, when he, at his farthest, in 1851, struck off to the westward.

The coast-line throughout was extremely low ; and in the thick, disagreeable weather which he almost constantly experienced, it was often a matter of great difficulty to prevent straying off the coast-line inland. He commenced his return on the 11th May, and reached the ship on 7th of June, in wretched health and depressed in spirits.

Directly his health was partially re-established, he, in spite of the Doctor's remonstrances, as I have before said, again set out on the 10th with his party of men and dogs, to complete the exploration of both shores of the continuation of Peel Sound, between the position of the 'Fox' and the points reached by Sir James Ross in 1849, and Lieutenant Browne in 1851. This he accomplished without finding any trace of the lost expedition, and the parties were again on board by 28th June. The ice traveled over in this last journey was almost all formed last autumn.

The extent of coast-line explored by Captain Young amounts to 380 miles, whilst that discovered by Hobson and myself amounts to nearly 420 miles, making a total of 800 geographical miles of new coast-line which we have laid down.

Hobson's report is a minute record of all that occurred during his journey of seventy-four days, and includes a list of all the relics brought on board, or seen by him. He suffered very severely in health : when only ten days out from the ship, traces of scurvy appeared ; when a month absent he walked lame; towards the latter end of the journey he was compelled to allow himself to be dragged upon the sledge, not being able to walk more than a few yards at a time ; and on arriving at the ship on the 14th of June, poor Hobson was unable to stand. How strongly this bears upon the last sad march of the lost crews ! And yet Hobson's food throughout the whole journey was pemmican of the very best quality, the most nutritious description of food that we know of, and varied occasionally by such game as they were able to shoot. In spite of this fresh-meat diet, scurvy advanced with rapid strides.

After leaving me at Cape Victoria, he says—" No difficulty was experienced in crossing James Ross' Strait. The ice appeared to be of but one year's growth ; and although it was in many places much crushed up, we easily found smooth leads through the lines of hummocks ; many very heavy masses of ice, evidently of foreign formation, have been here arrested in their drift: so large are they that, in the gloomy weather we experienced, they were often taken for islands."

Again, at Cape Felix, he observes,—" The pressure of the ice is severe, but the ice itself is not remarkably heavy in character ; the shoalness of the coast keeps the line of pressure at considerable distance from the beach ; to the northward of the island the ice, as far as I could see, was very rough, and crushed up into large masses." Here we notice the gradual change in the character of the ice as

17

Hobson left the Boothian shore and advanced towards Victoria Strait. The "very heavy masses of ice, evidently of foreign formation," had drifted in from the N. W. through M'Clure Strait; Victoria Strait was full of it; and Hobson's description of the ice he passed over clearly illustrates how Franklin, leaving clear water behind him, pressed his ships into the pack when he attempted to force through Victoria Strait. How very different the result *might* and probably *would* have been had he known of the existence of a ship-channel, skeltered by King William Island from this tremendous "polar pack"!

Hobson left King William's Island on the last day of May, having spent thirty-one days on its desolate shores. During that period one bear and five willow grouse were shot; one wolf and a few foxes were seen. One poor fox was either so desperately hungry, or so charmed with the rare sight of animated beings, that he played about the party until the dogs snapped him up, although in harness and dragging the sledge at the time. A few gulls were seen, but not until after the first week in June.

I have already explained how Hobson found the records and the boat: he exercised his discretionary power with sound judgment, and completed his search so well, that in coming over the same ground after him, I could not discover any trace that had escaped him.

I quite agree with him that there may be many small articles beneath the snow; but that cairns, graves, or any conspicuous objects could exist upon so low and uniform a shore, without our having seen them, is *almost* impossible.

Sunday evening, 29th.—Calm, warm, lovely weather; and we are thoroughly enjoying it in the quiet security of Lively harbor, or Godhavn. Although Friday night was dark, we managed to find out the harbor's mouth, and slowly steamed into it. The inhabitants were awoke by Petersen demanding our letters, but great indeed was our disappointment at finding only a very few letters and two or three papers, and these for the officers only! It appears that on the arrival of the whalers in early spring, the ice prevented their usual communication with the settlement, therefore the letters on board of them were unavoidably carried northward. Some few, however, which came out in the 'Truelove,' were landed at the neighboring settlement of Noursoak, and from thence were sent back to Godhavn.

It is rather a nervous thing opening the first letters after a lapse of more than two years. We received them in our beds at three o'clock in the morning; and when we met at breakfast were able, thank God! to congratulate each other upon the receipt of cheering home news. Lady Franklin and Miss Cracroft wrote to me from Bournemouth in March last. They have traveled more than we have, I think, having visited almost all the countries bordering the Mediterranean and Black Seas, posted through the Crimea, and steamed up the Danube! I am much gratified to learn that I have been elected a member of the Royal Yacht Squadron during my absence.

Yesterday morning I called upon the inspector, Mr. Olrik, who has been home to Denmark since I saw him last spring. In the autumn he took Mrs. Olrik and his family to Copenhagen, and had but just returned alone. He received me with his usual kindness, and promised me such supplies as we require. It so happens that none of my expected business letters have arrived, so that I am not accredited in the slightest degree, nor is there any hint thrown out as to where I am to take the 'Fox.' Mr. Olrik gave me a large bundle of 'Illustrated London News,' which was exceedingly acceptable, and told us that Austria was at war with France and Sardinia. By the latest news a battle had been fought and won by the latter Powers. Most fortunately a 'Navy List,' had come out to Hobson, otherwise I think we should have been utterly brokenhearted. We study

its pages daily, and delight in noticing the advancement of
our many friends.

1st Sept., Thursday night.—At sea, on *the passage*, and
already enjoying by anticipation, the pleasures of home!
Five busy days were spent in Godhavn, supplying our little
wants, in as far as they could be supplied, including 100
gallons of light beer. The natives were very useful, the
men bringing off water, stone-ballast, and sand, and a
troop of Esquimaux girls scrubbing the paintwork and the
decks.

Each evening the men went on shore, taking with them
a very limited quantity of rum-punch for the ladies, and
danced for several hours in a large store; whilst the officers
and myself spent the time with Mr. Olrik or the other
Danish gentlemen—Messrs. Andersen, Bulbrue, and Tyner.
Nothing could exceed their kindness to us, whilst their
good humor and their anecdotes, sometimes expressed in
quaint English, greatly amused us. We shall always retain
very agreeable recollections of Godhavn; twice has it been
to us an Arctic home.

Mr. Petersen's nieces, the belles of the place, came on
board (Miss Sophia with scented cambric handkerchief and
gloves—in other respects, she adheres to the Esquimaux
costume); they were pleased with the organ, although it is
out of repair, and they sang together very sweetly for us.
Our Esquimaux shipmates, Christian and Samuel, were discharged, and, by their own request their wages given in
charge to Mr. Olrik and Mr. Bulbrue; they seemed to understand the importance of husbanding their wealth. Christian said he thought it would not be all spent under three
years. First of all he intended buying a rifle for his
brother, and then some wood to build a house for himself.

I was gratified very much when I heard them say that
the men had treated them very well—"all the same as
brothers;" and they really seemed sorry to leave the ship;

they would come on board and look gravely about at every
thing as if regretting the coming separation. Even our
poor dogs seemed to think the ship their natural abode;
although landed at the settlement, they soon ran round the
harbor to the point nearest the ship, and there, upon the
rocks, spent the whole period of our stay.

On Tuesday night we set off some fireworks on shore to
amuse the natives, for I intended sailing next day, but the
wind prevented my doing so. The last day was spent in
the interchange of presents between our Danish friends and
ourselves; indeed, the sincere hearty good feeling which
existed between every individual in the 'Fox' and the inhabitants of the settlement was as gratifying as apparent.
Almost the only fresh supplies obtained here were rock-cod
and salmon-trout from Disco fiord. During our stay the
weather was delightful; indeed it was the first really fine
weather they had experienced at Godhavn during the present season, the summer having been cold and wet.

10th Sept., Saturday night.—To-day we passed to the
eastward of Cape Farewell, but about 100 miles to the
south of it. The last iceberg was seen to-day; and now
we are running along swiftly before a pleasant N. W. breeze.
Hitherto we have had every variety of wind and weather,
from a calm to a gale, but generally the wind has been favorable. The change of temperature is already perceptible.

Saturday night, 17th Sept.—A week of favorable gales
has brought us from Cape Farewell to within 400 miles of
Land's End, or about 1100 miles of distance. But such
rough weather is not pleasant in so small a vessel, however
much "like a duck" she may be; and our two years' sojourn
in the still waters of the frozen North has made us very
susceptible of the change.

CONCLUSION.

WE sailed all the way home from Greenland, yet the 'Fox' made the passage in only nineteen days, arriving in the English Channel on the 20th September; on the evening of the 21st I reached London (having landed at Portsmouth), and made known to the Admiralty the result of my voyage.

On the 23d September the 'Fox' was taken into dock at Blackwall; and, through the kindness and promptitude of the Lords of the Admiralty, I was enabled on the 27th, when the crew were assembled for the last time, to present the Arctic medal to such of my companions as had not already received it for previous Arctic service, and also to inform Lieutenant Hobson that his promotion to the rank of Commander would speedily take place.

I will not intrude upon the reader, who has followed me through the pages of this simple narrative, any description of my feelings on finding the enthusiasm with which we were all received on landing upon our native shores. The blessing of Providence had attended our efforts, and more than a full measure of approval from our friends and countrymen has been our reward. For myself the testimonial given me by the officers and crew of the 'Fox' has touched me perhaps more than all. The purchase of a gold chronometer, for presentation to me, was the first use the men made of their earnings; and as long as I live it will remind me of that perfect harmony, that mutual esteem and goodwill, which made our ship's company a happy little community, and contributed materially to the success of the expedition.

The names I have given to my discoveries are, with the exception of those by which I have endeavored to honor the members of the lost expedition, the names of active supporters of the recent search, and friends of Franklin and his companions, though such names are far from exhausting the number of those who have the highest claims to distinction on both grounds.

It will be observed that I have refrained from repeating names which have already been commemorated by preceding commanders, and which therefore are already in our charts. Besides the individuals already mentioned in the narrative, Sir Thomas D. Acland, one of the most zealous promoters of the search, both in and out of the House of Commons; Monsieur De la Roquette, Vice-President of the Geographical Society of Paris, and author of an interesting biography of Franklin; Rear-Admiral Fitzroy; and Major-General Pasley, R. E., stand high amongst those whom it has been my privilege to honor.

Although much talent has been brought to bear upon the deciphering of the letters found in a pocketbook near Cape Herschell (page 248 *ante*), yet, from their being so very much defaced by time, only a few detached sentences have been made out, and these do not in the slightest degree refer to the proceedings of the lost expedition.

It will be seen that I have noticed (page 260) the discrepancy between the number of souls accounted for by the Point Victory Record, and the generally received opinion that 138 individuals sailed in the 'Erebus' and ' Terror.'

I am now enabled to state, on the authority of the Admiralty, that only one hundred and thirty-four individuals left the United Kingdom, and of these five men subsequently returned: one by H. M. S. 'Rattler,' and four by the transport 'Baretto Junior;' so that only one hundred and

twenty-nine—the exact number mentioned in the record—
actually entered the ice.   The five invalids were —

From H. M. S. ‘ Terror,’ John Brown, Able seaman.
        “   Robert Carr, Armorer.
        “   James Elliot, Sailmaker.
        “   William Aitken, Marine.
From H. M. S. ‘ Erebus,’ Thomas Birt, Armorer.

The relics we have brought home have been deposited by
the Admiralty in the United Service Institution, and now
form a national memento—the most simple and most touching—of those heroic men who perished in the path of duty,
but not until they had achieved the grand object of their
voyage,—the *Discovery of the North-West Passage.*

London, 24th Nov. 1859,

APPENDIX.

No. I.

A LETTER TO VISCOUNT PALMERSTON, K. G., &c.,
FROM LADY FRANKLIN.

60 Pall Mall, December 2, 1856.

My Lord,—

I trust I may be permitted, as the widow of Sir John Franklin, to draw the attention of Her Majesty's Government to the unsettled state of a question which a few months ago was under their consideration, and to express a well-grounded hope that a final effort may be made to ascertain the fate and recover the remains of my husband's expedition.

Your Lordship will allow me to remind you that a Memorial * with this object in view (of which I enclose a printed copy) was early in June last presented to, and kindly received by you. It had been signed within forty-eight hours by all the leading men of science then in London who had an opportunity of seeing it, and might have received an indefinite augmentation of worthy names had not the urgency of the question forbidden delay. To the above names were appended those of the Arctic officers who had been personally engaged in the search, and who, though absent, were known to be favorable to another

---

* See Appendix II.

effort for its completion. And though that united application obtained no immediate result, it was felt, and by no one more strongly than myself, that it never could be utterly wasted.

I venture also to allude to a letter of my own addressed to the Lords Commissioners of the Admiralty in April last, and a copy of which accompanied, I believe, the Memorial to your Lordship, wherein I earnestly deprecated any premature adjudication of the reward claimed by Dr. Rae, on the ground that the fate of my husband's expedition was not yet ascertained, and that it was due both to the living and the dead to complete a search which had been hitherto pursued under the greatest disadvantage, for want of the clue which was now for the first time in our hands.

The Memorial above alluded to, and my own letter of earlier date, had not yet received any reply, when, in the month of July, the Lords of the Admiralty caused prompt inquiries to be made as to the possibility of equipping a ship at that advanced season, in time for effective operations in the field of search. The result was that it was pronounced to be too late, and the subject was dismissed for that season.

Upon this I addressed a letter to the Board (of which I take the liberty to enclose a copy), respectfully showing that by this unfortunate delay the opportunity had also been taken from me of sending out a vessel at my own cost, a measure which I had previously felt myself obliged to state to their Lordships would be the alternative of any adverse decision on their part. I pleaded therefore, as the only remedy for the loss of an entire summer season, that the route by Behring Straits was by some of the most competent Arctic officers considered preferable to the eastern route, and that the equipment of a vessel for this direction need not take place before the close of the year.

In reply, their Lordships caused me to be informed that

WALRUSES—A FAMILY PARTY.
From a Sketch by Captain Allen Young.

"they had come to the decision not to send any expedition to the Arctic regions in the present year."

This communication, however, was in answer merely to my own letter. The Memorialists had as yet received no reply, and accordingly the President of the Royal Society put a question respecting the Memorial in the House of Lords at the close of the session, which drew from one of Her Majesty's Ministers (Lord Stanley), after some preliminary observations, the assurance that Her Majesty's Government would give the subject their serious consideration during the recess. I may be permitted to add, that, in the conversation which followed, Lord Stanley expressed himself as very favorably disposed towards a proposition made to him by Lord Wrottesley, that, in the event of there being no Government expedition, I should be assisted in fitting out my own expedition; an assurance which Lord Wrottesley had the kindness to communicate to me by letter.

But, my Lord, as nothing has occurred within the last few months to weaken the reasons which induced the Admiralty, early in July last, to contemplate another final effort, and as they put it aside at that time on the sole ground that it was too late to equip a vessel for that season, I trust it will be felt that I am not endeavoring to re-open a closed question, but merely to obtain the settlement of one which has not ceased to be, and is even now, under favorable consideration. The time has arrived, however, when I trust I may be pardoned for pressing your Lordship, with whom I believe the question rests, for a decision, since by further delay even my own efforts may be paralyzed.

I have cherished the hope, in common with others, that we are not waiting in vain. Should, however, that decision unfortunately throw upon me the responsibility and the cost of sending out a vessel myself, I beg to assure your Lordship that I shall not shrink, either from that weighty responsibility, or from the sacrifice of my entire available fortune for the purpose, supported as I am in my convictions by such high authorities as those whose opinions are on record in your Lordship's hands, and by the hearty sympathy of many more.

But before I take upon myself so heavy an obligation, it is my bounden duty to entreat her Majesty's Government not to disregard the arguments which have led so many competent and honorable men to feel that our country's honor is not satisfied, whilst a mystery which has excited the sympathy of the civilized world, remains uncleared. Nor less would I entreat you to consider what must be the unsatisfactory consequences, if any endeavors should be made to quench all further efforts for this object.

It cannot be that this long-vexed question would thereby be set at rest, for it would still be true that in a certain circumscribed area within the Arctic circle, approachable alike from the east, and from the west, and sure to be attained by a combination of both movements, lies the solution of our unhappy countrymen's fate. While such is the case, the question will never die. I believe that again and again would efforts be made to reach that spot, and that the Government could not look on as unconcerned spectators, nor be relieved in public opinion of the responsibility they had prematurely cast off.

But I refrain from pursuing this argument, though, if any illustration were wanting of its truth, I think it might be found in the events that are passing before our eyes.

It is now about two years ago that one of Her Majesty's Arctic ships was abandoned in the ice. In due time this ship floated away, was picked up by an American whaler, carried into an American port, and (all property in her having been relinquished by the Admiralty) was purchased of her rescuers by the American Government, by whom she has been lavishly re-equipped, and is now on her passage to

England, a free gift to the Queen. The 'Resolute' is about
to be delivered up in Portsmouth harbor, not merely in evidence of the cordial relation existing between the two countries, but as a lively token of the deep interest and sympathy of the Americans in that great cause of humanity
in which they have so nobly borne their part. The resolution of Congress expressly states this motive, and indeed
there could be no other, as it is well known that for any
other purpose but the Arctic service those equipments would
be perfectly useless and require removal.

My Lord, you will not let this rescued and restored ship,
emblematic of so many enlightened and generous sentiments,
fail, even partially, in her significant mission. I venture to
hope that she will be accepted in the spirit in which she is
sent. I humbly trust that the American people, and especially that philanthropic citizen who has spent so largely of
his private fortune in the search for the lost ships, and to
whom was committed by his Government the entire charge
of the equipment of the 'Resolute,' will be rewarded for
this signal act of sympathy, by seeing her restored to her
original vocation, so that she may bring back from the
Arctic seas, if not some living remnant of our long-lost
countrymen, yet at least the *proofs* that they have nobly
perished.

I need not add that we have as yet no proofs, whatever
may be our melancholy forebodings. That such is the fact,
in a legal point of view, is shown by a case now or lately
pending in the Scotch courts, in which the right of succession to a considerable property is not admitted, on account
of the absence of all but conjectural testimony. In this
aspect of the question I have no personal interest, but it is
one that may not be deemed unworthy of your Lordship's
attention, combined as it must be with the fact that our
most experienced Arctic officers are willing to stake their
reputation upon the feasibility of reaching the spot where so

many secrets lie buried, if only they are supplied with the adequate means.

It would be a waste of words to attempt to refute again the main objections that have been urged against a renewed search, as involving extraordinary danger and risking life. The safe return of our officers and men cannot be denied, neither will it be disputed that each succeeding year diminishes the risk of casualty; and indeed, I feel it would be especially superfluous and unseasonable to argue against this particular objection, or against the financial one which generally accompanies it, at a moment when new expeditions for the glorious interests of science, and which every true lover of science and of his country must rejoice in, are contemplated for the interior of Africa and other parts which are far less favorable to human life than the icy regions of the north.

But with respect to expenditure, I may perhaps be allowed, as I have alluded to that topic, again to call to your Lordship's attention that the 'Resolute' is ready equipped for Arctic service by the munificence of another nation, and to add that other Arctic ships, equally well fitted for the purpose, are lying useless in Her Majesty's dockyards, along with accumulated Arctic stores brought back by the late expeditions, and therefore long since included in the navy estimates; and which, besides, are available only for Arctic service, and, if sold, would be bought at only nominal prices. In addition to the above sources of supply are those already existing on the Arctic shores, which are now studded with depots of provisions and fuel, left from the last and former expeditions, and fit as ever for use, because of the conservative properties of the climate.

But even were the expenditure greater than can thus reasonably be expected, I submit to your Lordship that this is a case of no ordinary exigency. These 135 men of the 'Erebus' and 'Terror' (or perhaps I should rather say the greater part of them, since we do not yet know that there are no survivors) have laid down their lives, after sufferings doubtless of unexampled severity, in the service of their country, as truly as if they had perished by the rifle, the cannon-ball, or the bayonet. Nay, more — by attaining the northern and already-surveyed coast of America, it is clear that they solved the problem which was the object of their labors, or, in the beautiful words of Sir John Richardson, that "they forged the last link of the North-West passage with their lives."

Surely, then, I may plead for such men, that a careful search be made for any possible survivor, that the bones of the dead be sought for and gathered together, that their buried records be unearthed, or recovered from the hands of the Esquimaux, and above all, that their last written words, so precious to their bereaved families and friends, be saved from destruction. A mission so sacred is worthy of a government which has grudged and spared nothing for its heroic soldiers and sailors in other fields of warfare, and will surely be approved by our gracious Queen, who overlooks none of Her loyal subjects suffering and dying for their country's honor.

This final and exhausting search is all I seek in behalf of the first and only martyrs to Arctic discovery in modern times, and it is all I ever intend to ask.

But if, notwithstanding all I have presumed to urge, Her Majesty's Government decline to complete the work they have carried on up to this critical moment, but leave it to private hands to finish, I must then respectfully request that measure of assistance in behalf of my own expedition which I have been led to expect on the authority of Lord Stanley, as communicated to me by Lord Wrottesley, and on that of the First Lord of the Admiralty, as communicated to Colonel Phipps in a letter in my possession.

It is with no desire to avert from myself the sacrifice of

my own funds, which I devote without reserve to the object
in view, that I plead for a liberal interpretation of those
communications, but I owe it to the conscientious and high-
minded Arctic officers who have generously offered me their
services, that my expedition should be made as efficient as
possible, however restricted it may be in extent.   The Admiralty, I feel sure, will not deny me what may be necessary
for this purpose, since, if I do all I can with my own means,
any deficiences and shortcomings of a private expedition
cannot I think be justly laid to my charge.

In conclusion, I would earnestly entreat of Her Majesty's
Government, while this subject is still under deliberation,
that they would be pleased to obtain the opinions of those
persons who, in consequence of their practical knowledge
and vast experience, may be considered best qualified to
express them in the present emergency.   And as it must be
in the ranks of those officers who would naturally be selected
for command of any final expedition that these qualifications
will most assuredly be found, I trust I may be pardoned for
directing your Lordship's attention to the names (which I
put down in the order of their seniority) of Captains Collinson, Richards, McClintock, Maguire, and Osborn.   All
these officers have passed winter after winter in Arctic service,
have carried out those skillful sledge operations which have
added so much to our knowledge of Arctic Geography,
and have ever, in the exercise of combined courage and
discretion, avoided disaster, and brought home their crews
in health and safety.

I commit the prayer of this letter, for the length of which
I beg much to apologize, to your Lordship's patient and
kind consideration, feeling assured that, however the burden
of it may pall upon the ear of some, who apparently judge
of it neither by the heart nor by the head, you will not on
that or on any light ground, hastily dismiss it.   Rather
may you be impelled to feel that the shortest and surest

way to set the importunate question at rest, is to submit it
to that final investigation which will satisfy the yearnings
of surviving relatives and friends, and, what is justly of
higher import to your Lordship, the credit and honor of
the country.

I have the honor to be, etc.,

JANE FRANKLIN.

The Right Hon. Viscount Palmerston, K.G.

18

No. II.

MEMORIAL TO THE RIGHT HON. VISCOUNT PALMERSTON, M. P., G.C.B.

London, June 5th, 1856.

IMPRESSED with the belief that Her Majesty's missing ships, the 'Erebus' and 'Terror,' or their remains, are still frozen up at no great distance from the spot whence certain relics of Sir John Franklin and his crews were obtained by Dr. Rae,—we whose names are undersigned, whether men of science and others who have taken a deep interest in Arctic discovery, or explorers who have been employed in the search for our lost countrymen, beg earnestly to impress upon your Lordship the desirableness of sending out an Expedition to satisfy the honor of our country, and clear up a mystery which has excited the sympathy of the civilized world.

This request is supported by many persons well versed in Arctic surveys, who, seeing that the proposed Expedition is to be directed *to one limited area only*, are of opinion that the object is attainable, and with little risk.

We can scarcely believe that the British Government, which to its great credit has made so many efforts in various directions to discover even the route pursued by Franklin, should cease to prosecute research, now that the locality has been clearly indicated where the vessels or their remains must lie,—including, as we hope, records which will throw fresh light on Arctic geography, and dispel the obscurity in which the voyage and fate of our countrymen are still involved.

Although most persons have arrived at the conclusion that there can now be no survivors of Franklin's Expedition, yet there are eminent men in our own country and in

America who hold a contrary opinion.   Dr. Kane, of the United States, for example, who has distinguished himself by pushing farther to the north in search of Franklin than any other individual, and to whom the Royal Geographical Society has recently awarded its Founder's Gold Medal, thus speaks (in a letter to the benevolent Mr. Grinnell) :— "I am really in doubt as to the preservation of human life. I well know how glad I would have been, had my duty to others permitted me, to have taken refuge among the Esquimaux of Smith Strait and Etah Bay.   Strange as it may seem to you, we regarded the coarse life of these people with eyes of envy, and did not doubt but that we could have lived in comfort upon their resources.   It re-quired all my powers, moral and physical, to prevent my men from deserting to the Walrus Settlements, and it was my final intention to have taken to Esquimaux life had Providence not carried us through in our hazardous escape."

But passing from speculation, and confining ourselves alone to the question of finding the missing ships or their records, we would observe that no land Expedition down the Back River, like that which, with great difficulty, re-cently reached Montreal Island, can satisfactorily accom-plish the end we have in view.   The frail birch-bark canoes in which Mr. Anderson conducted his search with so much ability, the dangers of the river, the sterile nature of the tract near its embouchure, and the necessary failure of provisions, prevented the commence-ment, even, of such a search as can alone be satisfactorily and thoroughly accomplished by the crew of a man-of-war, —to say nothing of the moral influence of a strong armed party remaining in the vicinity of the spot until the confi-dence of the natives be obtained.

Many Arctic explorers, independent of those whose names are appended, and who are absent on service, have expressed their belief that there are several routes by which a *screw*-vessel could so closely approach the area in question as to clear up all doubt.

In respect to one of these courses, or that by Behring Strait, along the coast of North America, we know that a single sailing vessel passed to Cambridge Bay, within 150 miles of the mouth of the Back River, and returned home unscathed,—its commander having expressed his conviction that the passage in question is so constantly open that ships can navigate it without difficulty in one season. Other routes, whether by Regent Inlet, Peel Sound, or across from Repulse Bay, are preferred by officers whose experience in Arctic matters entitles them to every consideration; whilst in reference to two of these routes it is right to state that vast quantities of provisions have been left in their vicinity.

Without venturing to suggest which of these plans should be adopted, we earnestly beg your Lordship to sanction without delay such an expedition as, in the judgment of a Committee of Arctic voyagers and Geographers, may be considered best adapted to secure the object.

We would ask your Lordship to reflect upon the great difference between a clearly-defined voyage to a narrow and circumscribed area, within which the missing vessels or their remains must lie, and those formerly necessarily tentative explorations in various directions, the frequent allusions to the difficulty of which, in regions far to the north of the voyage now contemplated, have led persons unacquainted with geography to suppose that such a modified and limited attempt as that which we propose involves farther risk and may call for future researches. The very nature of the former expeditions exposed them, it is true, to risk, since regions had to be traversed which were totally unknown; while the search we ask for is to be directed to a circumscribed area, the confines of which have already been reached without difficulty by one of Her Majesty's vessels.

Now, inasmuch as France, after repeated fruitless efforts to ascertain the fate of La Perouse, no sooner heard of the discovery of some relics of that eminent navigator, than she sent out a Searching Expedition to collect every fragment pertaining to his vessels, so we trust that those Arctic researches which have reflected much honor upon our country may not be abandoned at the very moment when an explanation of the wanderings and fate of our lost navigators seems to be within our grasp.

In conclusion, we further earnestly pray that it may not be left to the efforts of individuals of another and kindred nation, already so distinguished in this cause, nor yet to the noble-minded widow of our lamented friend, to make an endeavor which can be so much more effectively carried out by the British Government.

We have the honor to be, &c.,

F. Beaufort,
R. I. Murchison,
F. W. Beechey,
Wrottesley,
E. Sabine,
Egerton Ellsmere,
W. Whewell,
R. Collinson,
W. H. Sykes
C. Daubeny,
J. Fergus,
P. E. de Stzrelecki,
W. H. Smyth,
A. Majendie,
R. Fitzroy,
E. Gardiner Fishbourne,
R. Brown,
G. Macartney.

L. Horner,
W. H. Fitton,
Lyon Playfair,
T. Thorp.
C. Wheatstone,
W. J. Hooker,
J. D. Hooker,
J. Arrowsmith,
P. La Trobe,
W. A. B. Hamilton,
R. Stephenson,
J. E. Portlock,
C. Piazzi Smyth,
C. W. Pasley,
G. Rennie,
J. P. Gassiot,
G. B. Airy,
J. F. Burgoyne.

The following officers of the Royal Navy, who have been employed in the search after Franklin, and who are now absent from London, have previously expressed themselves to be favorable to the final expedition above recommended :—

Captains Sir JAMES C. Ross, and Sir EDWARD BELCHER;
Commodore KELLETT;
Captains AUSTIN,
 BIRD,
 OMANNEY,
 Sir ROBERT M'CLURE,
 SHERARD OSBORN,
 INGLEFIELD,

Captains MAGUIRE,
 M'CLINTOCK, and
 RICHARDS;
Commanders ALDRICH,
 MECHAM,
 TROLLOPE, and
 CRESSWELL;
Lieutenants HAMILTON
 and PIM.

No. III.

LIST OF RELICS OF THE FRANKLIN EXPEDITION,

Brought to England in the 'Fox,' by Captain M'CLINTOCK.

RELICS brought from the boat found in lat. 69° 08′ 43″ N., long. 99° 24′ 42″ W., upon the West Coast of King William Island, May 30, 1859 :—

Two double-barrelled guns, one barrel in each is loaded. Found standing up against the side in the after part of the boat.

A small Prayer Book; cover of a small book of 'Family Prayers;' 'Christian Melodies,' an inscription within the cover to "G. G." (Graham Gore?); 'Vicar of Wakefield;' a small Bible, interlined in many places, and with numerous references written in the margin; a New Testament in the French language.

Two table knives with white handles—one is marked "W. R. ;" a gimlet; an awl; two iron stanchions, 9 inches long, for supporting a weather cloth, which was round the boat.

26 pieces of silver plate—11 spoons, 11 forks, and 4 teaspoons; 3 pieces of thin elmboard (tingles) for repairing the boat, and measuring 11 inches by 6 inches, and 3-10ths inch thick.

Piece of canvas :—Bristles for shoemaker's use, bullets, short clay pipe, roll of waxed twine, a wooden button, small piece of a port-fire, two charges of shot tied up in the finger of a kid glove, fragment of a seaman's blue serge frock. Covers of a small Testament and Prayer Book, part of a grass cigar-case, fragment of a silk handkerchief, thread-case, piece of scented soap, three shot charges in kid glove fingers, a belted bullet, a piece of silk pocket handkerchief. Two pairs of goggles, made of stout leather and wire gauze, instead of glass; a sailmaker's palm, two small brass pocket compasses, a snooding line rolled up on a piece of leather, a needle and thread case, a bayonet scabbard altered into a sheath for a knife, tin water bottle for the pocket, two shot pouches (full of shot).

The spring hooks of sword belts, a gold lace band, a piece of thin gold twist or cord, a pair of leather goggles with crape instead of glass; a small green crape veil.

Two small packets of blank cartridge in green paper, part of a cherry-stick pipe stem, piece of a port-fire, a few copper nails, a leather bootlace, a seaman's clasp-knife, two small glass stoppered bottles (full), three glasses of spectacles, part of a broken pair of silver spectacles, German silver pencil case, a pair of silver (?) forceps, such as a naturalist might use for holding or seizing small insects, etc.; a small pair of scissors rolled up in blank paper, and to which adheres a printed government paper, such as an officer's warrant or appointment; a spring hook of a sword belt, a brass charger for holding two charges of shot.

A small bead purse, piece of red sealing-wax, stopper of a pocket flask, German silver top and ring, brass matchbox, one of the glasses of a telescope, a small tin cylinder, probably made to hold lucifer matches; a linen bag of percussion caps of three sizes, a very large and old-fashioned kind, stamped "Smith's patent;" a cap with a flange similar to the present musket caps used by Government, but smaller; and ordinary sporting caps of the smallest size.

Five watches.

A pair of blue glass spectacles, or goggles, with steel frame, and wire gauze encircling the glasses, in a tin case.

A pemmican tin, painted lead color, and marked "E." (Erebus) in black. From its size it must have contained 20lb. or 22lb.

Two yellow glass beads, a glass seal with symbol of Freemasonry.

A 4-inch block, strapped, with copper hook and thimble, probably for the boat's sheet.

Relics seen in lat. 69° 09′ N., long. 99° 24′ W., not brought away, 30th of May, 1859 :—

A large boat measuring 28 ft. in extreme length, 7 ft. 3 in. in breadth, 2 ft. 4 in. in depth. The markings on her stem were—"XXI. W. Con. N61., APr. 184." It appears that the fore part of the stem has been cut away, probably to reduce weight, and part of the letters and figures removed. An oak sledge under the boat, 23 ft. 4 in. long, and 2 ft. wide; 6 paddles, about 60 fathoms of deep-sea lead line, ammunition, 4 cakes of navy chocolate, shoemaker's box with implements complete, small quantities of tobacco, a small pair of very stout shooting boots, a pair of very heavy iron-shod knee boots, carpet boots, sea boots and shoes—in all seven or eight pairs; two rolls of sheet lead, elm tingles for repairing the boat, nails of various sizes for boat, and sledge irons, three small axes, a broken saw, leather cover of a sextant case, a chain-cable punch, silk handkerchiefs (black, white, and colored), towels, sponge, tooth-brush, hair comb, a mackintosh gun cover (marked in paint "A. 12 "), twine, files, knives; a small worsted-work slipper, lined with calf-skin, bound with red riband; a great quantity of clothing, and a wolf-skin robe; part of a boat's sail of No. 8 canvas, whale-line rope with yellow mark, and white line with red mark; 24 iron stanchions, 9 1-2 inches high, for supporting a weather cloth round the boat; a stanchion for supporting a ridge pole at a height of 3 ft. 9 in. above the gunwale.

Relics found about Ross Cairn, on Point Victory, May and June, 1859, brought away :—

A 6-inch dip circle by Robinson, marked I 22. A case of medicines, consisting of 25 small bottles, canister of pills, ointment, plaster, oiled silk, etc. A 2-foot rule, two joints of the cleaning rod of a gun, and two small copper spindles, probably for dog-vanes of boats. The circular brass plate broken out of a wooden gun-case, and engraved " C. H. Osmer, R. N." The field glass and German silver top of a 2-foot telescope, a coffee canister, a piece of a brass curtain rod. The record tin and the record, dated 25th of April, 1848. A 6-inch double frame sextant, on which the owner's name is engraved, " Frederick Hornby, R. N."

Found in a small cairn on the south side of Back Bay :—

A tin record case and record.

Seen about Ross Cairn, Point Victory, not brought away :—

Four sets of boat's cooking apparatus complete, iron hoops, 4 feet of a copper lightning conductor, hollow brass curtain-rod three quarters of an inch in diameter, 3 pickaxes, 1 shovel, old canvas, a pile of warm clothing and blankets 4 feet high, 2 tin canteens stamped " 89 Co., Wm. Hedges," " 88 Co., Wm. Heather," and a third one not marked. A small pannikin, made on board out of a 2lb. preserved-meat tin, marked " W. Mark ;" a small deal box for gun wadding, the heavy iron work of a large boat, part of a canvas tent, part of an oar sawed longitudinally and a blanket nailed to its flat side, three boat-hook staves, strips of copper, a 9-inch single block strapped, a piece of rope and spunyarn. Among the clothing was found a stocking marked " W." green, and a fragment of one marked " W. S."

Relics obtained at the Northern Cairn, near Cape Felix, May, 1859 :

Fragments of a boat's ensign, metal lid of a powder-case, two eye pieces of sextant tubes, brass button ; worsted glove, colors red, white and blue ; bung-stave of a marine's water keg or bottle, brass ornaments to a marine's shako ; brass screw for screwing down lid, also a copper hinge of the lid of powder-case ; a few patent wire cartridges containing large shot ; part of a pair of steel spectacles, glass being replaced by wood, having a narrow slit in it : two small rib bones, probably out of salt pork ; six or eight packets of needles ; small flannel cartridge containing an ounce of damaged powder ; a small, roughly made copper apparatus for cooking; some brimstone matches; piece of white paper folded up found in the North Cairn, two pike-heads, narrow strip of white paper, found under one of the tent places : their tent places were within a few yards of the cairn.

Beside a small cairn, about three miles north of Point Victory, was a pickaxe, with broken handle; brought away an empty tea or coffee canister.

Articles noticed about the North Cairn, not brought away :

Fragments of two broken bottles, several pieces of broken basins or cups, blue and white delfware, hoops of marine's water keg, small iron hoops, fragments of white line, spun yarn, canvas, and twine; three small canvas tents, under which lay a bearskin and fragments of blankets; two blanket frocks, several old mitts, stockings, gloves, pilot cloth, and box cloth jackets and trousers, large shot, piece of tobacco and broken pipe, metal part of powder-case, top of tin canister, marked "cheese," preserved-potato tin, feathers of ptarmigan, and salt meat bones.

Seen near Cape Maria Louisa :

Part of a drift tree, white spruce fir, 18 feet long, 10 inches in diameter; it appeared to have but recently (i. e. since thrown on the coast) been sawed longitudinally down the centre, and one-half of it removed.

Relics obtained from the Boothian Esquimaux, near the Magnetic Pole, in March and April, 1859.

Seven knives made by the natives out of materials obtained from the last expedition, one knife without a handle, one spear-head and staff (the latter has broken off), two files, a large spoon or scoop, the handle of pine or bone, the bowl of musk-ox horn; six silver spoons and forks, the property of Sir John Franklin, Lieutenants H. D. Vescomte and Fairholme, A. M'Donald, Assistant-Surgeon, and Lieutenant F. Couch (supposed from the initial letter T and crest a lion's head); a small portion of a gold watch-chain, a broken piece of ornamental work apparently silver gilt, a few small naval and other metal buttons, a silver medal obtained by Mr. M'Donald as a prize for superior attainments at a medical examination in Edinburg, April, 1838; some bows and arrows, in which wood, iron, or copper has been used in the construction—of no other interest.

REMARKS UPON THESE ARTICLES.

The spear-staff measures 6 feet 3 inches in length, and appears to have been part of a light boat's gunwale; it measured (before being partially rounded to adapt it to its present use,) about 1½ by 1¾ inches, is made of English oak, and upon the side has been painted white over green. The spear-head is of steel, riveted to two pieces of hoop, with bone between, and lashed on to the staff. The rivets are of copper nails. The native who sold it said he himself got it from the boat in Fish River. Another spear of the same kind was seen. The knives are made either of iron or steel, riveted to two strips of hoop, between which the handle of wood is inserted, and rivets passed through, securing them together.

The rivets are almost all made out of copper nails, such as would be found in a copper-fastened boat, but those which have been examined do not bear the Government mark. It is probable that most of the boats of the 'Erebus' and 'Terror' were built by contract, and therefore would not have the broad arrow stamped upon their iron and copper work. One small knife appears to have been a surgical instrument. A large knife obtained in April bears some marking, such as a sword or a cutlass might have. The man who sold it said he bought it from another, who picked it up on the land where the ship was driven ashore by the ice, and where the white people had thrown it away; it was then about as long as his arm. This was the first information he received of one of the ships having drifted on shore. One knife and one file are stamped with the broad arrow. The handles are variously composed of oak, ash, pine, mahogany, elm, and bone. The spoons and forks were readily sold for a few needles each, also the buttons, which they wore as ornaments on their dresses. Bows and arrows were readily exchanged for knives. Previously to the stranding on the neighboring shore of the last expedition these people must have been almost destitute of wood or iron. Some of them had even got only bone knives and spear-points. Some of their sledges were seen, consisting of two rolls of seal-skin, flattened and frozen, to serve as runners, and connected together by cross-bars of bones. Many more knives, bows and buttons, similar to those brought away might have been obtained, but no personal or important relics.

Seen in a Snow Hut in lat. 70½ deg. N., 20th of April, 1859, not brought away :

Two wooden shovels, one of them made of mahogany board, some spear-handles and a bow of English wood, a deal case which might have served for a telescope or barometer. Its external dimensions were :— length, 3 ft. 1 in.; depth, 3½ in.; width, 9 in.; two brass hinges remained attached to it.

Relics obtained from the Esquimaux near Cape Norton, upon the East Coast of King William Island, in May, 1859 :

Two tablespoons ; upon one is scratched "W. W.," on the other "W. G. ;" these bear the Franklin crest ; two table forks, one bearing the Franklin crest ; the other is also crested, probably Captain Crozier's ; silversmith's name is " L. West ;" two teaspoons, one engraved "A. M. D." (A. M'Donald), the other bears the Fairholme crest and motto ; handle of a dessert knife, into which had been inserted a razor (since broken off) by Milliken, Strand ; buttons, wood and iron, were here in abundance, but as enough of these had already been obtained, no more were purchased.

Taken out of some deserted snow-huts near here, some scraps of different kinds of wood, such as could not be obtained from a boat—teak or African oak.

Found lying about the skeleton, 9 miles eastward of Cape Herschel, May, 1859 :—The tie of black silk neckerchief ; fragments of a double-breasted blue cloth waistcoat, with covered silk buttons, and edged with braid ; a scrap of a colored cotton shirt, silk-covered buttons of blue cloth great-coat ; a small clothes-brush ; a horn pocket-comb ; a leathern pocket-book, which fell to pieces when thawed and dried ; it contained 9 or 10 letters, a few leaves apparently blank ; a sixpence, dated 1831 ; and a half-sovereign, dated 1844.

Articles seen among the natives at Cape Norton, not purchased : Bows made of wood, knives, uniform and plain buttons, a sledge made of two long pieces of hard wood.

From beside an Esquimaux stone mark, on the east side of Montreal Island :—Part of a preserved-meat tin, painted red ; part of the rim of some strong copper case or vessel ; pieces of iron hoop, two pieces of flat iron, and iron hook bolt, a piece of sheet copper.

Articles seen about a snow-hut near Point Booth, not purchased : Eight or ten fir poles, varying from 5 feet to 10 feet in length, the stoutest being 2½ inches in diameter. Two wooden snow shovels, about 3½ feet long, and made of pieces of plank painted white or pale yellow ; it occurred to me that the pieces of plank might have been the bottom boards of a boat. There was abundance of wood fashioned into smaller articles.

Contents of Boat's Medicine Chest.

One bottle labeled as zinzib. R. pulv., full ; ditto, spirit. rect., empty ; ditto, mur. hydrarg., seven-eighths full ; ditto, ol. caryphyll., one-fifth full ; ditto, ipec. P. co., full ; ditto, ol. menth. pip., empty ; ditto. liq. am-mon. fort., three-quarters full; ditto, ol. olivac., full; ditto, tinct. opii. camph., three-quarters full; ditto, vin. sem. colch., full; ditto, quarter full; ditto, calomel, full (broken); ditto, hydrarg. bit. oxyd., full; ditto, pulv. gregor, full (broken); ditto, magnes. carb., full; ditto, camphor, full; two bottles tinc. tolut., each quarter full; one bottle ipec. R. pulv., full; ditto, jalap R. pulv., full; ditto, scammon. pulv., full; ditto, quinac bisulph., empty; ditto (not labeled), tinct. opii., three quarters full; one box (apparently) purgative pills, full; ditto, ointment, shrunk; ditto, emp. adhesiv., full; one probang, one pen wrapped up in lint, one lead pencil, one pewter syringe, two small tubes (test) wrapped up in lint, one farthing, bandages oil silk, lint, thread.

No. IV.

GEOLOGICAL ACCOUNT OF THE ARCTIC ARCHIPELAGO.

DRAWN UP PRINCIPALLY FROM THE SPECIMENS COLLECTED BY

CAPTAIN F. L. M'CLINTOCK, R. N.

From 1849 to 1859.

BY THE REV. SAMUEL HAUGHTON, F. R. S.,

Fellow of Trinity College, Professor of Geology in the University of Dublin, and
President of the Geological Society of Dublin.

THE map which accompanies this geological description
is arranged from the specimens brought home by Captain
F. L. M'Clintock, R. N., from the four Arctic Expeditions
in which he served from 1848 to 1859. These specimens
are all deposited in the Museum of the Royal Dublin Society, and form a more extensive and better collection of
Arctic rocks and fossils than is to be found in any other
museum in Europe.

It will be most convenient to describe the geology of the
Arctic Islands by the formations which are to be found
there, which are the following :—

1. The Granitic and Granitoid Rocks.
2. The Upper Silurian Rocks.
3. The Carboniferous Rocks.
4. The Lias Rocks.
5. The Superficial deposits.

I shall describe these successive formations briefly, and
add a few remarks of a theoretical character, to indicate
the important inferences which may be drawn from the facts
respecting them made known to us by M'Clintock's discoveries.

I.—*The Granitic and Granitoid Rocks.*

These rocks form a considerable part of North Greenland, on the east side of Baffin's Bay, and constitute the rock of the country at the east side of the island of North Devon, which forms a portion of the coast-line of the west of Baffin's Bay, and the north side of the entrance into Lancaster Sound.

1. *Whale Fish Islands*, lat. 69° N., are composed of a very fine-grained, flaggy, black mica schist, composed of black mica in very small plates, occasionally putting on a hornblendic lustre, and minute grains of quartz interstratified with the mica. The softer varieties are cut by the natives into grissets and cooking utensils of various shapes, some of which resemble the cambstones found in Ireland, which are made from a kind of potstone, abundant in parts of the County Donegal.

2. *Upernavik*, lat. 72° N., Greenland.—This district is famous for the occurrence of large quantities of plumbago, which is found in a metamorphic rock of the following character. Fine-grained, amorphous, granitoid rock, composed of minute particles of grey quartz; a honey-colored felspar of waxy lustre, of unknown composition: minute particles of red semitransparent garnet, of conchoidal fracture; and small particles, with occasional large nests, of plumbago. The plumbago occurs both amorphous, and in long acicular crystals. Sometimes the rock becomes of coarser texture and more crystalline, and the yellow color of the felspar gives place to a greenish tinge; and it sometimes also becomes a felspar of perfect cleavage, semitransparent, and white. The dodecahedral crystals of garnet reach the diameter of one inch.

The general character of the rocks near Upernavik is different from that of the rock in which the plumbago is found; they consist of a fine-grained black mica schist, with very little felspar or quartz, and intersected by thin veins of elvan composed of quartz and white felspar. The cooking utensils of the natives are made from this fine schist, in preference to any other description of rock.

3. *Woman's Islands.*—These islands, off the west coast of Greenland, are composed of a garnetiferous mica slate, formed of black mica in layers, with alternating plates composed of white felspar and quartz, and filled with fine garnets, rose-colored, vitreous in fracture, and transparent.

4. *Cape York*, lat. 76° N., Greenland.—This cape is composed of a fine-grained granite, consisting of quartz, white felspar, with minute specks of a black mineral, of pitchy lustre, composition not yet determined.

5. *Wolstenholme and Whale Sounds*, lat. 77° N., Greenland.—At Wolstenholme Sound the granitoid rocks of Greenland become converted into mica slate and actinolite slate of a remarkable character. The mica slate is composed of large plates of an intimate mixture of black and white mica, the chemical examination of which will doubtless prove of interest. These plates of mica are separated by bands of pure white felspar. The actinolite slate is dark green, and formed by an almost insensible gradation from the mica slate. In the low ground between Wolstenholme and Whale Sounds, the granitic rocks cease, and are covered by deposits of fine red gritty sandstone, of a banded structure, and a remarkable coarse white conglomerate. The boundary between these formations is also marked by the development of masses of dolerite and clayey basalt.

6. *Carey's Islands*, 76° 40′ N., Greenland, lie to the westward of Wolstenholme Sound, and are composed of a remarkable gneissose mica schist, formed of successive thin layers of quartz granules, containing scarcely any felspar, and layers of jet black mica, with occasional facets of white mica. This mica schist passes into a white gneiss, composed of quartz, white felspar, and black mica penetrated

by veins, coarsely crystalised, of the same minerals. Yellow and white sandstones are also found in small quantity on the islands, reposing upon the granitoid rocks.

7. *Capes Osborn and Warrender*, lat. 74° 30' N., North Devon.—The granitoid rocks between these two capes are composed of graphic granite, consisting of quartz (grey) and white felspar; this graphic granite passes into a laminated gneiss, consisting of layers of black mica and white translucent felspar, sparingly mixed with quartz: with the gneiss are interstratified beds of garnetiferous mica slate, consisting of quartz, pale greenish white felspar, black and white mica in minute spangles, and crystals of garnet, rose-colored, disseminated regularly through the mass. Quartziferous bands of epidotic hornstone occur with the foregoing beds; and the whole series is overlaid by red sandstones, of banded structure, which bear a striking resemblance to those that overlie the granitoid beds of Wolstenholme Sound.

8. *North Somerset.*—The granitoid rocks are found again on the west side of the island of North Somerset, where they form the eastern boundary of Peel Sound. Boulders of granite are found at a considerable distance (100 miles) to the north-eastward of the rock *in situ*, as at Port Leopold, Cape Rennell, etc. The general character of the granitic rocks in the north and west of North Somerset are thus described by Captain M'Clintock:—

Near Cape Rennell we passed a very remarkable rounded boulder of gneiss or granite; it was 6 yards in circumference, and stood near the beach, and some 15 or 20 yards above it; one or two masses of rounded gneiss, although very much smaller, had arrested our attention at Port Leopold, as then we knew of no such formation nearer than Cape Warrender, 130 miles to the north-east; subsequently we found it to commence *in situ* at Cape Granite, nearly 100 miles to the southwest of Port Leopold.

19

"The granite of Cape Warrender differs considerably from that of North Somerset; the former being a graphic granite, composed of grey quartz and white felspar, the quartz predominating; while the latter, or North Somerset granite, is composed of grey quartz red felspar, and green chloritic mica, the latter in large flakes; both the granite and gneiss of North Somerset are remarkable for their soapy feel."*

To the east of Cape Bunny, where the Silurian limestone ceases, and south of which the granite commences, is a remarkable valley called Transition Valley, from the junction of sandstone and limestone that takes place there. The sandstone is red, and of the same general character as that which rests upon the granitoid rocks at Cape Warrender and at Wolstenholme Sound. Owing to the mode of travelling, by sledge, on the ice, round the coast, no information was obtained of the geology of the interior of the country, but it appears highly probable that the granite of North Somerset, as well as that of the other localities mentioned, is overlaid by a group of sandstones and conglomerates, on which the Upper Silurian limestones repose directly. A low, sandy beach marks the termination of the valley northwards, and on this beach were found numerous pebbles, washed from the hills of the interior, composed

Cape Bunny, Peel Sound.

---

* Journal of the Royal Dublin Society, 1857.

of quartzose sandstone, carnelian, and Silurian limestone. The accompanying sketch was made by Captain M'Clintock, on the spot, in 1849, and afterwards finished by Lieutenant Browne. It represents the island called Cape Bunny, which forms the eastern headland of the entrance of the now famous Peel Sound, down which the 'Erebus' and 'Terror' sailed, three years before it was visited by Sir James C. Ross and Lieutenant M'Clintock, in their first sledge journey on the ice. Cape Granite is the northern boundary of the granite, which retains the same character as far as Howe Harbor. It is composed of quartz, red felspar, and dark green chlorite; and is accompanied with gneiss of the same composition. I have in my possession a specimen of this granite, found as a pebble at Graham Moore Bay, Bathurst Island, S. W., a locality 135 knots distant from Cape Granite, to the N. W.

9. *Bellot's Straits*, lat. 72° N., separate North Somerset from Boothia Felix. The 'Fox' Expedition wintered here in 1858, and had abundant means of ascertaining the geological structure of the neighborhood. The junction of the granitoid and Silurian rocks occurs in these straits, the low ground to the east being horizontal beds of Silurian limestone, while on the west the granite hills of West Somerset rise to a height of 1600 feet above the narrow straits. The granite here is of three varieties.

α. Blackish grey, fine grained, gneissose granite, composed of quartz, white felspar, and large quantities of fine grains and flakes of hornblende, passing into black mica. The gneissose beds of this granite dip 13° S. E.

β. A red granite, graphic texture, composed of quartz and red felspar, coarse grained.

λ. Syenite, composed of honey-yellow felspar and hornblende, in very large crystals, the felspar passing into red and pink, and the whole rock mass penetrated by veins of the same material, but fine grained. This variety of igne ous rock was met with principally at Pemmican Rock, western inlet of Bellot's Straits. Large quantities of hornblende are also met with at Leveque Harbor, Bellot's Straits, composed of facetted crystals agglutinated together into large masses, forming a crystalline hornblendic gneiss.

10. *Pond's Bay, Baffin's Bay*, lat. 72° 40' N.—In this locality a quartziferous black mica schist underlies the Silurian limestone, and is interstratified with gneiss and garnetiferous quartz rock, all in beds, inclined 38° W. S. W. (true).

11. *Montreal Island*, mouth of the Fish River, lat. 67° 45' N.—The granitoid rocks, which everywhere, in the Arctic Archipelago, underlie the Silurian limestone, appear at Montreal Island as a gneiss, composed of bands of felspar (pink) and quartz ($\frac{1}{4}$ inch thick), separated by thin plates composed altogether of black mica; the whole rock exhibiting the phenomena of foliation in a marked degree.

The east side of King William's Island, though composed of Silurian limestone like the rest of the island, is strewed with boulders of black and red micaceous gneiss, like that of Montreal Island, and black metamorphic clay slate, in which the crystals of mica (qu. Ottrelite) are just commencing to be developed. It is probable that the granitoid rocks appear at the surface somewhat to the eastward of this locality.

12. *Prince of Wales' Island*, west of Peel Sound.—The granitoid rocks extend across Peel Sound into Prince of Wales' Island, in the form of a dark syenite composed of quartz, greenish white felspar passing into yellow, and hornblende. This rock is massive and eruptive at Cape M'Clure, lat. 72° 52' N., and occasionally gneissose, as at lat. 72° 13' N. Between these two points, at lat. 72° 37' N., a limestone bluff occurs containing the characteristic Silurian fossils, and is succeeded at 72° 40' by a ferruginous limestone, bright red, and a few beds of fine red sandstone,

like those observed by M'Clintock at Transition Valley,
North Somerset. The entire western portion of Prince of
Wales' Land is composed of Silurian limestone, which in
the extreme west, at Cape Acworth, becomes chalky in character, and non-fossiliferous, resembling the peculiar Silurian limestone found on the West side of Boothia Felix.

II.—*The Silurian Rocks.*

The Silurian rocks of the Arctic Archipelago rest everywhere directly on the granitoid rocks, with a remarkable
red sandstone, passing into coarse grit for their base. This
sandstone is succeeded by ferruginous limestone, containing
rounded particles of quartz, which rapidly pass into a
fine greyish green earthy limestone, abounding in fossils,
and occasionally into a chalky limestone, of a cream color,
for the most part devoid of fossils. The average dip of
the Silurian limestone varies from 0° to 5° N. N. W., and
it forms occasionally high cliffs, and occasionally low flat
plains, terraced by the action of the ice as the ground
rose from beneath the sea. The general appearance of the
rocks is similar to the Dudley limestone, and would strike
even an observer who was not a geologist. This resemblance to the Upper Silurian beds extends to the structure
of the rocks on the large scale. Alternations of hard limestone and soft shale, so characteristic of the Upper Silurian
beds of England and America, arranged in horizontal layers, give to the cliffs around Port Leopold the peculiar appearance which has been described by different Polar navigators as "buttress-like," "castellated;" this appearance
is produced by the unequal weathering of the cliff, which
causes the hard limestone to stand out in bands. Excellent
sketches of this remarkable appearance, drawn by Lieutenant
Beechey, are figured at page 35 of Parry's First Voyage,
'Hecla' and 'Griper,' 1819–20. The Western side of King

William's Island (now, alas! invested with so sad an interest) is a good example of the low terraced form which the limestone rocks assume at times.

The following list contains the names of the principal fossils brought home by Captain M'Clintock :—

No. I. GARNIER BAY (Lat. 74° N.; Long. 91° W.)

1. *Cyathophyllum helianthoides,* several specimens.
2. *Heliolites porosa.* Garnier Bay. Another specimen from near Cape Bunny.
3. Specimens of carnelian, gneiss, chalcedony, etc., etc., from the shingle near Cape Bunny.
4. *Cromus Arcticus,* several specimens.
5. *Atrypa phoca* (Salter).
6. *Atrypa reticularis.*
7. Brachiopoda on slab (various).
8. Cyathophyllum.
9. *Columnaria Sutherlandi* (Salter). Several specimens.

No. II. PORT LEOPOLD (Lat. 73° 50' N.; Long. 90° 15' W.)

1. Limestone containing numerous fossils of the Upper Silurian type : *Calmopora Gothlandica,* Goldf. *Rhynchonella cuneata ?* Dalm. *Cyathophyllum,* sp.
2. Dark earthy limestone, containing multitudes of the *Loxonema M'Clintocki,* as casts—1000 feet above sea level on North-east Cape.
3. Fine specimens of selenite from shaly beds in cliff.
4. Fibrous gypsum from same.

No. III. GRIFFITH'S ISLAND (Lat. 74° 35' N.; Long. 95° 30' W.)

1. Beautiful specimens of the *Cromus Arcticus.* Pl. VI. Fig. 5, Journ. R. D. S., Vol. I.
2. *Orthoceras Griffithi.* Pl. V. Fig. 1, Journ. R. D. S., Vol. I.
3. An Orthoceras with lateral siphuncle, and simple circular outline of septa.
4. *Loxonema Rossi.* Pl. V. Figs. 6, 8, 9, 10, 11, Jour. R. D. S., Vol. I.
5. Numerous specimens of crinodial limestone.
6. *Strophomena Donnetti* (Salter). Sutherland's Voyage ; Pl. V. Figs. 11, 12.
7. *Atrypa phoca* (Salter). Pl. V. Figs. 3, 4, 7, Journ. R. D. S., Vol. 1; and a ribbed Atrypa, not identified with European species, and undescribed.
8. An undescribed bryozoan Zoophyte. Pl. VII. Fig. 6, Journ. R. D. S., Vol. I.

9. *Calophyllum Pragmoceras* (Salter).   Sutherland; Pl VI. Fig. 4.
10. *Syringopora geniculata.*
11. An undescribed species of *Macrocheilus.*

No. IV. BEECHEY ISLAND. (Lat. 74° 40' N.; Long. 92° W.)

1. Orthoceras (species).
2. Great multitudes of *Atrypa phoca*, forming, in fact, a dark-colored earthy Atrypa limestone.
3. With these were associated many species of Loxonema, sometimes so abundant as to form a pale pink and whitish Loxonema limestone.
4. A species of ribbed Atrypa.
5. Crinodial limestone in abundance.
6. *Syringopora reticulata.*
7. *Calophyllum phragmoceras* (Salter).   Sutherland; Pl. VI. Fig. 4.
8. *Cyathophyllum cœspitosum.*
9. *Cyathophyllnm articulatum* (Edwardes and Haime.)
10. *Calamopora Gothlandica.*
11. *Calamopora alveolaris.*
*12. *Favistella Franklini* (Salter).   Sutherland; Pl. VI. Fig. 3.
13. *Clisiophyllum Salteri.*   Sutherland; Pl. VI. Fig. 7.
14. *Cyathophyllum* (species).
15. *Loxonema Salteri*, described by Mr. Slater in Sutherland's 'Voyage to Wellington Channel;' Pl. V. Fig. 19.

This is a fine slab of limestone, almost altogether composed of the remains of *Loxonema Salteri* and *Atrypa phoca*. It appears to have been quietly deposited at the bottom of a deep submarine depression, swarming with the Pyramidellidæ and deep-water Brachiopoda. The physical conditions indicated by the fossils are also rendered probable by the rock itself, which consists of fine grey limestone, subcrystalline, and intimately blended with the finest and most delicate description of mud, such as could only be found where the water was deep, and all currents far removed.

No. V. CORNWALLIS ISLAND, Assistance Bay (Lat. 74° 40' N.; Long. 94° W.)

1. *Orthoceras Ommaneyi* (Salter).   Sutherland; Pl. V. Figs. 16, 17.
2. *Pentamerus conchidium* (Dalman).   Sutherland; Pl. V. Figs. 9, 10
3. Pentamerus limestone.
4. *Cromus Arcticus.*   Journ. R. D. S., Vol. I. Pl. VI.
5. *Cardiola Salteri.*   Pl. VII. Fig. 5.   Journ. R. D. S., Vol. I.
6. *Syringopora geniculata.*

No. VI.   CAPE YORK, Lancaster Sound (Lat. 73° 50′ N.; Long. 87° W.)

A specimen of the same fossil coral which I have named, doubtfully, from Beechey Island, as Favosites or *Calamopora Gothlandica;* it is not impossible, however, that it is not a Calamopora at all, but a species of Chætctes.

No. VII.   POSSESSION BAY; South entrance into Lancaster Sound (Lat. 73° 30′ N.; Long: 77° 20′ W.)

Specimens of brown earthy limestone, with a fetid smell when struck with a hammer; resembles closely the limestone of Cape York, Lancaster Sound.

No. VIII.   DEPOT BAY, Bellot's Straits (Lat. 72° N.; Long. 94° W.)

1. *Maclurea* sp.
2. *Cyathophyllum helianthoides* (Goldfuss).
   The limestone of this locality is white and saccharoid, with large rhombohedral crystals of calcspar.

* No. IX.   CAPE FARRAND, East side of Boothia (Lat. 71° 38′; Long. 93° 35′ W.)

1. *Atrypa phoca* (Salter).   Sutherland; Pl. V. Fig. 3.
2. *Loxonema Rossi.*   Journ. R. D, S., Vol. I. Pl. V.
3. *Atrypa* (ribbed sp.)
4. *Calamopora Gothlandica* (Goldfuss).
5. *Cyrtoceras* sp.
   The rock at this locality is grey mud limestone.

No. X. WEST SHORE OF BOOTHIA (Lat. 70° to 71° N.), containing the Magnetic Pole.

1. *Atrypa phoca* (Salter).
2. *Loxonema Rossi.*   Journ. R. D. S., Vol. I. Pl. V.
3. *Favistella Franklini* (Salter).   Journ. R. D. S., Vol. I. Pl. XI.
4. *Loxonema Salteri.*   Sutherland; Pl. V. Fig. 18.
   The cream-colored chalky limestone found on the west side of Prince of Wales' Island here occurs, and is generally destitute of fossils. like that of Prince of Wales' Land.

† No. XI. FURY POINT (Lat. 72° 50′ N.; Long. 92° W.)

1. *Cromus Arcticus.*   Journ. R. D. S., Vol. I. Pl. VI.
2. *Maclurea* sp.

---

* Collected by Dr. Walker, surgeon to the 'Fox' Expedition.
† Collected by Dr. Walker, surgeon to the 'Fox' Expedition.

3. *Mya rotundata* (?).
4. *Stromatopora concentrica*.
5. *Cyathophyllum helianthoides* (Goldfuss).
6 *Petraia bina*.
7 *Calamopora Gothlandica* (Goldfuss).
8 *Favosites megastoma* (?)
9. *Cyathophyllum cœspitosum*.
10. *Facistella Franklini* (Salter).   Sutherland; Pl. VI. Fig. 3.
11. *Strephodes Austini* (Salter).   Sutherland; Pl. VI. Fig. 6.
12. *Atrypa phoca* (Salter).

    The limestone here is of the same grey earthy aspect as at Beechey Island and Port Leopold.

* No. XII.   PRINCE OF WALES' LAND (Lat. 72° 88′ N.; Long.
                    97° 15′ W.)   —
1. *Cyathophyllum* sp.
2. *Calamopora Gothlandica* (Goldfuss).
3. *Stromatopora concentrica*.

    These fossils occur in grey earthy limestone, near its junction with the red arenaceous limestone already described.

No. XIII.   WEST COAST OF KING WILLIAM'S ISLAND.

1. *Loxonema Rossi*.   Journ. R. D. S., Vol. I. Pl. V.
2. *Catenipora escharoides*.
3. *Orthoceras* sp.
4. *Maclurea* sp.
5. *Atrypa* sp.
6. *Syringopora geniculata*.
7. *Clisiophyllum* sp.
8. *Orthis elegantula*.

III.—*The Carboniferous Rocks.*

The Upper Silurian limestones already described are suc-ceeded by a most remarkable series of close-grained white sandstones, containing numerous beds of highly bituminous coal, and but few marine fossils.   In fact, the only fossil shell found in these beds, so far as I know, in any part of the Arctic Archipelago, is a species of ribbed *Atrypa*, which I believe to be identical with the *Atrypa fallax* of the car-boniferous slate of Ireland.   These sandstone beds are suc-

---

* Collected by Captain Allen Young.

ceeded by a series of blue limestone beds, containing an
abundance of the marine shells commonly found in all parts
of the world where the carboniferous deposits are at all developed.   The line of junction of these deposits with the
Silurians on which they rest is N. E. to E. N. E. (true).
Like the former they occur in low flat beds, sometimes rising
into cliffs, but never reaching the elevation attained by the
Silurian rocks in Lancaster Sound.

The following lists contain the principal fossils and specimens presented to the Royal Dublin Society by Captain
M'Clintock and by Captain Sir Robert M'Clure :

> Coal, sandstone, clay ironstone, and brown hematite, were found
> along a line stretching E. N. E. from Baring Island, through the
> south of Melville Island, Byam Martin's Island, and the whole of
> Bathurst Island.   Carboniferous limestone, with characteristic fos-
> sils, was found along the north coast of Bathurst Island, and at Hil-
> lock Point, Melville Island.

I have marked on the map the coal-beds of the Parry
Islands, which appear to be prolonged into Baring Island,
as observed by Captain M'Clure.   The discovery of coal in
these islands is due to Parry, but the evidence of the extent
and quantity in which it may be found was obtained during
the expeditions of Austin and Belcher.   In addition to the
localities surveyed by himself, Captain M'Clintock has given
me specimens of the coal found at other places by other
explorers ; and it is from a comparison of all these specimens that I have ventured to lay down the out-crop of the
coal-beds, which agrees remarkably well with the boundary
of the formations laid down from totally different data.

No. I.   HILLOCK POINT, Melville Island (Lat. 76° N.; Long. 111°
45′ W.)

Productus sulcatus.   Journ. R. D. S., Vol. I. Pl. VII. Figs. 1, 2, 3,
4, 7.
Spirifer Arcticus.   Journ. R. D. S., Vol. I. Pl. IX.

No. II. BATHURST ISLAND, North Coast, Cape Lady Franklin (?)
(Lat. 76° 40' N.; Long. 98° 45' W.)

Spirifer Arcticus. Jour. R. D. S., Vol. I. Pl. IX. Fig. 1.
Lithostrotion basaltiforme.

* No. III. BALLAST BEACH, Baring Island (Lat. 74° 30' N.; Long.
121° W.)

1. Wood fossilized by brown hematite; structure quite distinct.
2. Cone of the spruce fir, fossilized by brown hematite.

No. IV. PRINCESS ROYAL ISLANDS, Prince of Wales' Strait, Baring Island (Lat. 72° 45' N.; Long. 117° 30' W.)

1. Nodules of clay ironstone, converted partially into brown hematite.
2. Native copper in large masses, procured from the Esquimaux in
Prince of Wales' Strait.
3. Brown hematite, pisolitic.
4. Greyish yellow sandstone, same as Cape Hamilton and Byam Martin's
Island.
5. *Terebratula aspera* (Schlotheim). Journ. R. D. S., Vol. I. Pl. IX.
Fig. 4.

This interesting brachiopod was found in the limestone
by Captain M'Clure, at the Princess Royal Islands, in the
Prince of Wales' Strait, between Baring Island and Prince
Albert Land. I have no hesitation in pronouncing it to be
identical with Schlotheim's fossil, which is found in the
greatest abundance at Gerolstein, in the Eifel. Banks'
Land, or Baring Island, is composed of sandstone, similar
to that at Byam Martin's Island, and at the Bay of Mercy.
This sandstone contains beds of coal, apparently the continuation of the well-known coal-beds of Melville Island.
It is a remarkable fact, that these carboniferous sandstones
underlie beds of undoubtedly the carboniferous limestone
type, and that at Byam Martin's Island, where fossils are
found in this sandstone, they are allied to *Atrypa fallax*
and other forms characteristic of the lower sandstones of
the carboniferous epoch. It is, therefore, highly probable

---

* These specimens are "*Drift*," but are mentioned here as they were
found on the carboniferous sandstone area.

that the coal-beds of Melville Island are very low down in the series, and do not correspond in geological position with the coal-beds of Europe, which rest on the summit of the carboniferous beds. It is interesting to find at Princess Royal Island, where, from the general strike of the beds, we should expect to find the Silurian limestone underlying the coal-bearing sandstones,˙that this limestone does occur, and contains a fossil, *T. aspera*, eminently characteristic of the Eifelian beds of Germany, which form, in that country, the Upper Silurian Strata.

No. V. CAPE HAMILTON, Baring Island (Lat. 74° 15′ N. · Long. 117ʳ 30′ W.).

1. Greyish-yellow sandstone, like that found *in situ* in Byam Martin's Island.

2. *Coal.*—The coal found in the Arctic regions, excepting that brought from Disco Island, West Greenland, which is of tertiary origin, presents everywhere the same characters, which are somewhat re-markable. It is of a brownish color and lignaceous texture, in fine layers of brown coal and jet-black glossy coal interstratified in delicate bands not thicker than paper. It has a woody ring under the hammer, recalling the peculiar clink of some of the valuable gas coals of Scotland. It burns with a dense smoke and brilliant flame, and would make an excellent gas coal; and, in fact, it re-sembles in many respects some varieties of the ˙coal which has acquired such celebrity in the Scotch and Prussian law-courts, under the title of the Torbane Hill mineral.

No. VI. CAPE DUNDAS, Melville Island (Lat. 74° 30′ N.; Long. 113° 46′ W.).

Fine specimens of coal.

No. VII. CAPE SIR JAMES ROSS, Melville Island (Lat. 74° 45′ N.; Long. 114° 30′ W.).

Sandstone passing into blue quartzite.

No. VIII. CAPE PROVIDENCE, Melville Island (Lat. 74° 20′ N.; Long. 112° 30′ W.).

A specimen of crinoidal limestone, apparently similar to that occur-ring in Griffith's Island, from which, however, it could not have been brought by the present drift of the floating ice, as the set of

the currents is constant from the west. If brought to its present position by ice, it must have been under circumstances differing considerably from those now prevailing in Barrow's Strait.
Yellowish-grey sandstone.
Clay ironstone passing into pisolitic hematite.

No. IX. WINTER HARBOR, Melville Island (Lat. 74° 35 N'.; Long. 110° 45' W.).

Fine yellow and grey sandstone.

No. X. BRIDPORT INLET, Melville Island (Lat. 75° N.; Long. 109° W.).

Coal, with impressions of Sphenopteris.
Ferruginous spotted white sandstone.
Clay ironstone, passing into brown hematite.

No. XI. SKENE BAY, Melville Island (Lat. 75° N.; Long. 108° W.).

Bituminous coal, with finely divided laminæ, associated with brown crystalline limestone, with cherty beds, and grey-yellowish sandstone, passing into brownish-red sandstone.

No. XII. HOOPER ISLAND, Liddon's Gulf, Melville Island (Lat. 75° 5' N.; Long. 112° W.).

Nodules of clay ironstone, very pure and heavy, associated with ferruginous fine sandstone and coal of the usual description.

The hill-tops and sides along the south shore of Liddon's Gulf, and as far as Cape Dundas, are generally bare, composed of frozen mud, arising from the disintegration of shale, the annual dissolving snows washing them down and giving them a rounded form. The southern slopes generally support vegetation. Fragments of coal are very frequently met with, and at the mouth of a ravine on the south shore of Liddon's Gulf there is abundance, of very good quality; it contains a considerable quantity of pyrites or bisulphuret of iron.

No. XIII. BYAM MARTIN'S ISLAND (Lat. 75° 10' N.; Long. 104° 15' W.).

Yellowish-grey sandstone, *in situ*, containing a ribbed *Atrypa*, allied to the *A. primipilaris* of V. Buch, and the *A fallax* of the carboniferous rocks of Ireland.

Reddish limestone, with broken fragments of shells, of the same
description of brachiopod as the last.

Coal of the usual description.

Fine-grained red sandstone, passing into red slate.

Scoriaceous hornblendic trap (boulders).

The sandstone of Byam Martin's Island is of two kinds—
one red, finely stratified, passing into purple slate, and very
like the red sandstone of Cape Bunny, North Somerset, and
some varieties of the red sandstone and slate found between
Wolstenholme Sound and Whale Sound, West Greenland,
lat. 77° N. The other sandstone of Byam Martin's Island
is fine, pale-greenish, or rather greyish-yellow, and not distinguishable in hand specimens from the sandstone of Cape
Hamilton, Baring Island. It contains numerous shells and
casts of a terebratuliform brachiopod, closely allied to the
Terebratula primipilaris of Von Buch, found abundantly
at Gerolstein in the Eifel. On the whole, I incline to the
opinion that the sandstones, limestone, and coal of Byam
Martin's Island, are the corresponding rocks of Melville
Island, Baring Island, and Bathurst Island, are low down
in the Carboniferous System, and that there is in these
northern coal-fields no subdivision into red sandstone, limestone, and coal-measures, such as prevails in the west of
Europe. If the different points where coal was found be
laid down on a map, we have in order, proceeding from the
south-west—Cape Hamilton, Baring Island; Cape Dundas,
Melville Island, south; Bridport Inlet and Skene Bay, Melville Island; Schomberg Point, Graham Moore Bay, Bathurst Island; a line joining all these points is the outcrop
of the coal-beds of the south of Melville Island, and runs
E. N. E. At all the localities above mentioned, and, indeed, in every place where coal was found, it was accompanied by the greyish-yellow and yellow sandstone already
described, and by nodules of clay ironstone, passing into
brown hematite, sometimes nodular and sometimes pisolitic
in structure.

No. XIV. GRAHAM MOORE'S BAY, Bathurst Island (Lat 75° 30′ N.; Long. 102° W.).

Coal of the usual quality.

At Cape Lady Franklin, and at many other localities along the north shore of Bathurst Island, carboniferous fossils in limestone, clay ironstone balls passing into brown hematite, cherty limestone, and earthy fossiliferous limestone, with the same species of *Atrypa* as at Byam Martin's Island, were found in abundance by Sherard Osborn, Esq., Commander of H. M. S. 'Pioneer,' in whose journal the following note respecting them may be found :—

"The above collection was delivered over to Captain Sir Edward Belcher, C. B., by Commander Richards, at 2 P. M., on 7th Nov., 1853." *

It is to be hoped that they may soon be made available for the elucidation of the geology of this most interesting portion of the Arctic discoveries.

No. XV. BATHURST ISLAND, Bedford Bay (Lat. 75° N.; Long. 95° 50′ W.).

In this locality abundance of vesicular scoriaceous trap rocks were found by Captain M'Clintock; they appear to me to be the representatives of the volcanic rocks found everywhere at the commencement of the carboniferous period.

No. XVI. CORNWALLIS ISLAND, M'Dougall Bay.

1. *Syringopora geniculata.* Journ. R. D. S., Vol. I. Pl. XI. Fig. 2.
2. *Cardiola Salteri.* Journ. R. D. S., Vol. I. Pl. VII. Fig. 5.

The Syringopore found at Cornwallis Island appears to be identical with the variety of the Irish carboniferous *S. geniculata,* in which the corallites are at a distance from each other somewhat exceeding their diameters, and in which the connecting tubes are about two diameters apart.

A question of very considerable geological interest is

---

* *Vide* Arctic Expeditions, 1854–55, p. 254.

raised by the occurrence together of coral, in the same locality, of silurian and carboniferous forms.

I entertain no doubt of their being *in situ*, and occurring in the same beds, for the following reasons :

1st. The Syringopores of Griffith's Island were found at an elevation of 400 feet above the sea, and, therefore, could not be brought by drifting ice.

2nd. The specimens were apparently of the same texture and composition as the native rock, whenever the latter was visible from under the snow.

3rd. I do not believe in the lapse of a long interval of time between the silurian and carboniferous deposits,—in fact, in a Devonian period.

4. The same blending of corals has been found in Ireland, the Bas Boulonnais, and in Devonshire, where silurian and carboniferous forms are of common occurrence in the same localities.

5th. In the carboniferous beds proper of Melville Island and Bathurst Island, there were not found, so far as I am aware, any corals of the same character as those at Griffith's Island, Cornwallis Island, and Beechey Island, which could give a supply to be drifted to the latter localities in a Pleistocene sea. It is plain, from the height at which the corals were found that, if they were brought to their present localities by ice, it must have been during the period known as Post-tertiary, as the present conditions of drift-ice in Barrow's Straits do not permit us to suppose them to have been placed where we now find them by existing causes.

The occurrence of coal-beds in such high latitudes has been speculated on by many geologists—in my opinion, not very satisfactorily ; as it is very difficult to conceive how, even if the question of temperature was settled, plants even of the fern and lycopodium type could exist during the darkness of the long winter's night at Melville Island. This difficulty is increased by the facts made known to us by the discovery of ammonites and lias fossils in Prince Patrick's Island by Captain M'Clintock.

IV.—*The Lias Rocks.*

Many years ago it was asserted by Lieutenant Anjou, of the Russian Navy, that ammonites had been found by him in the cliffs on the south shore of the island of New Siberia, off the north coast of Asia, in lat 74° N. This statement, which was published in Admiral Von Wrangle's journal, attracted but little attention, until it was confirmed, as far as probability of such fossils occurring at so high a latitude is concerned, by the remarkable discovery of smilar fossils by Captain M'Clintock, in lat. 76° 20′ N., at Point Wilkie, in Prince Patrick's Island.

In a paper, published by the Royal Dublin Society, in the first volume of their journal, p. 223, Captain M'Clintock thus describes the finding of these fossils:

"After returning to Cape de Bray, we took up the provisions that the officer after whom it is called had left for us, and crossed the strait to Point Wilkie; reached it on the 14th May. This traverse was the more difficult from the great load upon our sledge, and the unfavorable state of the ice and snow. The freshly fallen snow was soft and deep, and beneath it the older snow lay in furrows across our route, hardened and polished by the winter gales and drifts, so that it resembled marble.

"On landing I found the beach low, composed of mud, with the foot-prints of animals frozen in it. A few hundred yards from the beach there are steep hills, about 150 feet in height, and upon the sides of these, in reddish-colored limestone, casts of fossil shells abound. Inland of these, the ordinary pale carboniferous sandstone and cherty limestone reappeared. The fossils are all small, and of only a few varieties, some being ammonites, but the greater part

20

bivalves. They differed from any I had met with before, and the rock was almost brick-red; I picked up what appeared to be fossil bone (*Ilchthyosaurus?*), only part of it appearing out of the fragment of the rock.

"Point Wilkie appears to be an isolated patch of liassic age, resting upon carboniferous sandstones and limestones, with bands of chert, of the same age as the limestones and sandstones of Melville Island. The eastern shores of Intrepid Inlet is composed of this formation; while the western, rising into hills and terraces, is of the underlying carboniferous epoch. At the western side of Intrepid Inlet I found upon the ice a considerable quantity of white asbestos, but did not ascertain from whence it had been brought."

The fossils thus found *in situ*, I have no doubt, belong to the liassic period; and as their geological interest is indubitable, I offer no apology for inserting here the following description, written by me on Captain M'Clintock's return to Dublin from his third Arctic expedition.

No. 1. WILKIE POINT, Prince Patrick's Land (Lat. 76° 20' N.; Long. 117° 20' W.).

LIAS FOSSILS,

(*a*) *Ammonites M'Clintocki*, Journ. R. D. S., Vol. I. Pl. IX. Figs. 2, 3, 4.
Monotis septentrionalis. Journ. R. D. S., Vol. I. Pl. IX. Figs. 6, 7.
Pleurotomaria, sp. Journ. R. D. S., Vol I. Pl. IX. Fig. 8.
Cast of some Univalve. Journ. R. D. S., Vol. I. Pl. IX. Fig. 7.
Nucula, sp.

(*a*) Ammonites M'Clintocki (Haughton).—*Testâ compressâ, carinatâ, anfractibus latis, lateribus, complanatis, transversim undato-costatis; costis simplicibus, juxtâ marginem interiorem levigatis; dorso carinato acuto; aperturâ sagittatâ, compressâ, antice carinatâ; septis lateribus 4-lobatis.*

This fine ammonite resembles several species common in the upper lias of the Plateau de Larzac, Sevennes, in France. It approaches *A. concavus* of the lower Oolite, but is distinguished by having only four lobes on the lateral margins of the septa, and by its showing no tendency to a tricarinated keel. The following measurements give an exact idea of its form, as compared with that of the species mentioned :

	Diameter, Inches.	Width of last Spire. Diam=100	Thickness of last Spire.	Overlapping of last Spire.	Width of Umbilic.
A. M'Clintocki,	1.83	$\frac{51}{100}$	$\frac{24}{100}$	$\frac{20}{100}$	$\frac{20}{100}$
A. concavus, .	2.95	$\frac{50}{100}$	$\frac{24}{100}$	$\frac{19}{100}$	$\frac{16}{100}$

The principal difference here observable is in the somewhat greater size of *A. concavus*, and the larger umbilic of *A. M'Clintocki*. It certainly resembles this well-known ammonite very closely; and it appears to me difficult to imagine the possibility of such a fossil living in a frozen, or even a temperate sea.

The discovery of such fossils *in situ*, in 76° north latitude, is calculated to throw considerable doubt upon the theories of climate which would account for all past changes of temperature by changes in the relative position of land and water on the earth's surface. No attempt, that I am aware of, has ever been made to calculate the number of degrees of change possible in consequence of changes of position of land and water; and from some incomplete calculations I have myself made on the subject, I think it highly improbable that such causes could have ever produced a temperature in the sea at 76° north latitude which would allow of the existence of ammonites, especially ammonites so like those that lived at the same time in the tropical warm seas of the south of England and France, at the close of the Liassic, and commencement of the lower Oolitic period.

During the course of the same Arctic expedition in which these organic remains were found, Captain Sir Edward Belcher discovered in some loose rubble, of which a cairn was built on Exmouth Island (lat. 77° 12′ N., lon. 96° W.), vertebral bones of, apparently, some liassic enaliosaurian. All doubt as to the reality of this discovery, and all idea of accounting for the occurrence of such remains by drift, must be abandoned, as the fossils found by M'Clintock were unquestionably *in situ,* and it is impossible to evade the consequences that follow to geological theory from their discovery.

Captain Sherard Osborn, also, found broken vertebræ of an ichthyosaurus, 150 feet up Rendezvous Hill, the north-west extreme of Bathurst Island : of these specimens, one lay among a mass of stone that had slipped from the N. W. face of the hill; the other was by the side of a ravine or deep watercourse on the southern face of the same elevation. I have no doubt but that they were *in situ.*

I am well aware that the question of light in the Arctic seas will be disposed of by some geologists, who will remind us that the saurians, and probably the ammonites, were endowed with a complicated optical apparatus, rendering them capable of using their eyes, not only for the distinct vision of objects differing greatly in distance, but also of using them, under widely differing conditions of light and darkness ; and I readily admit the force of such observations.

But what are we to say as to the question of temperature ? It was certainly necessary for an ammonite to have a sea free from ice, on which to float and bask in the pale rays of the Arctic sun ; and therefore I claim a temperature for those seas, at least similar to that which now prevails in the British Islands : and I may add that the ammonite, from its habits, was essentially dependent on the temperature of the air, as well as on that of the water.

There is at present a difference of 49° 5 F. between the mean annual temperature of Point Wilkie and Dublin ; and if this change of temperature be supposed to be caused by a change of the relative positions of land and water, the temperature of Dublin, or of some place on the same parallel of latitude, must be supposed to be raised to 99° 5 F. ; while the temperature of the thermal equator will exceed 124°—a temperature only a few degrees below that requisite to boil an egg ! I reject, without scruple, a theory that requires such a result, which must be considered as a minimum ; as it is probable that the ammonite required a finer climate than that of Britain for the full enjoyment of his existence.

The theory of central heat, also, appears to me to be open to the same objection, as a mode of explaining this remarkable geological fact; for it will simply add a constant to our present climates, leaving the differences to remain, as at present, to be accounted for by latitude and distribution of land and water. The astronomical theory of Herschel, also, which would account for former changes of climate by changes in the radiating power of the sun, would only increase the temperature at each latitude, leaving the differences as at present.

The only speculation with which I am acquainted, which is capable of solving this *opprobrium geologicorum*, is the hypothesis of a change in the axis of rotation of the earth, the admission of which, as a geological possibility, is mathematically demonstrable, and which has recently had some singular evidence in its favor advanced by geologists. In 1851, I brought forward, at the Geological Society of Dublin, a case of angular fragments of granite occurring in the carboniferous limestone of the County Dublin ; and explained the phenomena by the supposition of the transporting power of ice. In 1855, Professor Ramsay laid before the Geological Society of London a full and detailed theory of glaciers and ice as agents concerned in the formation of a remarkable breccia, of Permian age, occurring in the central counties of England; and still more recently the same agent has been employed by the geological surveyors of

India to account for the transport of materials at geological periods long antecedent to those in which ice transport is commonly supposed to have commenced. The motion of the earth's axis would reconcile all the facts known, and it must be regarded as a geological desideratum to determine its amount and direction, and to assign the cause of such a movement. The solution of this problem I regard as quite possible.

It is well worthy of remark, that the arguments from the occurrence of coal-plants and ammonites strengthen each other; the coal-plants rendering the question of *light*, and the ammonites that of *heat*, insuperable objections to the admission of any received geological hypothesis to account for the finding of such remains, *in situ*, in latitudes so high as those of Melville Island, Prince Patrick's Island, and Exmouth Island.

V.—*The Superficial Deposits.*

The surface of the ground, where exposed, throughout the Arctic Archipelago, does not appear to be covered with thick deposits of clay or gravel, such as are found generally in the north of Europe, and referred by geologists to what they call "the Glacial Epoch." There are not, however, wanting abundant evidences of the transport of drift materials, and there is some good evidence, collected by Captain M'Clintock, of the direction in which the drift was moved.

Specimens of granite, which I have no hesitation in referring to the characteristic granite of the west side of North Somerset, were found at Leopold Harbor (North Somerset) and at Graham Moore Bay (Bathurst Island); one of these localities is N. E. and the other N. W. of the granite of North Somerset, from which I infer that there was no constant prevailing direction for the drift ice that carried these boulders, but that they were transported to the northward in various directions, according to the varying motion of the currents that moved the ice. The boulder of granite at Port Leopold is 100 miles N. E. of the granite which gave origin to it; and the specimens from Graham Moore Bay are 190 miles to the N. W. of their source.

At Cape Rennell (North Somerset), in a direction intermediate between the two former directions, a remarkable boulder of the same granite was found, confirming the general direction of the transporting force from south to north. Its position and size are thus recorded by Captain M'Clintock :—" Near Cape Rennell we passed a very remarkable rounded boulder of gneiss or granite; it was 6 yards in circumference, and stood near the beach, and some 15 or 20 yards above it; one or two masses of rounded gneiss, although very much smaller, had arrested our attention at Port Leopold."

It is well known that Captain Sir Robert M'Clure brought home specimens of pine-trees found in the greatest abundance in the ravines on the west coast of Baring Island; one of his specimens preserved in the museum of the Royal Dublin Society measures 15 inches by 12 inches, and contains three knots that prove it formed a portion of the stem high above its root. The bark is not found on this specimen, which does not represent the full thickness of the tree; I have estimated that this fragment contains 70 rings of annual growth.

Similar remains were found by Captain M'Clintock and Lieutenant Mecham in Prince Patrick's Island, and in Wellington Channel by Sir Edward Belcher. On the coast of New Siberia, Lieutenant Anjou found a clay cliff containing stems of trees still capable of being used as fuel. The original observers all agree in thinking that these trees grew where they are now found; and Captain Osborne, in mentioning Sir Roderick I. Murchison's opinion that they are drift timber, justly adds the remark, that a sea sufficiently free from ice to allow of their being drifted from the south would indicate also a climate sufficiently mild to allow of their having grown upon the land where they now occur. Mr. Hopkins, in his anniversary address as President of the Geological Society of London, has published a remarkable geological speculation, which would account for the facts above mentioned.* So far as the evidence of drift boulders is concerned, I have shown that the direction of the currents was from the south; a fact which falls in with the drift theory, so far as it goes.

We cannot, however, dissociate these trees from the facts connected with the distribution of the remains of the Siberian Mammoth in Asia and America. It is now known that this elephant was provided with a warm fur, and that his food was of a kind which grows even now in Northern Siberia; so that the drift theory, which was formerly supposed necessary to account for the occurrence of these remains, has now been quietly dropped, *sub silentio*, by the geologists. Many other drift theories have, in like manner, lived their short day, and gone the way of all false hypotheses; among others, the drift theory of the origin of coal. Further investigation may show that the glacial epoch of Europe was one of a very different character in Asia and America, and that, while glaciers clothed the sides of Snowdon and Lugnaquillia, pine forests flourished in the Parry Islands, and the Siberian elephants wandered on the shores of a sea washed by the waves of an ocean that carried no drifting ice.

There is abundant evidence, however, that the Arctic Archipelago was submerged in very recent geological periods; for we know that subfossil shells, of species that now inhabit the waters of the neighboring seas, and found

* Journ. Geol. Soc. Lond., vol. VIII. p. lxiv.

at considerable heights throughout the whole group of islands. M'Clure found shells of the *Cyprina Islandica,* at the summit of the Coxcomb range, in Baring Island, at an elevation of 500 feet above the sea-level; Captain Parry, also, has recorded the occurrence of *Venus* (probably *Cyprina Islandica*) on Byam Martin's Island ; and in the recent voyage of the ' Fox,' Dr. Walker, the Surgeon of the expedition, found the following subfossil shells at Port Kenedy, at elevations of from 100 to 500 feet :—

1. *Saxicava rugosa.*
2. *Tellina proxima.*
3. *Astarte Arctica* (Borealis.)
4. *Mya Uddevallensis.*
5. *Mya Truncata.*
6. *Cardium* sp.
7. *Buccinum undatum.*
8. *Acmea testudinalis.*
9. *Balanus Uddevallensis.*

At the same place a portion of the palate-bone of a whale (Right Whale) was found at an elevation of 150 feet.

All these facts indicate the former submergence of the Arctic Archipelago, but this submergence must have been anterior to the period when pine forests clothed the low sandy shores of the slowly emerging islands, the remains of which forests now occupy a position at least 100 feet above high-water mark.

The geolgical map which I am enabled to publish from the data collected by Captains M'Clintock, M'Clure, Osborne, &c., is an enlargement of that which was published in 1857 by the Royal Society of Dublin, to illustrate the fine collection of Arctic fossils and minerals deposited in the museum of that body by Captains M'Clintock and M'Clure. In perfecting it for its present purpose I have availed myself of all the other sources of information within my reach, among which I am bound to mention in particular the exellent appendix to Dr. Sutherland's 'Voyage of the Lady Franklin and Sophia,' written by Mr. Salter, Palæontologist of the Geological Survey of Great Britain.

Many of the mineral specimens of Greenland, and the fossils from Cape Riley, Cape Farrand, Point Fury, and Brentford Bay, were collected by Dr. David Walker, surgeon and naturalist to the 'Fox' Expedition.

No. V.

LIST OF SUBSCRIBERS TO THE 'FOX' EXPEDITION.

Name	£	s.	d.
Acland, Sir T. D. Bart.........	100	0	0
Adams, Dr.Walter, Edinburg.	3	3	0
Aldrich, Captain R.N...........	1	1	0
Allan, Rob. M., Esq.............	1	1	0
Allen, Captain Robert...........	5	5	0
Allen, Captain, R.N..............	2	2	0
Ames, Mrs...........................	5	0	0
Ames, Miss	1	0	0
Anon.................................	5	0	0
Armstrong, Mrs....................·	1	1	0
Armstrong, children of Mrs...	0	8	9
Arnold, Mrs.........................	1	1	0
Arrowsmith, John, Esq.........	5	0	0
Austin, Rear-Adm. Horatio T. R.N., C.B........................	5	0	0
Babbage, Charles, Esq.........	10	0	0
Baikie, Dr..........................	1	1	0
Baker, Mrs..........................	5	0	0
Barkworth, Geo., Esq...........	5	0	0
Barras, Miss........................	1	1	0
Barrett, H. J., Esq...............	1	0	0
Barrow, John, Esq...............	25	0	0
Barstow, Lieutenant, R.N.....	1	0	0
Barth, Dr. Henry	5	5	0
Bath, W. J. C., Esq.............	0	2	6
Batty, Mrs. J. M	1	1	0
Beaufort, Rear-Adm. Sir Francis, K.C.B.........................	50	0	0
Bell, Thos., Esq., Pres. Linn Society	10	10	0
Bennett, John S., Esq...........	5	0	0
Birch, J. W. N., Esq.............	10	0	0
Bird, Captain, R.N...............	5	0	0
Birmingham, small sums collected at Evans' Library....	3	1	0
Booth, Mrs..........................	5	0	0
Borton, Mrs., collected by.....	1	10	0
Boston, collected at, by Mr. Morton ....,	4	4	0
Bovill, Walter, Esq..............	5	0	0
Boyer, Lieut. R.N.	0	10	0
Boyle, the Hon. Carolina C...	1	0	0
Brigg, collected at................	1	1	0
Brine, Captain, R.E..............	1	1	0
Brooking, J. Holdsworth, Esq.	10	0	0
Brown, Robt., Esq., V.P.L.S.	20	0	0
Brown, John, Esq.,..............	5	5	0
Brown, J. E., Esq., R.N........	0	5	0
Bruce, the Rev. C................	1	1	0
Burgoyne, Captain, R.N.......	1	0	0
Burton, Alfred, Esq..............	1	1	0
Byron, the Hon. Fred...........	5	0	0
Chesney, Major-General.......	2	2	0
Collinson, Capt., R.N., C.B...	20	0	0
Coningham, W., Esq., M.P....	100	0	0
Coote, C. W., Esq................	1	0	0
Coote, Charles, Esq..............	10	0	0
Courtauld, Samuel, Esq.........	25	0	0

Name	£	s.	d.
Courtauld, George, Esq.........	15	0	0
Coutts, Messrs. & Co..............	50	0	0
Crasp, J., Esq., Surgeon, 63rd Regt. ....,,......	1	0	0
Cranford, John, Esq..............	5	0	0
Cresswell, S. Gurney, Commander, R.N......................	5	0	0
Dalgety, F. T., Esq	10	10	0
De la Roquette, M., V.P. of Geog. Soc. of Paris, 1000 fr..	40	0	0
Dilke, C. W., Esq.................	5	0	0
Dixon, James, Esq.................	10	0	0
Doxat, Alexis, J., Esq...........	10	10	0
Doxat, Miss H., collected by..	4	0	0
" Dubious"..........................	0	2	6
Dufferin, Lord.....................	25	0	0
Edgar, Mrs., collected by......	5	0	0
Ellesmere, the Earl of...........	15	0	0
Elphinstone, the Hon. Mount-Stewart............................	10	0	0
Elton, Sir Arthur H., Bart.....	5	5	0
Emanuel, Ezekiel, Esq...........	1	0	0
Fairholme, the Hon. Mrs.......	150	0	0
Filliter, George, Esq.............	10	0	0
Fitton, Dr...........................	21	0	0
Fortescue, Rev. T. F. G.........	2	2	0
Garling, H., Esq....................	1	1	0
Gassiot, J. P., Esq................	25	0	0
Gimingham, W., Esq., & Mrs.	2	2	0
Gipps, Lady..........................	5	0	0
Gowen, J, R., Esq.................	5	0	0
Graves, Messrs. Pall Mall......	1	1	0
Griffiths, G. H., Esq..............	5	5	0
Gruneisen, Ch. Lewis, Esq....	1	1	0
Gruneisen, Mrs.....................	1	1	0
Guillemard, the Rev. W. H...	5	0	0
Guillemard, Miss..................	1	0	0
Hall, James, Esq..................	5	0	0
Hanbury, Mrs.......................	1	1	0
Hardinge, Commander, R.N..	0	10	0
Hardwicke, Philip, Esq.........	5	0	0
Harney, Julian, Esq., collected by, at Jersey................	50	0	0
Heales, Alfred, Esq..·...........	5	5	0
Hereing, Miss.	2	2	0
Hicks, John, Esq...................	2	0	0
Hill, Col. 63d Regt...............	1	0	0
Hodgson, Mrs.......................	10	0	0
Holland, Commander, R.N...	5	0	0
Hollingsworth, H., Esq.........	2	2	0
Holland, Rob., Esq................	10	10	0
Hooker, Dr. J. D...................	5	5	0
Hornby, Miss Georgina.........	100	0	0
Hornby, the Rev. Edward.....	25	0	0
Hornby, Mrs. Edmund........,,	5	0	0

	£	s.	d.
Hornby, Miss Georgina, collected by	13	4	0
Hovell, W. H., Esq	5	5	0
Hughes, Lieutenant, R.N	2	0	0
Inglis, Lady	10	1	0
Irby, T. W., Esq	1	0	0
Jackson, N. Ward, Esq	21	0	0
Jauson, J. C., Esq	5	5	0
Jeanes, H. W., Esq., R.N	0	10	0
Jersey "Times"	2	10	0
Kellett, Commodore, C.B.	10	0	0
Kendall, Mrs	1	0	0
Kendall, the Rev. Professor	1	0	0
Key, Lieutenant, R.N	0	5	0
King, William, Esq	5	0	0
Laird, Macgregor, Esq	50	0	0
Laird, John, Esq	25	0	0
L. and N. W	1	4	0
Lanford, J., Esq., Quartermaster 63d Regiment	0	10	0
Langhorne, A., Esq	1	1	0
Larcom, Mrs	1	0	0
Leach, William, Esq	5	5	0
Le Feuvre, W. J., Esq	50	0	0
Lefroy, C. E., Esq	2	0	0
Leicester, the Rev. F	1	1	0
Lethbridge, Lieut., R.N	0	5	0
"Lochmaben Castle," Owners of the	5	5	0
Lyall, D., Esq., R.N., M.D.	5	0	0
Mackintosh, Eneas, Esq	10	0	0
Maguire, Captain, R.N	3	3	0
Maitland, Capt. Sir Thos. R.N.	1	0	0
Majendie, Ashhurst, Esq., and Mrs.	100	0	0
Servants of the above	0	14	0
Malby, Messrs.	5	0	0
Malby, Messrs. Workmen in their Establishment by a 6d. Subscription	4	11	6
Mansfield, W. H. S., Esq	0	10	0
Mantell, Dr A. A	1	0	0
Markham, Clements, Esq	1	1	0
Markman, Mrs	1	0	0
M'Rea, Captain, R.N	0	10	0
M'Kinlay, Miss	1	0	0
M'Kinlay, Miss Elizabeth	1	0	0
M'William, Dr., R.N	1	1	0
Merry, W. L., Esq	1	1	0
Morris, Rev. F. B	1	0	0
Morris, Sir Armine, Bart.	5	0	0
Murchison, Sir Roderick Impey, G. C. St. S., President of the Royal Geog. Soc.	100	0	0
Murray, John, Esq	20	0	0
Nares, Fras., Esq.	2	2	0
Newall, W. L., Esq	100	0	0
Nicholson, Sir Charles	5	0	0
N. J	2	2	0
Norwood, collected at, by a Lady	7	15	0

	£	s.	d.
Ommanney, Captain Erasmus, R.N.	2	0	0
Osborn, Sir George, Bart	1	0	0
Paget, A. F., Esq	0	10	6
Paget, C. H. M., Esq	1	1	0
Pasley, Gen. Sir Charles W., K.C.B.	10	0	0
Second Subscription	10	0	0
Third Subscription	5	0	0
Pattison, H. L., Esq	50	0	0
Pearce, Stephen, Esq	2	2	0
Phillimore, Captain, R.N	2	2	0
Pigou, Fred., Esq	10	0	0
Prescott, Vice-Adm. Sir Henry, K.C.B.	5	0	0
Rawnsley, the Rev. Drummond	5	0	0
Rawnsley, Mrs., collected by.	1	0	0
Rawnsley, William, Franklin collected by, at Uppingham School	0	10	0
Raynsford, Mrs.	1	1	0
Reynardson, H. B., Esq	5	0	0
Rogers, Lieut., R.N	1	0	0
Roget, Dr. P. M.	5	0	0
Roper, George, Esq	5	5	0
Ross, Rear-Adm. Sir Jas. C	21	0	0
Rupert's Land, Bishop of	5	0	0
Sabine, Major-General	25	0	0
Sadler, W. F., Esq	10	10	0
Sefton, the Countess of	10	0	0
Shearley, W., Esq.	2	0	0
Sheil, Sir Justin	5	0	0
Shewell, John Tulmin, Esq	5	5	0
Simpson, J., Esq., R.N	1	10	0
Skey, Dr	2	2	0
Smith, Eric E., Esq	2	0	0
Smith, John Henry, Esq	10	10	0
Smith, Osborn, Esq	2	2	0
Smith, Archibald, Esq	5	5	0
Sparrow, James, Esq	5	0	0
St. Asaph, the Bishop of	10	0	0
St. David's, the Bishop of	10	0	0
St. Selger, A. B	5	0	0
Stainton, J. J., Esq	3	3	0
Statham, J. L., Esq	1	1	0
Stephenson, Robert, Esq	20	0	0
Stirling, Commander, R..N	0	10	0
Strzelecki, Count P. de	25	0	0
Swinburne, Rear-Admiral	30	0	0
Sykes, Col., M.P	5	0	0
Taylor, William, Esq	5	0	0
Tennant, James, Esq	2	0	0
T. H., collected in shillings by.	2	0	0
Thackeray, W. M., Esq	5	0	0
Thompson, J., Esq	1	1	0
Tindal, Commander, R.N	2	2	0
Tinney, W. H., Esq., Q.C.	20	0	0
Tite, W., Esq., M.P	50	0	0
Trevelyan, Sir W. C., Bart.	40	0	0
Trevelyan, Lady	10	0	0
Trevilian, M. C., Esq	2	2	0
Trollope, Commander, R.N	2	2	0

	£	s.	d.		£	s.	d.
Tuckett, Fred., Esq	6	0	9	Wrottesley, Lord	50	0	0
Tudor, J., Esq	0	10	0				
Turner, Alfred, Esq	15	0	0	Young, Charles F., Esq	5	0	0
Tweedie, W. M., Esq	5	0	0	Young, Miss	5	0	0
				Young, A. Verity, Esq	2	2	0
Vincent, John, Esq	1	0	0	Yule, Mrs. H	5	0	0
				The brother and sisters of the			
Walker, James, Esq	21	0	0	late John and Thomas Hart-			
Washington, Capt., R.N., Hy-				nell, of HMS. 'Erebus,' bu-			
drographer of the Navy	21	0	0	ried at Beechey Island	5	0	0
Waterfield, Edward, Esq	5	0	0	A Commander, R.N	0	5	0
Wayse, the Rev. J. W	5	0	0	A Commander in the Mer-			
Weld, Charles R., Esq	5	0	0	chant Service	500	0	0
Wheatstone, Professor	5	0	0	A Friend, C. H	0	5	0
Willes, Hon. Mr. Justice	21	0	0	A Friend	1	0	0
Wilson, Robert, Esq	1	1	6	The daughters of a retired			
Wittenoom, Mess	1	1	0	Commander	2	0	0
Wodehouse, Commander	1	10	0	A Sympathiser	1	0	0
Woodcock, J. Parry, Esq	5	0	0				
Worsley, Marcus, Esq	10	0	0		£2981	8	9
Wright, the Rev. R. F	2	2	0				

----◄•◦•►----

A life-boat, presented by Messrs. White of Cowes.

A large quantity of preserved potatoes, by Messrs. King, late Edwards.

Apparatus for lowering a boat at sea, presented by Mr. Clifford, the inventor.

Three traveling tents, by Messrs. Winsor and Newton.

A stove, by Mr. Rettie.

20 dozen " Isle of White sance," by Mr. Tucker of Newport.

Apparatus for reefing topsails, from Mr. Cunningham, the inventor.

THE END.

GODFREY TRAVELING 90 MILES IN A SNOW STORM, TAKING PROVISIONS TO HIS DYING COMRADES.

GODFREY'S NARRATIVE

OF THE

LAST GRINNELL

Arctic Exploring Expedition,

IN SEARCH OF

SIR JOHN FRANKLIN,

1853—4—5.

WITH A

BIOGRAPHY OF DR. ELISHA K. KANE,

FROM THE

CRADLE TO THE GRAVE.

BY

WM. C. GODFREY.

ONE OF THE SURVIVORS OF THE EXPEDITION.

SUPERBLY ILLUSTRATED.

PHILADELPHIA:

J. T. LLOYD & CO.

1857.

PHILADELPHIA:
STEREOTYPED BY GEORGE CHARLES.

PREFACE.

It has been a cause of deep regret with the author and publisher of this Narrative, that the circumstances referred to in the last chapter of the book, have delayed the publication. As some passages in this volume are very much at variance with the common accounts we have of the temper and character of Dr. Kane, and likewise reflect somewhat on his conduct as a Naval Commander, it would have been more satisfactory if these charges had appeared during the Doctor's lifetime. But the explanations given by Godfrey himself show that the earlier publication of his book was impossible ; however anxiously he might desire to vindicate himself, and to remove the stains affixed to his character by the unfavorable mention made of him in Dr. Kane's book. It may be remarked that, if Dr. Kane were now living, he could not repel Godfrey's charges without a negation of his own statements. He has fully admitted, in his journal, the most material facts connected with that extraordinary affair—the attempt to take Godfrey's life. He has not only related those facts distinctly, and with very little difference from Godfrey's own account ; but he has related them in a manner which seems to call for public approbation. This last-mentioned circumstance

1*

satisfies us that Dr. Kane *thought* that he was doing his duty on that occasion. Perhaps very few persons who read his book attentively will come to the same conclusion. The circumstances to be considered in connection with this matter are : 1. That Godfrey had formerly been dismissed by his Commander, with permission to return to the United States. Did this permission release him from his compact to serve for a certain term on board of the *Advance*? 2. When, under the pressure of starvation, he returned with his companions, to solicit relief from Dr. Kane, did this return renew his original obligations and restore him to his former position on board of the vessel? 3. Could he reasonably be suspected of an intention to desert in such a country as Northern Greenland and in the midst of an Arctic winter? If he did desert, in such circumstances, would his example be likely to be followed by others of the brig's company? 4. Was his return to the vessel with a load of provisions such an act as might be expected from a deserter? 5. Was the Commander justified in shooting a man for a mere refusal to come on board? 6. It appears that, according to the contract made with the seamen before their departure from New York, the strict regulations of the Naval service were to be dispensed with on this Expedition; the discipline of the brig could not, therefore, justify the Commander in resorting to such an extreme measure as shooting a man to enforce an order.

But, as the time has past when Dr. Kane could be held responsible for this act, we are disposed to consider it as an error of the judgment; and it may be easier to excuse him on that score than to overlook the deliberate wrong which he has done to William C. Godfrey by making vague charges of delinquency against this man, who appears, even from the Doctor's own statements, to nave oeen the constant friend and benefactor of the whole brig's company.

It is a remarkable fact that Godfrey appears, in the Doctor's narrative, only as a half-pardoned criminal, even when accounts are given of signal services performed by him at the imminent hazard of his own life ! And yet we have found scarcely any specification of a fault of sufficient magnitude to call for a private reprimand ; nevertheless, this unfortunate person has been rebuked by his commanding officer before the whole world, and he may even be handed down to *posterity* as an object of distrust and abhorrence.

The death of Dr. Kane does not make it less incumbent on our author to clear himself from undeserved censure. If any of the Doctor's fellow-voyagers, who profess so much love and reverence for the Doctor's memory, can show how Godfrey merited the harsh treatment he has received, they can do so as easily as Dr. Kane himself could, if he were now alive.

Although the two parties to this singular controversy occupied very different positions on board of the exploring brig *Advance,* at the bar of the American public there is no recognizable distinction between Elisha K. Kane and William C. Godfrey. We feel confident that the decision of the public in this case will be in accordance with the dictates of "even-handed justice."

The merits of this work, as a complete and circumstantial history of the last Arctic Exploring Expedition, will be acknowledged, we think, by every candid and intelligent reader.

Philadelphia May 30, 1857.

PORTRAIT OF DR. KANE.

WM. C. GODFREY.

CHAPTER XVII.

SEVERAL TRAVELING PARTIES SENT OUT—THEIR ILL
SUCCESS—MORTON AND HANS CHRISTIAN TRAVEL
NORTHWARD—THEIR FAMOUS DISCOVERIES—A SEPA-
RATION OF OUR COMPANY—THE AUTHOR, WITH SEVEN
COMPANIONS, PERMITTED TO LEAVE THE BRIG—THEY
TRAVEL SOUTHWARD—ARE OVERTAKEN BY THE WIN-
TER—THEIR UNPARALLELED SUFFERINGS FROM COLD
AND FAMINE—THE AUTHOR VISITS AN ESQUIMAUX
SETTLEMENT—THE GENEROSITY AND BENEVOLENCE OF
THESE "BARBARIANS"—THEIR HOUSES, MODES OF
LIVING, &C.

FOR about two weeks after our unsuccessful attempt
to reach the Humboldt Glacier, the serious illness of
Dr. Kane prevented him from undertaking any new
enterprise. As soon as he was well enough to travel,
he made two unsuccessful attempts to cross the Sound
with Esquimaux guides.

Early in June two traveling parties were sent out.
One of these parties, under the direction of McGarry
and Bonsall, came to the foot of the Humboldt Glacier,
which is a perpendicular wall of ice, 250 feet high and
50 miles long. Finding it impossible to scale this stu-

15*

pendous embankment, or to proceed any further, they returned to the brig. The other traveling party consisted of two persons only, viz., Mr. Morton and Hans Christian. They reached the foot of the glacier on the 15th day of June, and traveled in their dog-sledge on the land-ice of the Sound, crossing Peabody's Bay, and so found a practicable road along the base of the vast wall of ice spoken of above. They proceeded, according to Morton's statement, in a direction as nearly northward as possible, passing along the edge of Kenneday Channel, which extends from the 80th to the 81st parallel. Here, as they report, the ice was found broken up and the water in a navigable condition. They also saw "flocks of geese, ducks, and dovekies," and gulls probably; and Mr. Morton—having ascended a berg or knob of ice five hundred feet high—beheld "a boundless waste of water, stretching away toward the pole."

If this account given by Morton is correct, it is probable that the pole is covered by water. In that case it might be difficult for a navigator to put his foot on the " earth's pivot," according to the earnest desire of Captain Ross, unless the adventurer should happen to have more faith than St. Peter, and be able to walk on the surface of the sea. I sincerely hope that, for the benefit of future explorers, there may be some better means of access to this "open polar sea" than by the way of Smith's Sound; otherwise no vessel of considerable size will ever be able to reach it.

As the summer drew near its close, it became evident

that the American brig *Advance* was one of the permanent fixtures or "institutions" of the ice-regions. All hope of moving her had been pretty nearly abandoned, and we began to contemplate the sad necessity of remaining another winter in this gloomy clime. Among other troubles in prospect was a scarcity of provisions. In order to increase our supplies of eatables, Hans, Petersen, and I were almost constantly engaged in hunting. We caught or shot a number of white rabbits, foxes of both varieties, white and blue, and a few seals. The flesh of these animals, by being allowed to freeze, was easily preserved for future use.

About the latter part of August all hands were summoned on deck, and Dr. Kane, in a formal speech, announced that such of the men as wished to leave the brig for the purpose of traveling homeward, had full permission to do so. I perceived that the apprehended scarcity of provisions led to this generous offer. As I had never enjoyed much comfort, or experienced much kindness, on board of the *Advance*, I was one of the first to embrace this opportunity to depart. A majority of the brig's company, viz., Sonntag, Dr. Hayes, Petersen, Bonsall, Blake, Riley, Whipple, and Stevenson, came to the same conclusion. Our withdrawal left but eight persons on board.

Dr. Kane furnished us with a boat placed on sledge-runners, and some few cooking utensils and other articles which could be spared from the brig. We bade our comrades who stayed behind an affectionate adieu, and started on the 28th of August—rather too late in

the season for such an undertaking. Our purpose was
to proceed by boat or sledge conveyance, as we best
could, to Upernavick, the most northern Danish settlement, from whence we expected to find a passage in
some vessel to our own country. We traveled southward on the ice some three hundred and fifty miles,
when the severity of the weather compelled us to go on
shore and build ourselves a hut. This habitation was
made of stones, in the Esquimaux style of architecture.
We covered it, according to our best ability, with oars
and sails; nevertheless, it was a rather airy place of
residence. We were entirely destitute of provisions,
and were obliged to gather the lichen or rock-moss and
boil it for our maintenance, although the taste of the
herb is extremely nauseating, and its nature is decidedly
unwholesome. We hunted every day, but could find
no game. Meanwhile, the dark season was coming on
very rapidly, and our situation became exceedingly pre-
carious. I constructed several fox-traps, and although
foxes were very scarce in this neighborhood we had the
good fortune to catch two of them. As all of our ship
biscuit had been consumed, we had nothing of the bread
kind to eat with our fox-meat. In other circumstances,
we might have thought the taste of this meat unpleasant,
as it has somewhat of a fishy flavor, but long abstinence
enabled us to eat it with a good relish. We called our
hut the "Wanderers' Home," and we made a strong
effort to feel comfortable and contented in our domestic
establishment, designing to spend the winter there, if
possible, and to pursue our journey early in the spring.

The average temperature was 50° below zero; a greater degree of cold than we had ever experienced in the more northern latitude where the brig was harbored.

When we had been about a week in this pleasant location, we were visited by a party of Esquimaux, who were migrating to Cape York, having been starved out of their former place of residence, about fifty miles further to the North. Although we ourselves were rather " hard up" for something to eat, we gave these poor wanderers a morsel of food, without any expectation that they would ever have it in their power to reciprocate our kindness. But a good deed, even in this "naughty world," often meets with its reward in a most unexpected manner. Several days after, the same party, with some other Esquimaux, men, women and children, making altogether eighteen persons, called on us again, having a good stock of provisions, which they offered to sell us at our own valuation. The commodities which they wished to dispose of consisted of seal and walrus meat, eider-ducks, loons, and other water-fowls.

Before we began to trade, we had a grand entertainment, our Esquimaux guests supplying the viands and we cooking them. It was neither " a feast of reason" nor " a flow of soul," for we all ate in the most unreasonable manner, and thought of nothing but the gratification of our corporal appetites. As a specimen of the way in which we used up the eatables at this banquet, I will mention that I myself consumed two eider-ducks, each of which was larger than any wild duck ever seen

in the United States. Dr. Kane, when we were about
to separate ourselves from his company, had supplied
us with some beads, needles, and other trifling articles,
suitable for trading with the natives ; and this was supposed to be our main resource for supplying ourselves
with provisions. On the morning after the arrival of
our native guests, we applied ourselves to business and
obtained a good stock of food and other necessaries on
very easy terms. I "swapped" an old jack-knife with
one of the Esquimaux gentlemen for a pair of excellent
bear-skin boots, each of us believing that we had got
the best of the bargain. A string of small beads, worth
about two cents in the United States, was considered
as a fair price for a pair of eider-ducks or a good
large lump of walrus-meat. When our visitors were
about to depart, after we had traded to our mutual satisfaction, they invited me to accompany them to their
settlement. I did so with a great deal of pleasure, as
I wished to examine their modes of life; however,
having some speculation in my eyes, I took with me
some large sewing needles, several articles of cheap
jewelry, some beads, &c., which I designed to barter
with the inhabitants of the settlement for articles of
food and clothing. Our Esquimaux friends traveled in
dog-sledges, six of which they had with them and a
team of four dogs to each sled. One of the company,
named Colootna, offered me a seat in his vehicle, and we
set out in very high spirits, although the thermometer
was 48° below zero. The settlement was sixty miles
from our hut, and we reached it in about eighteen

hours. On the way, we gave chase to a bear, who kept us in pursuit of him for six hours, and then escaped by a very "cute trick," diving under an ice floe and appearing on the other side, entirely beyond our reach. He looked back at us, as I imagined, with a comical expression of countenance, as if he would have said, "You couldn't come it that time, my boys." He was a fine fat old fellow and promised to afford some capital eating. His escape was a source of bitter disappointment to my Esquimaux companions, and some of the women and children of the party cried very heartily when the bear gave us the slip.

When we arrived at the settlement, the "barbarous people showed me not a little kindness," treating me in the most generous and hospitable manner. I remained with them for two or three days, in order to cultivate their acquaintance and open the way for a regular trade, which might be the means of supplying our party with food during the winter. The habitations of the Esquimaux savages are of a very singular construction. They are of a circular shape with round dome-like tops; the diameter of the building never exceeding eight or ten feet. The height of the dome, in the centre, is about equal to the diameter of the hut. The entrance consists of a low arched-way, two feet high and six feet in length. The opening of this archway is just large enough for a man to creep through on his hands and knees, and every one who enters must do so in this humiliating manner. Around the interior of the hut, half way between the floor and the ceiling, there

16

is a gallery made of stone, like all the other parts of the building—leaving in the centre of the hut an area not more than three feet in diameter. The occupants of the dwelling live and sleep in the gallery, where their bedding, consisting of moss and skins, is disposed. The cooking is done by a lamp, rudely constructed of stone, which stands on the edge of the platform or gallery whereon the family sit when they are awake and lie when they are asleep. The cooking lamp is fed with the blubber of the seal or walrus.

As the hut is made almost air-tight, having no aperture except the little door, partially guarded from the cold external atmosphere by the long arch-way described above, the interior of the dwelling is quite warm. The heat of the cooking-lamp, which is kept always burning, together with the breath and vital heat of the occupants, is sufficient to make the apartment comfortable; and indeed too warm for persons who are not accustomed to the Esquimaux modes of living.

When I had made all the purchases I desired, and signified my wish to return to my companions, my friend Colootna conveyed me home in his dog-sledge. My comrades were glad to see me, and (as I suspect,) were still better pleased to see the additional stock of provisions I had brought with me. Some of them were in very bad health, and all were, more or less, afflicted with the blue devils. They suffered considerably from the cold likewise, for our house was not as comfortable as the dwellings of the Esquimaux. My companions were very much divided in opinion respecting the proper course to be pursued. Some were for remaining where we were until Spring, and then proceeding on our way to Upernavick; some wished to pass the winter at the neighboring Esquimaux settlement; and some were desirous of returning immediately to the brig. The last-mentioned expedient was less acceptable to me then either of the others. I considered that we had, to all intents and purposes, been dismissed from our vessel, because our Commander thought that his family was larger than he could well maintain ; and as we had received our portions, like so many prodigal sons, and been set adrift, I preferred living on husks or moss, or any thing else, to going back with expressions of contrition and making a pitiful appeal to the benevolence of Dr. Kane.

A few weeks had passed away, and we had not yet resolved what to do. Our stock of provisions had nearly run out. Several of our men were sick, and nearly all were haunted by gloomy anticipations. Karl Petersen and I had some energy and resolution left, and we had health and strength enough to attempt something for the relief of our companions. We walked to the Esquimaux village, sixty miles over the ice, the thermometer fifty degrees below zero. Incessant exercise was necessary to keep us from frezing. We could not stop a moment for rest or refreshment, and we could not sleep on the way as we had no tent or bedding. We finished the journey in eighteen hours, traveling without intermision ; and this was extraordinary speed, considering our benumbed condition and the disabling effect of spare diet. Our only food on the way consisted of a little dried walrus-meat, on which we breakfasted, dined and supped, as we walked. When we arrived at the settlement, we staggered like drunkards, being completely unnerved by fatigue and exhaustion.

After all our labor we were doomed to meet with a great disappointment. The inhabitants of the settlement, according to the usual improvident habits of the Esquimaux, had exhausted nearly all their provisions by continual feasting, and they were now almost as badly provided with food as we ourselves were. The young men of the village were absent on a seal and walrus-hunting expedition; and as they had been away longer than usual, it was thought that they had met with but little success. Nevertheless, the benevolent savages took pity on our wretched condition, and spared us a little food from their scanty stores. As the principal men of the village were absent with their dog-sledges, we could obtain no conveyance back to our home, and were obliged to return on foot with the little meat we had obtained, after resting ourselves for a few hours. We made as little delay as possible, for those of our company who remained at the hut were suffering for want of victuals. We carried the small stock of walrus-meat we had obtained from the Esquimaux, strapped on our backs. The load was not very oppressive, it is true, but it added somewhat to the wearisomeness of our journey. When about half-way to our dwelling-place, I was unlucky enough to sprain my ankle while attempting to leap over a chasm in the ice ten feet wide. This accident added very much to my sufferings during the remainder of our walk; and my lameness was the cause of considerable delay, prolonging the journey to twenty-five hours.

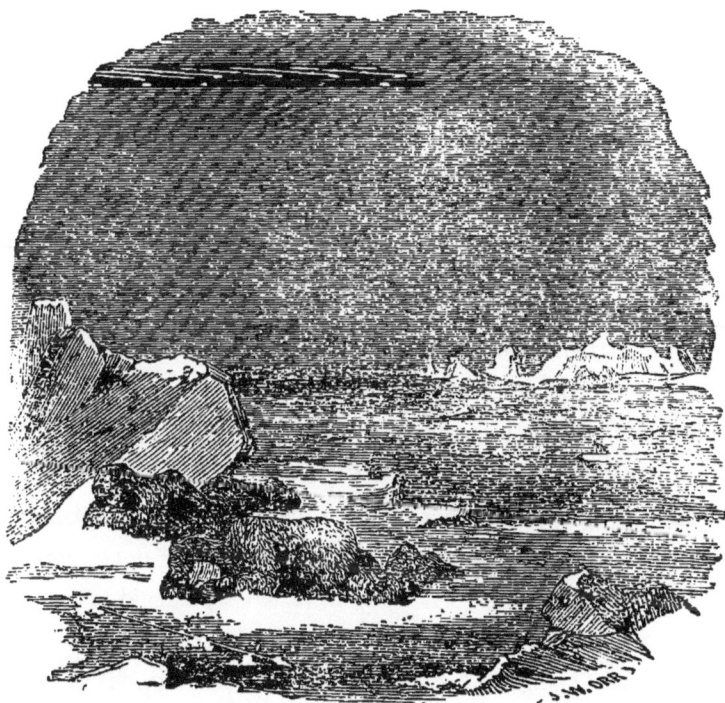

GODFREY'S CORDIAL PUTS THE ESQUIMAUX TO SLEEP.

16*

CHAPTER XVIII.

THE AUTHOR AND HIS PARTY ENDURE ALL THE HORRORS
OF FAMINE—THEY RESOLVE TO RETURN TO THE BRIG
—THE AUTHOR'S RELUCTANCE TO GO BACK—HE COM-
PLIES WITH THE WISHES OF THE MAJORITY—ANOTHER
TROUBLESOME JOURNEY—THE ESQUIMAUX TRY TO
OUT-YANKEE THE YANKEES—THEY MISS THEIR FIGURE
—VIRTUES OF "GODFREY'S CORDIAL"—THE AUTHOR'S
SUCCESSFUL STRATAGEM.

THE last supply of provisions obtained by Petersen
and I was consumed within two or three days, except
about fifteen pounds of walrus-meat, which, although
frozen, was in an advanced stage of putrefaction. The
mention of this circumstance may surprise the reader;
but while I remained in the polar regions, I had frequent proofs of the fact, that extreme cold is sometimes
almost as conducive as extreme heat to the decomposi-
tion of animal matter. On this meat, offensive as it
was, we were obliged to subsist for two days. At the
end of that time an Esquimaux hunter stopped at our
hut with his dog-sledge. As there was no hope of relief from any other quarter, my companions wished to
engage this Esquimaux to convey one or two of our
company to the brig, to solicit Dr Kane for a barrel

of ship-biscuit, or something else which might be the means of sustaining our lives. Petersen and I were requested to go on this mission; but I informed my fellow-sufferers that I could not on any account become a petitioner to Dr. Kane. I had reason to think that he was prejudiced against me, and I should prefer starving in that icy wilderness to becoming a pensioner on his bounty. I told them that I was willing to undertake any other journey, or to attempt any thing else for their relief, even if the attempt required the sacrifice of my own life, but they must find some other messenger to perform the errand they now had in contemplation. After some debate, it was determined that Bonsall and Petersen should be the begging embassadors to Dr. Kane. The Esquimaux, who undertook to carry them in his sledge, was promised a reward on his arrival at the vessel. I learned afterward that the strength of the dog-team proved inadequate to the conveyance of the three men; and at the end of the first eighty miles the animals were completely worn out, so that a sort of "rotation in office" became necessary, the dogs being placed *in* the sledge while the men hauled it.

In this unusual style of traveling they proceeded fifty miles further, when they fell in with a large party of Esquimaux hunters, and after some conversation it was agreed that they should all go to the brig together. The hunters had sledge-room enough to accommodate the whole party, and so our messengers sped much better than they had expected. Bonsall and Petersen **did** not return; but as soon as they gave Dr. Kane an account of our starving condition, that gentleman very promptly dispatched some provisions for us by the Esquimaux hunters, detaining one of their number as a "hostage" for the safe delivery of the articles.

In the meanwhile, I had been making all possible exertions to obtain food by hunting, trapping, &c., in which operations my remaining companions were too sickly or feeble to give me any assistance. Four or five days after the departure of the messengers, my comrades informed me that they themselves had come to the determination to go to the brig, and earnestly entreated me to accompany them. I consented, because I saw very plainly that they were not able to take care of themselves. After making all the preparation that was necessary we started; and, oh reader, how shall I give you the faintest idea of the tribulation I experienced on the way! When I had performed the part of dry-nurse for ten or twelve hours, and was almost distracted by the multiplicity of my cares and duties, we met the Esquimaux hunters who had been sent from the vessel with some provisions for our use. They had five sledges, with teams of six dogs each. Both parties came to a halt; and after the usual salutations, arrangements were made for cooking a meal. The Doctor had sent us some biscuit and salt pork, and we soon had a good kettle of "scouse" in the course of preparation. In the meanwhile, we tampered with our craving appetites by nibbling dry biscuit. As soon as the repast was finished, the Esquimaux divided our

company, consisting of six persons, into five lots, so
that four of the sleds should carry one man each, and
the fifth one two.   As soon as we were all on board,
we went off in gallant style, and put sixty miles behind
us in the first ten hours.   At the end of that time we
halted, pitched our tents, and enjoyed a most refreshing sleep, as the gnawings of conscience or hunger did
not interrupt our repose.

The next day our Esquimaux drivers held a consulta-
tion apart, and appeared to·be debating some subject
of importance, in their own estimation at least.   The
conference being over, they approached us and gave us
to understand that four of them, with the same number
of sledges, would be obliged to visit the place of their
abode on business of great consequence.   Two of their
men and one sledge would remain with us, until the
other members of their party should return.   They
would also leave us a tent and every thing necessary
for our comfort.   Though very much vexed at this detention, we felt that we had no right to object to the
proposed plans, as these people were certainly pri-
vileged to attend to their own affairs before ours.
Soon after, four of the hunters drove off in a different
direction from that we had lately been traveling.   They
had scarcely been gone an hour, before the two remaining Esquimaux announced that it had just come to
their recollection that they would be obliged to go too;
and they began to hitch up the last dog-team for that
purpose.   I new became suspicious of a trick, and resolved that these fellows should not out-jockey me.

Happening to have a small book of "Ethiopian Melodies" in my pocket, I took it out and examined a page
with the most earnest attention; then, putting on a
very gloomy aspect, I informed the two hunters that
they had chosen the most unlucky day in the whole
year for this new journey. "After we have slept once
more," said I, "the danger will be over, and you can
then start as soon as you please, without any fear of
the consequences." Finding that I had made some
impression on their superstitious feelings, I endeavored
to touch them on another assailable point, by promising
them a capital supper. The gluttonous proclivities of
the Esquimaux made this last argument a clincher.
Our two gentlemen were persuaded to pass the night
with us; and, while I prepared for them a bountiful
supper, according to promise, my mind was occupied
with painful reflections on the new embarrassments
which now presented themselves. I saw very plainly
that these Esquimaux, for some reason or other, wished
to desert us; and it was equally evident that, if we
should be abandoned in that place, the consequences
would be fatal to some of my sick companions. I could
see but one or two ways of extricating ourselves from
the difficulty. I did not doubt our ability to *compel*
these two savages to convey us to the brig; but knowing these people to be unwarlike and cowardly in their
disposition, I was unwilling to take advantage of these
defects of character. My intercourse with the native
tribes had taught me that all kinds of trickery with
them is considered fair and honorable. They are

GODFREY AND HIS SICK COMPANIONS DESERTED BY THE ESQUIMAUX.

always ready to practice a *ruse*, or to excuse others for the same propensity. I determined, therefore, to combat them with their own weapons; but nothing but the desperate circumstances in which I was placed could have induced me to use the stratagem, of which I am about to give an account. Convinced that it was an affair of life or death, for Dr. Hayes and two others of my party appeared to be almost in the last extremity, and were likely to die for want of medical assistance, I resolved that no time should be lost in the conveyance of these sufferers to the vessel, where alone they could meet with the attentions they required. I endeavored to touch the humane feelings of the two Esquimaux, by explaining to them the dangerous situation of my comrades; but these representations did not answer the purpose; it was plain that they had made up their minds not to go to the brig. Their obstinacy in this matter was unaccountable to me at that time, but the mystery was cleared up afterward. When these hunters and their associates conveyed Bonsall and Petersen to the brig, as I have previously related, Dr. Kane feasted them in his cabin, and they embraced that opportunity to steal some of the Doctor's knives, forks, spoons, and every other small article that could possibly be carried off without too much risk of detection. They had likewise committed another piece of knavery, by throwing away some of the provisions which they had engaged to carry to our party at "Wanderers' Home," notwithstanding they had left one of their company as a hostage for the safe delivery

17

of these provisions. These deeds of delinquency made them afraid to revisit the brig, where they might expect to be held accountable for their rascality.

Finding that the two native hunters could not be persuaded or induced to help us on our way, and being now satisfied that they had resolved to leave us on the ice, I perceived that it would be necessary to turn the joke on themselves. Among other trumpery in our baggage department, there were a few bottles of medicines. One of these nostrums, labeled " *Godfrey's Cordial*," appeared to have been invented by some namesake of mine, with whom I cannot claim the honor of a personal acquaintance. However, the physic is considered to be "a safe and pleasant remedy for colic, griping pains, and other diseases to which children are liable." I had known it to be given to peevish infants, to make them sleep, and its virtue as an *opiate* was the circumstance that chiefly recommended it to my notice at that time. Having prepared a pot of "scouse" expressly for the entertainment of our faithful Esquimaux carriers, I seasoned the mess with a pretty large dose of the anodyne mixture. This preparation was greedily swallowed by my two patients, who were too intent on gratifying their own appetites to observe that my companions and I did not partake of the same dish. After awhile, perceiving that they were becoming drowsy, I advised them to put themselves to bed in the tent. As an Esquimaux is always willing to eat or sleep, they readily took my counsel, and were soon locked up tightly in the embrace of the poppy-crowned deity. I then deposited in the tent provisions enough to serve them for two or three days,—(which was as much as I could spare,)—and having hitched up the dog-team, we placed our invalids in the sledge, wrapped them up well in buffalo skins and blankets, and started off at full speed. Hayes, Sonntag, and Stevenson occupied the sledge; and as the dogs could not conveniently drag a heavier load, Blake, Whipple, and I, being the healthiest men of the party, ran on behind and assisted the dogs, by pushing against the back of the sledge. I really am not casuist enough to know whether my conduct in this affair was justifiable or not. It was certainly an unjust act to take possession of a sled and dog-team which did not belong to us; but then the question arises, would it not have been a greater fault to allow our sick people to perish on the ice? I was placed between the horns of a moral dilemma, so that it was impossible for me to take any course with which my conscience would have been perfectly satisfied. Some time after this occurrence, I met with one of the natives whom I had tricked; he gave me full credit for my ingenuity, and was so excessively complimentary, as to say that I deserved to be an Esquimaux. He gave me a humorous account of the astonishment of himself and his comrade when they awoke, and found that they had been outwitted by the white men; and he begged me to supply him with some of the "sleepy stuff," as he thought it would be a good joke to try its effects on some of his countrymen.

When our party had traveled, in the manner I have

described, about eight hours, we came to an Esquimaux
settlement, where we stopped to repose. Here I met
with two of the hunters who had deserted us on the
preceding day. They were very much surprised to see
us at that place. I informed them that we had borrowed the sledge and dog-team from their associates,
who were waiting at the tent in expectation of their
arrival, according to promise. As they never had any
intention to go back, and knew that their friends did
not expect them, my story did not obtain much credit.
They appeared to be apprehensive that we had done
their companions some mischief, and when I parted
from them, they were about to start for the place where
we had left my two slumbering patients. I sent word
to the victimized hunters that whenever it suited their
convenience to come to the brig, their sledge and dog-
team would be returned, and the owners should be suita-
bly recompensed for the use of them.

CHAPTER XIX.

THE WANDERERS RETURN TO THE BRIG—SOME OF THEM ARE TAKEN SICK—DR. HAYES HAS HIS TOES CUT OFF —STARVATION ON SHIPBOARD—PREVALENCE OF THE SCURVY—THE MEN DYING FOR WANT OF FRESH PROVISIONS—SEVERAL PARTIES SENT OUT TO PROCURE FOOD—THE COLD DRIVES THEM BACK—THE AUTHOR'S SOLITARY JOURNEY OF NINETY-FIVE MILES—HIS DARING ENTERPRISE SUCCEEDS—HE OBTAINS A SUPPLY OF FRESH MEAT—MORE OF HANS CHRISTIAN'S LOVE AFFAIR.

WE traveled as rapidly as the strength of the dogs would permit, timing matters so as to stop for rest at the different Esquimaux settlements on the way. The natives treated us with uniform kindness at the several villages where we halted; and I believe that some of our invalids would have died on the way, but for the relief afforded them by the hospitality of the "savages." We reached the brig on the 12th of December, having been absent more than three months. Famine, disease, and long suffering had made such havoc in our personal appearance that our friends on board could scarcely recognize us; certainly a more ghastly company was never seen on the deck of an hermaphrodite brig. The

17*

sick people were immediately put to bed. Some of
them were found to be in a very bad condition. Sonntag, Blake, and Stevenson were quite ill for several
weeks; and Dr. Hayes was obliged to part with his
toes, as his feet had been badly frozen. This toeless
condition, by the way, was one of our arctic fashions,
as a considerable proportion of our company had been
subjected to that kind of trimming; though, (if a bad
pun may be excused,) few of us could well afford to
have our understandings retrenched.

We found that those of our men who had remained
on board had suffered rather severely, though their situation exposed them to much less hardship than our
party of wanderers had sustained. Our second winter
in the polar regions was more calamitous than the first.
Of course, the longer we remained there the more our
stock of provisions and fuel must become exhausted.
The commodities we had brought out for the purpose
of trading with the Esquimaux were nearly expended;
the consequence was, that the supplies of fresh meat
which we had hitherto obtained from the natives now
became more scanty. Latterly, these people had visited
us but seldom, as they never leave their houses in the
winter except in cases of absolute necessity. The want
of fresh meat caused the scurvy to prevail among us
more extensively than ever. In the latter part of December nearly all of our men were sick; and it was
very perceptible that unless they could have the benefit
of a salutary change of diet, the death of some of them
would be inevitable. The dogs were dying in great

numbers—literally starving to death. In this contingency, Dr. Kane and Petersen started in a dog-sledge for the nearest Esquimaux settlement, called Etah, with the hope of procuring some meat; but the severity of the cold compelled them to turn back before they had accomplished their purpose. Several other parties were sent out with the same result. At last Dr. Kane dispatched Hans Christian on a similar mission, having a notion that the hardihood of this young native would enable him to perform the task. Hans gave me an expressive glance when he took his departure, and I judged then that he did not intend to return. I mentioned in a former part of this narrative that he had entrusted me with the secret of a love affair in which he was engaged, and I suspected that he was now about to settle down as a married man. The event seemed to confirm my suspicions, for he remained absent for more than three weeks.

In the meanwhile, the state of affairs on board became almost desperate. Several of our men appeared to be at the point of death; their sufferings were most distressing; and all this misery proceeded from the want of suitable food; and it appeared to me that, with a little energetic exertion, this necessary article might be obtained. As I was in good health, and was always willing to undertake any labor for the good of our little community, I wondered that our commander did not send me on a provision-hunting expedition, as every other healthy man on board had been dispatched on this errand. The reason why he did not send me has

been subsequently explained by the Commander himself.
He was "afraid that I might meet or waylay Hans
Christian on the route and *murder* him!" Good heavens!
how could Dr. Kane have harbored the suspicion that it
was possible for me to perpetrate such a crime? Had
he ever seen any thing assassin-like in my conduct?
When the reader has accompanied me through this
narrative, he may come to the conclusion that Dr.
Kane himself was quite as likely to commit such a deed
of blood as William Godfrey. *I* never attempted to
shoot a man on a slight provocation, and without any
coloring of law or justice; nor have I ever shown a
disposition to assail the person or the reputation of a
man whom I supposed to be defenseless. Were Dr.
Kane now living, I should speak of the events I am
about to record in a manner which might be unpleasant
to the feelings of his enthusiastic admirers; but as the
man who was my enemy without a cause has gone to
his final account, I shall say no more than is absolutely
necessary for my own vindication.

Among other unwarrantable liberties which Dr.
Kane has taken with my name and character, I find
the following mention of me in his published journal:
"I had on board a couple of men, William Godfrey and
John Blake, whose former history I would like to know
—bad fellows both of them; but daring, energetic and
strong." If Dr. Kane had any curiosity to know my
"former history" he might have been gratified, if he
had merely hinted his wishes to myself. I could have
told him a tale, not of crime but of sorrow, which might

have disarmed his prejudices and ill-will. As the name of John Blake appears above, in an unfortunate connection, I must do him the justice to say, that I know no reason why he deserved to be called a " bad fellow," more than any other person on board of the brig *Advance*, except that it was his misfortune, as well as mine, not to please Dr. Kane. He was no hypocrite, no sycophant, he was not slavishly submissive to his superior, he would swear a little sometimes, and would occasionally go to sleep in the midst of one of the Doctor's religious exhortations ; and I believe that was the most damnable sin that the recording angel ever set down to his account. For all these things Blake did penance, and is therefore, (according to the Catholic doctrine,) entitled to forgiveness ; unless it should be urged that his penance was *involuntary*. Once, when he complained of being unwell, and showed a disinclination for some task which the Doctor imposed on him, our "mild and gentle" Commander struck him on the head with a handspike, inflicting a wound which placed his life at some hazard.

To show how apt Dr. Kane was to misconstrue a man's character, I will refer to the glowingly favorable account he has given of that " pious youth," Hans Christian. This sly and sedate individual had the audacity to fall in love without his Commander's permission, and while he was professing the most unbounded affection for the Doctor, and declaring his perfect satisfaction with his situation on board of the *Advance*, he was making preparations to " vamoose" at the first opportunity. I have confessed that he made me acquainted with his design ; for which I could not blame him, as his term of service had expired, and he had a right to follow his own inclinations. I thought so at least, and I did not choose to become an informer.

It was mentioned above that Hans had been sent to the settlement of Etah for provisions. He had been absent several weeks, and but one person on board could guess at the cause of his detention. Meanwhile the sickness and distress on board increased daily, until I could bear the sight of my comrades' misery no longer. As I had once been dismissed from the brig, and had never entered into any new contract with the Commander, I considered myself under no obligation to wait for the orders which I saw plainly that he did not intend to give. Believing that it was in my power to supply my companions with the means of health and comfort, I resolved to start forthwith for the Esquimaux village. I did not ask Dr. Kane's permission, for several reasons. 1. I thought that such an application to him would be an acknowledgment of his authority to control my movements. 2. I had reason to believe that he would not give his consent. 3. He might forbid me to go; and I judged that if it were a fault for me to go without orders, it would be a still greater fault to go *against* orders.

Without making any communication to Dr. Kane on the subject, I started on foot, about the latter part of February, 1854, and walked ninety-five miles over the ice to the Esquimaux village called Etah. Several of

our company, including Dr. Kane himself, had at different times, attempted to make this journey in dog-
sledges, but were driven back by the severity of the
cold. I traveled the whole distance *on foot*, without
pausing to rest but once, and with nothing to eat during
the whole walk except two hard biscuits. The reader
will observe that I was obliged to keep in constant
motion to avoid freezing, as I had no blanket or
buffalo-skin to wrap myself in if I felt disposed to sleep.
I had the ill-luck to encounter a severe snow-storm
when about half-way, and I took shelter under the lee
of an ice-hill, where I remained for two hours, at the
great risk of my life; for had I fallen asleep I might
have awaked in heaven. Had I kept on while the snow
was falling rapidly, I would probably have been struck
with snow-blindness; in that case I should have lost
my way, having no companion to guide me, and I must
have perished. Traveling alone in these regions is so
very dangerous, that unless a man knows well what he
can endure, he should never undertake it. I made
this journey in thirty hours.

On my arrival at Etah, I found our truant, Hans
Christian, domesticated in the hut of his intended
father-in-law. He excused himself for not coming
back with the sledge and provisions, by stating that he
had been very sick. I judged that he had merely been
love-sick; but knowing how to excuse a lover's foibles,
I did not reproach him. Kalutunah, Shangheu and
some other distinguished citizens of Etah, prepared a
rich banquet of seal-meat in honor of my arrival, and

they appeared to be much grieved when they understood that I could make but a short stay. When I made them acquainted with the destitution of my companions on shipboard, they made a contribution of seal and walrus-flesh, amounting to about 450 pounds, for which I was unable to offer them any recompense, and none was demanded. After resting myself for four hours, I took the sledge and dog-team which Hans had brought to the settlement with him, and having put the provisions which had been given me on board, I took leave of my friends and started on my return. Before I left, however, I advised Hans Christian to come back and stay with us a little while longer, as I thought it probably that the Expedition would proceed homeward in the Spring ; and in that case, Hans would be honorably dismissed from the service, as he would not be expected to leave his native country. In compliance with my advice, he promised to return to the brig as soon as an opportunity offered.

CHAPTER XX.

THE AUTHOR RETURNS TO THE BRIG WITH A LOAD OF
FRESH MEAT—HIS WARM RECEPTION—HE BECOMES A
TARGET FOR PISTOL AND RIFLE PRACTICE—REFUSES
TO COME ON BOARD—DR. KANE AND BONSALL TRY
TO COMPEL HIM—HE TREATS THE DOCTOR DISRE-
SPECTFULLY AND RETIRES UNDER A GALLING FIRE—
HIS DESPERATE JOURNEY BACK TO ETAH—HE IS
OVERPOWERED BY THE COLD, AND SINKS DOWN IN A
SNOW-DRIFT—HIS PROVIDENTIAL ESCAPE.

As my dogs were fresh and vigorous, after their long
rest at the settlement, they traveled very rapidly. As
my business was urgent, I stopped but two or three
times on the way, and then only long enough to feed
the animals and give them a little rest. I felt some
doubts arising as to the reception I should meet with
when I arrived at the vessel, but I hoped that my success in procuring food for the starving people would be
a sufficient apology for my unauthorized absence. I
made up mind, however, not to go on board until I was
assured of meeting with friendly treatment. When
about fifty yards from the vessel, I stopped and hailed
with the customary, "Ship ahoy!" Bonsall appeared
at the side, and I requested him to call up Dr. Kane.

18

The commander soon presented himself, and I accosted him as nearly as I can remember with the following words: "Dr. Kane, I have brought some fresh provisions for the use of my suffering companions. I am about to return for some more, and I hope you will send some of your men to take these on board." He did not answer me for several minutes, but appeared to be reflecting what he should do. At length he said, "William, you had better come on board." I replied, "That is unnecessary, Dr. Kane; here is the meat; will you be kind enough to send some of your people for it?" He then said, in a peremptory tone, "I tell you, you must come on board." To this I promptly answered, "I will not." "If you do not," said he, "I will shoot you!" During this conversation, Dr. Kane had descended from the vessel's side to the ice and approached me. I met him half way, and when he spoke of shooting me, we were scarcely two yards apart. He put his hand into his pocket, as if to draw out a pistol. "Dr. Kane," said I, "you cannot frighten me in this way, and I thought that you knew me too well to make the attempt. Hans was sick and not able to come with the provisions; I have brought them, and ask you to apply them to the relief of your starving crew. Is this an offense which deserves capital punishment?" He replied, "I do not punish you for bringing the provisions, but for leaving your vessel without permission." Said I: "I have been discharged from the brig, and am no longer under your command; but had you treated me in a proper manner, I would have remained

DR. KANE SHOOTING AT GODFREY.

with you as long as my services were required." To
this he answered, "If you will not come on board,
come nearer the side, while I try to convince you that
you are under a mistake."

I complied with this request, and, as soon as we came
near the companion-way, the Doctor called for Bonsall,
who immediately came down on the ice. The Doctor
then repeated, "You *must* go on board." Said I:
"If you choose to murder me, you may; but go on
board I will not." Dr. Kane then drew a pistol and
gave it to Bonsall, directing him to shoot me if I attempted to go away. The Doctor then ascended the
companion-ladder, and went on board. I turned to
Bonsall and said, "Comrade, do you intend to shoot
me?" He answered, "I will shoot you, if you offer to
leave the side of the brig." "Then," said I, "you
must shoot, for I am going this moment;" and I suited
the action to the word, walking very deliberately toward
my sledge. Bonsall presented his pistol and pulled the
trigger, but the cap exploded without communicating
with the charge. Dr. Kane now appeared on deck,
and seeing me in the act of walking off, he snatched a
rifle from the gun-stand, for the purpose of shooting
me, as he fully admits in his journal; but, owing to
his haste in handling the weapon, it went off before he
could bring it to bear. He caught up another rifle,
cocked it, took deliberate aim, and fired. The bullet
whistled as it passed my head; but God, being more
merciful than this amiable and saintly naval officer,
protected me from harm. I then bowed to the Doctor,

18*

in acknowledgment of his intended kindness, and advised him to go below and compose himself. "When your nerves are steadier," said I, "perhaps you may shoot with more effect." He stood gazing at me as if astonished at my audacity. I walked a few paces further, and then turned and addressed him again: "Dr. Kane, as you will not order your men to unload the sledge, I shall have to go back without it. But no matter; I have walked to Etah once, and I can do so again. I shall borrow a sledge there, and return with another load of meat. In the mean time, you can practice with the rifle until I come back and offer you a chance for another shot."

Then, leaving the sledge, with its load, on the ice, I bowed again to the Doctor and departed. My former journey on foot to Etah was one of unexampled hardship and danger, but the repetition of that journey, at a time when I was already exhausted with fatigue, was a desperate undertaking. I expected to die on the way; but I preferred this alternative to making that submission which my late Commander required. I felt revengeful enough against Dr. Kane to wish that he had killed me, so that he might experience the pangs of remorse. When I had plodded on my weary way for several hours, the thought suddenly occurred to me that I was without a morsel of food, and that it would be impossible for me to obtain any before I came to Etah. "But that matters little, (I soliloquized,) it is not likely that I shall die of *hunger*."

I made this journey at the coldest and darkest period

of the arctic winter. The temperature must have been
at least fifty degrees below zero. My limbs became
stiffer every moment, and a drowsy feeling crept over
me in spite of every effort to resist it. Often did I
feel strongly tempted to lie down,

"And with one dying glance upbraid the sky;"

but better feelings prevailed; and I looked up to
Heaven with affectionate confidence, remembering that
man alone was my enemy. I felt, however, that the
catastrophe was approaching. My physical energies
had been tried to their utmost powers of endurance,
and they failed at last. I felt an oppressive weight on
my brain; my limbs were immovable; I tottered and
sank into a deep snow-drift. Then I recognized the
certainty of my fate, recommended myself to Divine
mercy, and became insensible.

But a few minutes could have elapsed, I think, before I recovered my senses. I felt no pain—no unpleasant sensation of any kind—but was extremely
drowsy; and although quite conscious that sleep and
death, at that time, were one and the same thing, that
thought would not have prevented me from indulging
my somnolent inclination. In such circumstances sleep
is so fascinating and attractive, that the gloomy aspect
of his "half-brother" ceases to be terrible. A touch
of the ice-king's sceptre then becomes as potent and
irresistible as the somniferous influences of Prospero's
wand. But, while my physical powers succumbed to
the antagonism of natural causes, my spirit resisted,

and prompted me to attempt one more struggle for my life. I felt that it was unmanly to be victimized by any earthly power, without resisting to the last extremity. With a desperate effort I arose to my feet, and gave myself a severe buffet in the face, which effectually awakened me. In fact, the pain of the bruise kept me wide awake for three hours afterward. Strange as it may seem, when I again began to walk I found myself much refreshed. I judged that while my senses were absent I had enjoyed the benefit of a short sleep. I had, on several former occasions, observed the wonderfully renovating effect of a very short slumber, when arctic wayfarers appear to be completely overcome by cold and fatigue. One instance occurs to my remembrance. When the rescue party, mentioned in a former chapter, were returning to the brig, and the men seemed to be entirely worn out by toil and hardship, each was allowed to sleep for two minutes while sitting on the side of the sledge. They were aroused in time to prevent fatal consequences; but this sleep of only two minutes duration appeared to restore all their animation and vigor.

My falling into the deep snow-drift (as mentioned above,) was a providential circumstance, as a man is much less likely to freeze in a pile of snow than on the naked ice. After I had recovered my power of locomotion, I struggled onward with some degree of speed for the first twenty miles, but afterward with a slow and irregular pace, like the movements of a somnambulist. I have no recollection of any thing that occurred during the last forty miles of my journey, and I am totally unable to comprehend how it was possible for me to travel at all. It is a still greater mystery how I could keep in the right course. I learned afterward from the Esquimaux of Etah, that they saw me approaching their settlement, and ran out to meet me. They found that my eyes were closed, and that I was unable to answer any questions. The charitable natives took me into one of their huts, chafed my half-frozen limbs, and administered to my necessities with the most anxious attention. I slept fifteen hours without intermission, and, on awaking, found myself as well and as vigorous as ever.

GODFREY FAINTS FROM HARDSHIPS.

THE LIFE, TRAVELS, AND ADVENTURES OF

FERDINAND DE SOTO,

DISCOVERER OF THE MISSISSIPPI.

By LAMBERT A. WILMER.

Five Hundred and Fifty octavo pages, Seventy-nine admirable Engravings on Wood, and Six superb Steel Plates. All of these embellishments were executed by the most celebrated artists in the United States.

———— ◄•••► ————

THIS book is a complete biography of the renowned adventurer, containing the incidents of his birth and early life; his ambitious love, and the great dangers to which he was thereby exposed; his efforts to gain the object of his attachment by seeking wealth and celebrity in America; his many daring and chivalric deeds; his perilous enterprises and important discoveries; his crimes and misfortunes; his singular and mysterious death; and his burial under the waters of the Mississippi.

WILMER'S Life of Ferdinand de Soto is the only book ever published which gives a true and faithful account of the operations of the Spaniards in America. It exposes the errors and misrepresentations of the historians in general; and proves conclusively that a majority of the "mighty conquerors" were freebooters and villains of the most detestable and infamous character. It contains many thrilling accounts of

SPANISH BARBARITIES

AND

DEEDS OF THE MOST THRILLING ATROCITY,

It gives the only genuine narrative of the "CONQUEST OF PERU" which has ever yet appeared in the English language, and proves that the "illustrious hero, Francisco Pizarro," was in reality an odious and contemptible cut-throat and cowardly robber, who deserved to expiate his crimes on the gibbet.

(395)

Among other items of the most absorbing interest in this work is a *correct* account of the

CAPTURE AND BURNING OF THE PERUVIAN INCA,

AND THE MASSACRE OF THOUSANDS OF HIS SUBJECTS. We can declare most conscientiously that no American history ever published gives a true account of these transactions, and the other tyrannical deeds of Pizarro and his confederates. The narrative of these events in the "Life of De Soto" is taken principally from suppressed manuscripts in the Spanish libraries, which the kings of Spain would not allow to be published. The murder of the Inca is one of the most astounding and revolting deeds ever recorded in the history of the world.

This great work also gives a complete and truthful account of De Soto's discoveries and adventures on that part of the American continent now forming the States of *Florida, Georgia, South Carolina, North Carolina, Alabama, Mississip i, Arkansas, Louisiana,* and the *Indian Territory.* Some of these veritable details are far more wonderful than the wildest inventions of the novelist.

The futile but persevering search of the Spaniards after the imaginary FOUNTAIN OF YOUTH, and a Gold Region supposed to exist in some part of North America, is graphically related. The horriving cruelties of the Spaniards are faithfully detailed.

The whole of De Soto's route in North America is described as almost one continuous conflict with the natives. Several of his battles with the North American Indians, in sanguinary horror, surpass all similar events in the records of Indian warfare. His great battle fought at Mauvilla (the site of which is near Mobile, in the State of Alabama) occasioned a greater loss of human life than any other engagement which ever took place between the white race and the aboriginal tribes of America. The fearful sufferings of the Spaniards after this battle are described. All their baggage, clothes, camp equipments, plunder (including pearls and gold of great value), fell into the hands of the Indians. The subsequent adventures of De Soto are full of peril and hardship: many of his followers were frozen to death; many others were massacred by the Indians; a large number perished in a conflagration of the Spanish camp, and the survivors were left in the midst of a severe winter without clothes or shelter. In all these disasters, the indomitable resolution of De Soto excites the admiration of the reader. He sets all danger at defiance, overcomes every obstacle, and fights his way to the Mississippi. He builds boats, crosses that mighty stream in spite of the opposition of the natives, who assemble in great numbers along the banks of the river and harass the Spaniards with a continued attack. De Soto's progress through the wilderness to the foot of the Ozark Mountains is next given. His terrible conflicts with the original *Camanches* are described. This tribe proves to be unconquerable. De Soto returns to the Mississippi. His grief, disappointment and remorse. He is attacked with a severe disease. His biographer suspects that he was poisoned. Proofs adduced. He dies. A friendly chief offers to sacrifice his beautiful daughter on De Soto's tomb, and presents her to Louis de Moscoso for that purpose.

The work abounds with incidents of the most startling, extraordinary and romantic description, all of which are certified by references to authentic history. It comprises twelve episodes of Indian character and life. The work contains Six superb Steel Plate Engravings, one of which is a *Photograph of the $10,000 Painting ordered by Congress*, now adorning the Rotunda of the Capitol. The book is printed on the finest paper, and bound in good style. *It is a work indispensable to every Library. The Steel Engraving of the Burial of De Soto in the Mississippi is pronounced the finest work of art ever done in this country.*

Unbought Opinions of the Press.

From Washington Union.

Mr. Wilmer has produced a work which will obtain for him a lasting fame. Without any overstrained rhetoric, he tells the romantic story of De Soto's adventures in such a fascinating style, that the interest of the reader never flags till he has finished the volume. Differing from Prescott and Irving, the author of this work, while he apologizes for "De Soto," does not fall into the common error of eulogium.

We cannot help remarking the difference, in this particular, between the treatment of our author's subject and that which Mr. Abbott saw fit to bestow upon Napoleon; had the latter observed the same judiciousness in his history, it would have been invaluable, and would have done the justice to a great man which the fulsomeness of the eulogist, like the hatred of his detractors, has defeated.

The history of De Soto is presented to the public in a very attractive form; it contains over five hundred pages of clear, handsome print, and it is embellished by steel engravings from the skillful hands of the Sartains, and woodcuts by Orr & Telfer. The portraits of De Soto and Donna Isabella, are fine specimens of the art.

The book is one of the best that the American press has produced during the year, and we have no doubt it will become a standard work, and will well reward the scholarship of the author, and the enterprise of the publishers.

From Cincinnati Times.

"The Life and Adventures of Ferdinand De Soto." This is the title of a new and very interesting volume, just issued by J. T. Lloyd, Philadelphia. The author. L. A. Wilmer, has faithfully performed his task, and given us a work well worth taking its place in any library in the land, as authentic and reliable. To the city of the Great West, the history of the discovery of the Mississippi cannot fail to possess unbounded interest, and to be read with avidity wherever it is introduced. The volume is handsomely bound, and profusely illustrated.

From Memphis Eagle and Enquirer.

"The Life, Travels, and Adventures of Ferdinand De Soto, Discoverer of the Mississippi—by L. Wilmer—Philadelphia, J. T. Lloyd."

This interesting and splendidly illustrated work will have an immense sale; it is one of the popular works of the day. Embracing a period of forty-three years, from the birth to the death of De Soto. What marvels of adventures are here recorded. The work, in thrilling interest, surpasses any thing published in twenty years.

From N. O. Picayune.

"Life of De Soto—J. T. Lloyd, Publisher, Philadelphia." It is a work for every library in the land. De Soto, the discoverer of the Mississippi, and Pizarro's brother-conqueror of Peru. The wood and steel engravings are handsomely executed by J. W. Orr & R. Telfer, N. Y. It will have immense sale in the Mississippi Valley.

From N. O. Delta.

"Life, Travels, and Adventures of De Soto, Discoverer of the Mississippi." Of all those heroic adventurers who came to North and South America, with the sword, the cross, and the flag of Spain, De Soto is to us the most interesting. His life is a romance full of hair-breadth adventures, chivalrous deeds, and unequaled daring—his sword flashed from the waters of Tampa Bay to the banks of the Mississippi.

From Frank Leslie's Illustrated Newspaper.

"The Life, Travels, and Adventures of Ferdinand De Soto, Discoverer of the Mississippi, by L. A. Wilmer—J. T. Lloyd, Publisher, Philadelphia." This valuable addition to the literature of America we hail with pleasure. Bringing out the work in such elegant style reflects credit, in every respect, upon the taste and liberality of the publisher. It is written in a graceful, fluent style; indeed, so full of interest is the work, that we found it difficult to lay it aside after we had once commenced its perusal. It is illustrated with numerous fine steel and wood engravings.

From St. Louis Republican.

"The Life of Ferdinand De Soto, Discoverer of the Mississippi," by L. A. Wilmer, and published by J. T. Lloyd, Philadelphia. Perhaps there is no name connected with history so suggestive of daring adventure, of perilous enterprise, and romantic interest, as that of De Soto, the Discoverer of the Mississippi. There is something so attractive in this Life of De Soto, that we are reminded of reading Robinson Crusoe in our youthful days. The pages flow with the daring deeds of the hero, the splendor of his achievements, the celerity of his movements, and his fortitude, where disease and famine, and myriads of savage foes were all assailing him in a remote wilderness never trodden by white man before. The work Mr. Wilmer has given to the public is a good one. He has drawn freely from the many sources at his command. His style is clear and vigorous. The typographical appearance of the book is splendid, and the engravings striking and excellent.

From Willis's Home Journal.

"Life of De Soto, Discoverer of the Mississippi," by L. A. Wilmer, and bearing the imprint of J. T. Lloyd, Philadelphia. This is the most interesting work it has ever been our privilege to read. The author possesses tragic power of a high order. The account Mr. Wilmer gives of the capture and burning of the Peruvian Inca, and the massacre of thousands of his subjects, makes one's blood run cold. The volume has 550 pages, and profusely illustrated on steel and wood.

From Chicago Tribune.

"Life and Adventures of Ferdinand De Soto, Discoverer of the Mississippi," by L. A. Wilmer—J. T. Lloyd, Publisher, Philadelphia. From a cursory glance at this work, we are satisfied that it is a book of rare interest. It is handsomely printed and highly illustrated. Mr. Bamford, the agent here, has nearly *sixteen hundred* subscribers waiting for the work.

From N. Y. Courier and Enquirer.

"Life of De Soto, Discoverer of the Mississippi," by L. A. Wilmer—Philadelphia, J. T. Lloyd. As De Soto was among those Spaniards who arrived on this continent at an early period—as he was a companion of Pizarro in the conquest of Peru—always taking the lead in all the battles—and as he was afterward an adventurer in our own country, better materials from which a life could be written no author could wish. There are many parts of the volume from which we might take extracts; we might tell of De Soto's attachment to Donna Isabella, daughter of Governor De Avila—how he was repulsed by the haughty father, on account of his poverty—how he determined to seek wealth, and embarked in the Peruvian wars—his immense success in making millions of dollars by burning the Peruvian Inca—his returning to Spain and marrying the beautiful Isabella—his adventures in this country—his battles and hardships—his discovery of the Mississippi, and his burial under its turbulent waters. It is a work worth having.

☞ TEN THOUSAND AGENTS WANTED—To whom we will supply this book at the wholesale price of $ per copy, and give each Agent a certain district exclusively. Single copies will be sent by Mail, free of postage, on receipt of $1.50. By ordering one hundred copies at a time, the work will be put at $ per copy.

☞ THIS BOOK IS SOLD ONLY BY OUR AUTHORIZED AGENTS. POSTMASTERS are requested to act as our Agents; and if they cannot spare the time to do so, they will oblige us by handing this Circular to some energetic young man of their acquaintance.

☞ Enclose your money in a letter if there is no Express office convenient, and direct it plainly, taking care to write the name of your Post Office County and State. Registered letters are always at our risk. *Address,*

J. T. LLOYD, Publisher, Pa.

N. B.—As we allow Agents such large profits, it will not pay us to send Sample Books on time: the cash must accompany every order. Agents are furnished Circulars and fine Illustrated Showbills, to assist them in getting subscribers.

To the United States Senate and House of Representatives of the United States of America.

YOUR PETITIONER respectfully shows, that he is the Publisher and Proprietor of a new work recently issued in Philadelphia, and London, England, entitled, "THE LIFE, TRAVELS, AND ADVENTURES OF FERDINAND DE SOTO, THE DISCOVERER OF THE MISSISSIPPI RIVER," 1 vol. 8vo., 536 pages, 6 steel plates by JOHN SARTAIN, Philadelphia, and 89 fine wood engravings, by J. W. ORR, New York. That it is eminently a *National Work*, deserving of a wide circulation in the United States, and should be placed in every State and Public Library in the country. That it is the first authentic account of the discovery of the mighty Mississippi, whose waters wash nearly one-half of the States of this great Republic, and whose commerce contributes millions annually toward the support of this government. That the work traces out De Soto's whole route, from the landing at Tampa Bay, Florida, through the entire southern country, to the banks of the Mississippi, which he took possession of in an imposing manner, in the name of the King of Spain. His battles with the many ferocious Indian tribes inhabiting at that time the whole South, are graphically described. Their customs, religion, and belief are fully narrated by the author, who has spent many years of his life in searching the monasteries of Spain for authentic accounts of "De Soto's" explorations in this country, and many facts in regard to the extreme cruelty of the early Spanish explorers to the poor Indians are for the first time given to the light of day in this volume. That "De Soto," as is shown, was basely poisoned by his comrades, in order that they might return to their native country, and escape from a land which had cost them so many trials, hardships, and extreme sufferings. That the discoverer of the Mississippi was secretly and silently, at the dead of night, taken to the middle of the great river which had cost him his life, and sunk to the bottom. That his comrades attempted to escape by descending the Mississippi in rude boats, but were pursued by myriads of savages in canoes, and nearly all were slaughtered.

Your petitioner further says: That *there is no account of this interesting history of the "Discovery of the Mississippi," to be found in any Library in America* That Congress, to commemorate the "Discovery of the Mississippi," very wisely purchased a painting of the same, at a cost of $10,000, and placed it in the Rotunda of the Capitol. But how much more important to the people is this faithful history of the Life of De Soto, the discoverer of that great river, than a painting.

Therefore, your petitioner prays that you will pass a Bill for the purchase of ten thousand (10,000) copies of the Life of De Soto, for general distribution among the various State Libraries. THAT YOUR PETITIONER, THINKING MORE OF GIVING THIS WORK A LARGE CIRCULATION THAN MAKING MONEY ON IT, PROPOSES TO SELL THE BOOK TO CONGRESS AT COST, to wit, $1.50 per copy; $2.50 being the retail price, many members of both Houses having purchased the book at that price.

By passing this Bill, you will confer a benefit on your constituents, and your petitioner will ever pray, etc.

J. T. LLOYD.

PHILADELPHIA, 8TH JANUARY, 1859.

GODFREY'S THRILLING NARRATIVE

OF THE LAST

Grinnell Arctic Exploring Expedition

WM. C. GODFREY, (FROM A PHOTOGRAPH.)

IN SEARCH OF SIR JOHN FRANKLIN

By WM. C. GODFREY, One of the Survivors.

Three hundred pages and 80 Engravings.   Price in   Cloth Binding, $1.

J. T. LLOYD, Publisher, Philad'a.

(401)

A NEW AND SINGULAR CHAPTER

IN THE HISTORY OF

MRS. CUNNINGHAM-BURDELL.

She visits a Matrimonial Office in Forty-third Street—Is Introduced to Mr. Fitzgerald of St. Louis—Her Appearance and Dress—Her Opinion of Domestic Peace and of New York Ladies—She offers to find a Model Wife—Her Sentiments on Love, Marriage, and Divorce—Is a Free Lover—Mrs. Willis, the Broker—Discourse of Ghosts—She Relates the Wonderful Story of a Clock—Fitzgerald Makes a Remark about Dead Men, and Cunningham gets Nervous —An Important Confession about her Marriage—She Tells her Age—She Offers to Cure Fitzgerald of a Cold—Wants him to go and Drink a Punch of her Making—He thinks of the Bloody Work in Bond Street, and Declines—She Accepts Five Dollars as a Slight Token of Respect—She Discourses of Murders and Executions—Is Opposed to Capital Punishment—Denounces the Reporters as a Meddlesome, Lying Set of Vultures—Her Opinion of the Tombs as a Residence—A Decisive Meeting—Cunningham Wants a Set of Furs—She Offers to Take Charge of Fitzgerald's Household Affairs—Wants him to Take a House Up-town—Mr. Fitzgerald Attempts to Get Away, but is Seized by Cunningham and Detained by Force—He Makes another Present, and gets into the Hall, which is Dark—He Finds Himself Locked In—He Calls in Vain to be Released—He Gets into the Parlor—Resolves to Smash a Window—Interesting Denouement—Where Mrs. Cunningham Went after the Meeting.

In November last, a young man, giving the name of C. Frank Fitzgerald, of St. Louis, Mo., went to the Matrimonial Office of Mrs. Jessie Willis, No. — West Forty-third street, in this city—an office which was started in the summer of 1858, and has been quite extensively advertised. We copy the following specimen of the advertisements from the New York Herald, of January 27th:

"MRS. JESSIE WILLIS will give introduction to ladies and gentlemen with a view to matrimony, at her office, — West Forty-third street, from 3 to 8 P. M. Parties suited; references required. Gentlemen's fee $1: ladies free. Letters from the country must be post-paid, with return letter stamps. N. B.—All business confidential."

THE GREAT SENSATION BOOK,

JUST ISSUED,

MATRIMONIAL BROKERAGE IN THE METROPOLIS.

The most astounding volume issued in many years. 200 pp. Illustrated on Steel and Wood. Portraits of

A Fifth Avenue Belle, who answered a $50,000 Advertisement for a " Pretty Wife."

Portrait of Mrs. Willis, the Matrimonial Broker; List of Victims, Merchants, Lawyers, Southern Planters, and Fast Young Men: all introduced to beautiful but thoughtless Girls. A bushel of Love Letters and Daguerreotypes captured by the Police from Dr. Lyons, before he sailed for Europe. Over 3000 Matches made at Mrs. Willis' Office annually. John Dean and Miss Boker. Breach of Promise Cases, arising from Matrimonial Brokerage Offices, one for $10,000; another for $6,000; and for $11,000. Names of many of the Victims—Men well known.

Hear what the New York Evening Post says, (Wm. C. Bryant, Editor.)

MATRIMONIAL.—The subject was novel, and the writer of the articles is the first who has given it a thorough investigation. His inquiries have been long and laborious, and not always pleasant; but the results, as he has given them, are in every essential respect authentic. Some doubt has been expressed, by correspondents and others, as to the truth of his descriptions of the several interviews held in a recent instance, but we are assured, on the best of evidence, that they are nothing more nor less than a faithful report of what took place and was said. If we had not been convinced of this, the articles would not have been printed in this paper. The author, moreover, has many letters and documents that have fallen into his hands, and which we have seen, confirmatory of the stories he has narrated.

Many breach of promise cases arise from acquaintances formed in matrimonial offices, and by means of advertisements; a fact which is illustrated by the history of Mr. Gillette, in another number. In short, it may be taken for granted, in nearly every case, that these proceedings are designed to decoy unthinking, inexperienced, and heedless persons into some trap, either to wheedle them out of their money, or to put them in a position in which they will be completely in the power of the sharpers.

We believe that the writer who makes these exposures has rendered a service to the public, and the book which he proposes to form from his contributions will contain much valuable information.

200 Pages, Octavo. Price 50 Cents.

Address J. T. LLOYD, Publisher, Philada., Pa